"Does doing funky things with a mincess?
Absolutely not! There are plenty of tea[...]crazy
things. What the Columbus Chill had [...] was
soul. Their antics were genuine and tou[...]nan
anyone could expect. Their soul's divinity was to entertain the fans. Fun was
so imbedded into their DNA that their success amazingly spawned a major
league team. If I could get into a time machine I'd go back and enjoy those
Columbus Chill games."

—Jon Spoelstra, author of *Marketing Outrageously Redux* and coauthor with
Steve DeLay of *The Ultimate Toolkit*

"*Chill Factor* is both an entertaining tale of an underdog sports franchise
that beat the odds and a highly compelling marketing case study. At
times it reads like a novel—with fun characters both on the ice and in the
front office—but it really happened. It's a terrific story, well told, and the
marketing and leadership lessons will stay with you long after you put it
down."

—Kevin Sullivan, founder, Kevin Sullivan Communications, Inc.,
and White House Communications Director (2006–2009)

"My life as a rock star began in the fall 1991 and, for me, lasted through
the spring of 1993. At that time I was a player for the Chill and living in
the sudden, and shocking, hockey utopia of Columbus, Ohio. An eccentric
creation, the Chill was unconventional in every manner. Their whacky
approach to sports marketing and in-game operations roused the people of
the city, galvanized them to dream bigger, and in the process created a cult
following unlike anything I've seen in my twenty-plus years in the sports
business. *Chill Factor* is the intriguing story of this happening and the
mastermind behind it, team President David Paitson, whose approach in
life is akin to Jerry Seinfeld and his promotions like Bill Veeck on steroids."

—Don Granato, Assistant Coach, Buffalo Sabres

"The Columbus Chill grew the interest in hockey in Ohio, creating the opportunity for the NHL to expand there and without the hockey fanatics the Chill had created, I am not sure the NHL would be there now. *Chill Factor* is a great historical story of the game of hockey, from minors to majors in small town USA. David Paitson was a visionary when it came to running and marketing a minor league sports franchise. He knew how to put a great product on the ice and ran a first class program and knew how to survive as a franchise in a very volatile minor league climate. I once interviewed there for the coaching vacancy and came back to my wife and said "this program is first class and this guy is brilliant and, if I were to get into coaching, Columbus would be my first choice."

—Craig Laughlin, television analyst for the Washington Capitals

"I remember finishing up many a Blue Jacket Radio Network postgame show and then standing around the main concourse of Nationwide Arena to talk hockey with the hardcore fans—many of which used to be Chill fans. Many a story was told about the Chill, from the on-ice excitement and shenanigans to the off-ice marketing and promotions, which seemed to go from the bizarre to off the charts! The on-ice success of the Chill would eventually result in a minor league record for consecutive sellouts and help set the table for the arrival of the NHL Blue Jackets in the fall of 2000. You will find *Chill Factor* to be a fun and informative read on the running of a successful minor league franchise in Columbus, Ohio."

—George Matthews, original radio voice of the Columbus Blue Jackets

CHILL
FACTOR

CHILL
FACTOR

HOW A MINOR-LEAGUE HOCKEY
TEAM CHANGED A CITY FOREVER

Dr. DAVID PAITSON AND CRAIG MERZ

Foreword by Bob Hunter

**SPORTS
PUBLISHING**

Inquiries may be addressed to: www.DavidPaitsonPresents.com

For a complete listing of team and franchise information, visit
www.columbuschill.net, and for regular updates on Chill news join the Columbus
Chill Memories Facebook page.

Sports Publishing books may be purchased in bulk at special discounts for
sales promotion, corporate gifts, fund-raising, or educational purposes. Special
editions can also be created to specifications. For details, contact the Special Sales
Department, Sports Publishing, 307 West 36th Street, 11th Floor, New York, NY
10018 or sportspubbooks@skyhorsepublishing.com.

Sports Publishing® is a registered trademark of Skyhorse Publishing, Inc.®, a
Delaware corporation.

Visit our website at www.sportspubbooks.com.

10 9 8 7 6 5 4 3 2 1

Library of Congress Cataloging-in-Publication Data is available on file.

Cover design by Brian Peterson
Cover photo courtesy of Greg Bartram, Better Image Photography

Print ISBN: 978-1-68358-369-1
Ebook ISBN: 978-1-68358-370-7

Printed in the United States of America

To my wife, Lauren, and step daughters, Aubrey and Kristey,
for all of your patience, love, and support.

And to my father, Jim Paitson, for encouraging me to always follow
my instincts.
—DP

* * *

To my parents, Dave and Vicki, for instilling the work ethos
that allowed me to see this project to fruition. Somehow
my patience didn't match yours as you raised four rambunctious,
sports-crazed boys.

To my brothers David, Eric and Chris, thanks for all the great
memories growing up and the desire, like mine, to see the NHL
someday come to Columbus. And, for those epic two-on-two floor
hockey games in the basement.

I only wish Dad and David we're here to see this book published.
I hope I made you proud.

To Mary. When we met sixteen years ago you said I should someday
write a book. Thanks for your patience. We did it.
—CM

CONTENTS

Foreword　　　　　　　　　　　　　　　　　　　　　　xiii

Introduction: Greetings from Columbus, Ohio　　　　　xxi

Chapter One: Dark Shadows of Scarlet and Gray　　　1

Chapter Two: A First-Rate Second Choice　　　　　13

Chapter Three: Naysayers Be Damned　　　　　　24

Chapter Four: It's Not Your Common Cold　　　　33

Chapter Five: A Taylor-Made Problem　　　　　　43

Chapter Six: Opening Night Meltdown　　　　　　53

Chapter Seven: Magic and Mayhem　　　　　　　65

Chapter Eight: The Land of Misfit Toys　　　　　75

Chapter Nine: Mardi Gras Meets High Sticking　　85

Chapter Ten: America Discovers Columbus　　　　93

Chapter Eleven: A Born-Again Used-Car Salesman　103

Chapter Twelve: A Game-Changing Moment　　　113

Chapter Thirteen: Pipeline to the Show　　　　　123

Chapter Fourteen: The Big Sell　　　　　　　　137

Chapter Fifteen: Building for the Future　　　　155

Chapter Sixteen: The Walkout　　　　　　　　165

Chapter Seventeen: The Battle Lines Drawn　　　177

Chapter Eighteen: Moe Knows Hockey　　　　　187

Chapter Nineteen: A Seat at the Big Boys' Table　201

Chapter Twenty: The Evil Empire　　　　　　　207

Chapter Twenty-One: The Drive to the Finish　　219

Chapter Twenty-Two: Pucks, Politics, and the Art of the Power Play 231

Chapter Twenty-Three: The Enemies Within 243

Chapter Twenty-Four: Striking Back 251

Chapter Twenty-Five: Udder Madness 265

Chapter Twenty-Six: Last Call 275

Chapter Twenty-Seven: The Chill Factor 285

Acknowledgments 293

Overtime 295

Shootout 303

In a city that was named after Cristobal Colon,
There's a hard-hitting hockey team that calls the town home. (Hi home)
Well their sticks are stout and their blades are sharp,
You're gonna feel the Chill right through your heart.
OOOOOOOOOOOOO yes you will, call them the Columbus Chill.
OOOOOOOOOOOOO yes you will, you're gonna feel the Chill.
Gotta warn their opponents to make a Doctor's appointment,
'Cause they're gonna need a cast and crutch and some ointment.
Well they slice and slash and dice and trauma,
They're gonna send the other guys crying to their momma.
OOOOOOOOOOOOO yes you will, you're gonna feel the Columbus, the Columbus,
The Columbus Chill,
OOOOOOOOOOOOO call them the Columbus Chill.
—"The Chill Fight Song" by Heywood Banks

FOREWORD

At the time of the Chill's birth announcement in 1991, I must have been a bit underwhelmed. Professional teams had come and gone from Columbus like frenzied Christmas shoppers through a department store revolving door.

Almost thirty years later, the names still roll off the tongue like a bartender's beer menu, but affixing a league and a sport to these ghostly images is more of a challenge.

Magic . . . All-Americans . . . Golden Seals . . . Capitals . . . Bucks . . . Cagerz . . . Xoggz . . . Checkers . . . Stars . . .

It's not difficult to imagine the haunting echo of a "genius" on *Jeopardy!* who always has the principal export of Mauritania in his back pocket:

"I'll take Failed Columbus Sports Franchises for $200, Alex."

That's a joke, but it wasn't that funny when the Chill arrived; Columbus was a minor league city with a major league population, one that attracted minor league franchises in just about every sport that had them and "major league" franchises that were major only in name.

Many of those teams ended up with creditors stalking them to the ends of the earth, or at least to an abandoned office in a strip center in a deteriorating part of town. Teams arrived with a hail of superlatives, vanished amidst a storm of excuses, and ended up bouncing paychecks like basketballs all over town. With more than a million people and what seemed like a hundred teams in leagues and sports that didn't deserve much attention, Ohio's largest city was on its way to becoming the junk sport capital of the world.

What's hard to believe is that when the Chill arrived, there hadn't been a minor league hockey team in town for fourteen years.

The Columbus Owls were here when I came to the city to cover high school sports in 1975, and they didn't get much respect from the *Columbus Dispatch* sports department. One of our copy editors covered the team's home games, not because he was assigned to do it, but because he liked hockey and no one stopped him.

The team drew the same 1,500 to 2,000 hockey diehards to most of its home games at the 5,700-seat Ohio State Fairgrounds Coliseum, dedicated in 1917 and not seen as a viable venue for big events since the Ohio State basketball team moved out in 1956 and into the St. John Arena.

The Owls didn't have much visibility beyond that. When an Owls player and his wife knocked on the door of our townhouse apartment, said they lived a few doors down, didn't know anybody in town and desperately needed a babysitter for their infant daughter, my wife and I agreed to watch her. It wasn't until after our border collie snapped at their pesky little girl that I learned that the girl's father, Willie Trognitz, had piled up an incredible 305 penalty minutes as the Toledo Goaldiggers enforcer the previous season. It struck me then that if your dog is going to bite anybody's infant daughter, it's probably not a good idea for the mutt to attack the child of a guy who fought hockey enforcers for a living, especially one who two years later would be banned for life by the International Hockey League for whacking an opponent over the head with a hockey stick.

But the stupidity of putting myself in the line of fire of one of hockey's notorious villains obscures my original point: When the already-infamous Willie—a nice guy off the ice, by the way—banged on my door as a member of the Columbus Owls, it wasn't like getting a visit from Stan Mikita or Bobby Orr. The Owls existed in their own little world that didn't include most of us. They were the city's third professional hockey team in less than ten years, a perfect fit in a city that would soon have professional softball (All-Americans), women's pro basketball (Minks, twenty years ahead of their time), and indoor soccer (Capitals).

That's why the birth of the Chill wouldn't have made much of an impression on me. This was a different Columbus than today's Columbus, both in substance and in mind.

A hipster looking for nightlife in the city landed in either German Village or near Ohio State's campus and not in the after-five desert of empty office buildings and lonely, desolate streets in between. There was no Convention Center, no Arena District, and no row of crowded bars and restaurants on Gay Street. A big chunk of today's Arena District was occupied by the deteriorating structures of the abandoned Ohio Penitentiary. The Brewery District could have been called "The Brewery Graveyard"; long dead breweries left old brick buildings that oozed history but inspired no thoughts of the future entertainment district. There was no City Center Mall, which opened in 1989 on the site of today's Columbus Commons and was seen as the future; in a city that cried out for living, breathing bodies on the streets, it looked inward instead of outward and closed in 2009 after several years on its death bed.

Going to the Short North meant going to the Short North Tavern; Mellman's Corner, a popular stop at the southwest corner of High and Goodale Streets was replaced by the Greek Orthodox Cathedral in 1986, cutting the viable bar options in an area now teeming with bars, restaurants, and galleries in half.

When a big-name musical act came to the city, it stopped at Veterans Memorial or at Ohio State's St. John Arena, and events in St. John were relatively rare. The Triple-A baseball Columbus Clippers hosted an occasional concert in Cooper Stadium, located in its own little human desert on West Mound Street; the old ballpark was more memorable as a launching point for Franklin Delano Roosevelt's 1932 presidential campaign. There was no Columbus Crew and no Crew Stadium. Going shopping usually meant going to Northland, Eastland, or Westland malls; the big regional shopping areas—Easton, Polaris, and the Mall at Tuttle Crossing were still in the future. The fact that Scioto Downs was one of the city's top entertainment choices said a lot about the entertainment options that were available; the harness racing track ten miles south of the city often packed its grandstand and clubhouse without a racino because major league sports options were more than 100 miles away.

This dull environment spawned a city of small thinkers, many seemingly satisfied to think of us as an overgrown college town that couldn't measure up to other cities of our size. Mayor Buck Rinehart didn't belong to this group. He went after a major league baseball team when it became clear the big leagues might expand (Reds owner Marge Schott said Columbus would get a team over her dead body) and went to St. Louis in 1987 to meet with Bill Bidwell, owner of that city's football Cardinals, when the team was looking to relocate. Until he died in February 2015, Rinehart insisted that Bidwell was seriously thinking about Columbus before he moved his team to Arizona. It seems odd that he would have to defend himself almost thirty years later, especially with the Columbus metro area pushing two million, but at the time he was mostly derided for his efforts.

For some reason, we always seemed a little embarrassed by our interest in the majors, as if we were asking for the NHL or NBA to consider adding an expansion franchise in Biloxi, Mississippi, instead of to one of the largest and healthiest metro areas in North America. But Columbus always suffered from a bit of an inferiority complex when it came to stuff like this. We would look around, see the merits of other places, and tend to overlook the positives close to home. People would move here from other places and marvel at what a huge, thriving city this had become, but a lot of the folks who had lived here for years couldn't see it. They were trapped in the place this *used* to be.

When the Chill arrived, new minor league franchises weren't big news. The new teams often had the shelf life of a gallon of milk, so there was no reason to think the city's new East Coast Hockey League team would be different from the others and certainly no reason to believe that it would have a lasting impact on the city's sports landscape. In 1991, it looked like just another nomadic outfit that would rest its weary haunches in the city for a few seasons and move on; one that would play some games, win some hearts, and then disappear like a puff of smoke in a strong wind.

Except that it wasn't. That the Chill would be different from the others should have been clear from that first Opening Night, when the AA team held a frozen chicken shoot, using giant slingshots to propel frozen chickens into the goal. If you'll fire frozen chickens with giant slingshots, you'll probably do just about anything . . . and the Chill did.

An entertainment void existed in our big city, and the Chill helped fill it. Because of the team's savvy marketing, wacky promotions, and entertaining brand of hockey, Chill games quickly became a destination for the twenty-something set and the team cultivated a large following among local fans. People flocked to the old Coliseum the way they never had for the Owls, Golden Seals, or Checkers, and Columbus began to build their resume as a hockey town.

This wasn't as easy as it looks from a seat in Nationwide Arena at a Blue Jackets game in 2020. The late Moe Bartoli, who might be called the godfather of professional hockey in Columbus, once told me how he had a hockey school the first couple of years that the Checkers were in town in the mid-1960s, and some of the kids showed up wearing football helmets. Bartoli, player-coach of the city's first professional hockey team, didn't let that nod to King Football scare him off. He said from the beginning that he recognized the city as "a real sports town" and figured that if fans would come to the Fairgrounds for hockey games, they would go anywhere.

They went to Chill games—again and again and again—mostly because of the marketing genius of team president David Paitson, one of the co-authors of this book, and his staff. The team had a string of 83 consecutive sellouts during the team's early years, and the *Wall Street Journal*, *Sports Illustrated*, *USA Today* and the *Hockey News*, ESPN, and ABC's *World News Tonight* all came calling.

Despite all of that, the ice wasn't always smooth. The Chill had the same problems with the old Coliseum that previous hockey teams had; building managers had standard dates booked March and April, so local hockey teams that made the playoffs ended up playing their "home" games in other places.

I remember covering a game in Troy's Hobart Arena, which I described at the time as "the Fairgrounds Coliseum before its last three renovations," and wondering how in the name of Bobby Hull this could possibly happen in a huge, progressive city such as Columbus.

The column I wrote about it had a one-word ending—"Moo"—which is ironic given that a few seasons later the Chill opened the season as the Mad Cows, a one-night identity change replete with cow-spotted uniforms, a 40-foot inflatable cow, and a dunking-for-cow-tongues contest.

That's a taste (sorry) of the creativity that marked the Chill's eight years in the city and one reason why I knew that a book by the guy who came up with many of those zany ideas (Paitson) and the beat reporter who covered the team during those years for the *Columbus Dispatch* (Craig Merz) would be fascinating.

There is more to the Chill than a succession of funny stories, though. The franchise almost died before the start of its second season when the fairgrounds manager booked three events in the Coliseum in February and took the Chill's dates away. This happened after the ECHL schedule was released, and then Chill public relations director Brent Maurer said the league "tried to pull the plug" on the franchise.

Both because of that embarrassing issue and the team's remarkable success, Columbus mayor Greg Lashutka took notice and appointed three people to a committee to see if a study was needed for the possible construction of an arena, and from that a 10-man commission that included Paitson was eventually created that made the recommendation to put an arena issue on the ballot.

The timing for such a ballot issue was horrible. Taxpayers around the nation were rebelling at the thought of paying for a stadium or arena that would have a privately owned professional sports franchise as its primary tenant. Ohio State broke ground on its own 19,000-seat arena in 1996, in part to head off the city's efforts to build a venue that would offer the competition of major league sports.

Issue 1 lost at the polls on May 6, 1997, just days before the National Hockey League was to announce its decision on expansion. But such a compelling case for an NHL franchise had been made by the city's business titans, community leaders, and, yes, Paitson and the Chill, that the league granted Columbus and other expansion hopefuls more time to resolve their arena problems. Less than a month later, Nationwide Realty, Inc., announced it would build the arena privately and a couple of weeks after that the NHL announced that Columbus would get the major league franchise it sought, which would begin play in the fall of 2000.

Would the NHL's Blue Jackets be in Columbus today if the Chill hadn't blazed the trail for them in the 1990s? It's an intriguing question. I'm just glad it's a risk that we didn't have to take.

Bob Hunter was a sportswriter for the *Columbus Dispatch* for more than forty years (1975–2016), the last twenty-four as a columnist. During that time, he covered all sports—including hockey and the Columbus Chill. Hunter is the author of ten books, including *Saint Woody: The History and Fanaticism of Ohio State Football* and *Players, Teams and Stadium Ghosts*, and has won numerous writing awards. He resides in Westerville, Ohio.

Introduction:

GREETINGS FROM COLUMBUS, OHIO

The numbers on the scoreboard were breathtaking, a sight to behold:

Columbus 3, Chicago 0.

We're a mere ten minutes into the first period of our regular-season National Hockey League debut and we're pouring it on the Blackhawks—one of the league's Original Six franchises—blistering the nets with three goals in a span of just over two minutes. The scoring spree sends the stunned fans into pandemonium. I am exhilarated beyond belief.

"Welcome to the NHL, Columbus!"

That was the tag line of the ad campaign we ran in the months leading up to the Blue Jackets' inaugural season, in 2000. Our intention was to foster a sense of local pride as our city joined the big leagues, its brand-new hockey team set to compete against teams representing major North American metropolises from New York to Chicago to Los Angeles.

"Columbus, Ohio? Are you serious?" a Detroit Red Wings fan proclaimed in the television spot.

"See you in New York, losers," barked an obnoxious kid wearing his Rangers jersey.

The ad, created by Columbus ad agency Zero Based Marketing, challenged the perception that Columbus truly could support a major-league sports franchise. It was intended to stir our fans' passions, swell their collective pride, and help change the athletic identity of the city. Up until three years earlier, when Columbus and Nashville were surprisingly awarded NHL franchises, few outside of the area knew more about it than that it was Ohio's state capital and home to the Ohio State University and its fabled athletic teams, known as the Buckeyes.

Columbus residents had heard the dismissive comments before, but the truth was that their small town was quickly blossoming into a major city.[1] Still, when the Blue Jackets' name was unveiled in November 11, 1997, one famed hockey journalist's disdain for it was so fierce that he was rumored to have said, "What's [NHL Commissioner Gary] Bettman trying to do, ruin the league?"

But despite all the derision and skepticism, here we stood on opening night 2000, proudly witnessing it all as it played out on the ice like a scene from a movie.

You're damn right Columbus belongs!

Getting there, however, had been a wild ride. A little less than a decade earlier, I had come looking for a place to settle a minor-league hockey franchise in the burgeoning East Coast Hockey League, two levels below the NHL. Soon, I found myself at the helm of a team that took Columbus by storm. The Columbus Chill existed for only eight seasons and never advanced beyond the second round of the playoffs, but the team forever altered people's lives in this once-sleepy central Ohio town. It is not hyperbole to state that without the Chill there would be no Blue Jackets, nor would there be an entertainment and sports district serving as a model for reenergizing the core of a city, a plan that would be studied and revered by other municipalities across North America.

The Chill was like a brilliant meteor flashing across the northern sky, spectacular and beautiful and then gone in an instant. But its impact will last forever.

---

[1] As of the 2020 estimate by the US Census Bureau, Columbus was the 14th largest city in the United States, with a population of 922,533.

How did we do it?

We set out to get the public's attention by slapping Columbus directly across its face. We took high sticking to a new level with edgy and innovative marketing concepts created by a team of young sports marketing professionals with an attitude. We joked about your mother, your sister, and toothless goons. Those ideas captured the hearts of sports fans, advertising executives, local media, and the general public and then kept them coming back for more.

Thriving on creativity, we embraced the philosophy that the only way to know where the line is, is to step over it once in a while. This is how we ended up at No. 7 on the list of best pick-up lines by Chill players: "You know, French isn't all I learned in Quebec," and, in a nod to the Ohio State-Michigan rivalry, hosting a Leak on Blue contest, in which participants used water guns filled with yellow-dyed water to simulate peeing on the Michigan colors.

The Chill's irreverent game presentation was a three-ring circus drawing inspiration from popular culture of the day. We worshipped at the altar of David Letterman, and our high priests were Beavis and Butthead. Figure skaters Nancy Kerrigan and Tonya Harding's highly publicized feud and the O. J. Simpson murder trial were tabloid folly begging for mockery. There were on-ice marriages and divorces and contests poking fun at city figures and fading movie and TV stars.

Our un-PC methods helped us achieve what many thought was impossible: we'd broken Ohio State's stranglehold in the market and proved that there was room for professional sports in central Ohio, for a team people with no allegiance to OSU could call their own.

We struggled early on to gain acceptance, which is why we had to be innovative. A Chill game was once described by a local magazine as "the world's largest dorm party" and "Mardi Gras meets high sticking." At its height, the Chill surpassed the Buckeyes as the "best sporting event," according to a survey of *Columbus Monthly Magazine's* readers.

P. T. Barnum would have been proud.

The national media soon came calling as well. A *Wall Street Journal* article entitled "Hockey's Chill, Lukewarm on Ice, Scores with Puckish Promotions" ran just two months after our first home game, calling it "hockey for the hip." Three weeks later *ABC World News Sunday* did an extended feature of its own.

This is the story of a minor-league franchise that was trying to turn a college football town into a major-league city simply by giving the people something they didn't know they wanted.

In the fall of 1991, as was the case for most of the century, Ohio State athletics reigned supreme in Columbus. All pro franchises that landed in its wake were subservient. Heck, OSU's marching band had more sway in Columbus than any of the pro teams. Couples planned their weddings to avoid Ohio State home games because they knew some of their closest "friends" had something else to do that day and would not betray their beloved Buckeyes. Even funerals were carefully arranged around home football dates.

It was in that climate that the Chill entered into some fortunate timing. Minor league hockey was experiencing a national growth, and Ohio State football was meandering under head coach John Cooper, who was about to enter his fourth season leading the Buckeyes in the fall of 1991. During his short time in Columbus, he had already drawn considerable flak from the fandom and scrutiny by the media for his 19–14–2 record, which included losses in the past two bowl games and, to the disdain of the legions, three consecutive losses to their bitter rival, the University of Michigan.

This gave us the sliver of an opening we needed to body check our way into the consciousness of area news outlets and the paying public. The Chill took advantage of the situation and the fact that Columbus had grown into a metropolitan area of 1.3 million people, many of whom fell in the coveted 18–34 demographic (memo: sell them cheap beer) and had lots of disposable income.

Facing long odds, the Chill resorted to off-the-wall marketing in its attempt to avoid becoming yet another member of the Columbus graveyard for franchises, which included three previous stabs at hockey. The tombstones ranged from A (All-Americans) to almost Z (Xoggz—pronounced zogs, and don't bother asking what it means). They failed by land (Minks), sea (Seals) and air (Red Birds). Columbus was used to having well-intentioned but ultimately cash-strapped owners promise the Stars (hockey) but end up chasing Comets (basketball) in Jets (baseball).

The Buckeye hockey team had a modest fan base and there were a fair number of out-of-market hockey fans living in Columbus at the time; yet the result of our effort was that the whole city—not just hockey fans—gravitated to our then-75-year-old arena to watch unknown players compete.

By the end of the first season the Chill began a sellout streak that would eventually set a minor-league hockey standard that stood for more than a decade. Games were played in the cramped 5,700-seat barn but the Chill's home rink became known for its fresh, alternative music; wickedly derisive sound bites directed toward opposing teams, and in-game promotions such as "Headlocks and Wedlocks."

From that, the Chill built a formidable base that at its apex boasted 6,400 full and partial season ticket-holders—a figure that was more than double the average "announced" attendance during the best years of the prior Columbus-based hockey franchises. That achievement captured the imagination of the city and it wasn't long before the clamor for bigger and better grew louder, though many thought—and hoped (some publicly)—the fervor would die. It didn't.

Instead, the Chill organization, backed by its growing and impassioned fan base, forced city and county leaders to explore new alternatives toward funding an arena that could attract a major league franchise. The Chill led grassroots efforts to get a tax initiative approved and even pledged to be the main tenant of the new facility until the potential arrival of an NHL franchise, all the while knowing its existence would no longer be required once the dream was realized. It was an altruistic approach but in keeping with the franchise's desire to be more than just a hockey team for six months out of a year.

The Chill also had a long-range plan to make hockey successful in Columbus by building and operating the Chiller ice rinks to attract a new generation of hockey fans. In the ensuing years, the Chillers produced figure skating champions, Division I collegiate hockey players and NHL draftees. In the 2018–19 and 2019–20 seasons, five players with local ties played in the NHL: Sean Kuraly (Boston Bruins), Connor Murphy (Chicago Blackhawks), Jack Roslovic (Winnipeg Jets), and brothers Kole (Columbus Blue Jackets) and Kiefer (Anaheim Ducks) Sherwood. Yet despite all the success, the Chill was still David skating against Goliath. That's the way it was in Columbus for decades. Despite occasional gestures from ambitious community leaders to acquire a team in the big four of major league sports (baseball, basketball, football, and hockey) those forays were always met with skepticism within and outside the city: *Who needs big-time pro sports when we have our Buckeyes?*

But the city's old ways couldn't stop us.

Chill Factor is the story of how to succeed when nobody wants or expects you to. And have a laugh while doing it.

Chapter One

DARK SHADOWS OF SCARLET
AND GRAY

"Sure, you may think hockey is a violent, perverted example of male machismo. But for only $5, what's your point?"

"Assault somebody, in life you get five years, in hockey you get five minutes. Is this a great game or what?"

"A man's gotta do what a man's gotta do. And if that means busting some chops once in a while, so be it."

—Headlines appearing in print ads from the Chill's first season.

Mark LeClerc, the creative director at Indianapolis-based ad agency Concepts Marketing Group, was reading a series of potentially aggressive headlines for a print campaign we were considering as part of our inaugural season.

This was a new venture for me. Named President and General Manager at just thirty-one, it was my first opportunity to lead a professional sports team. Back in the 1980s I had spent six years working in public relations and marketing for the NBA's Indiana Pacers. Later I rejoined my friend and Pacers mentor Ray Compton, a former newspaperman turned legendary sports promoter, and helped re-launch minor league hockey in Indianapolis. This time, however, I was no longer part of the supporting cast. This was my chance and I didn't want to blow it. Ray's no-holds-barred marketing style influenced me greatly. I realized that we had to be bold.

It was late August 1991, barely a month after we announced the formation of the Columbus Chill and about two months from our first home game. From the outset we planned on being forceful with our marketing, but after some recently negative publicity of the OSU football team, I asked Mark to up the ante a bit.

He didn't disappoint, pitching a list of in-your-face headlines a few days later. Some of the lines made me cringe, but I loved it. If Columbus was going to notice us we'd have to slap the city across the face to get the public's attention. This was scarlet-and-gray Buckeye country and the shadow Ohio State athletics cast was long. We were cognizant of their market dominance and respected what they were doing but couldn't afford to be in awe of the university. In the past, minor league hockey and various professional sports teams had tried and failed more than twenty times, and all were swallowed up by the great Buckeye beast. If we were going to have any chance to break the trend we had to get the media and public to take notice of us any way we could.

Audacity isn't part of my personality, but we intended to define our team's image with a bit of a rebel attitude. To get there, I drew inspiration from Bill Veeck—the legendary maverick baseball owner and promoter best known for flamboyant publicity stunts—and his classic book, *Veeck—As in Wreck*. Veeck was a public relations and marketing pioneer who, as the owner of the St. Louis Browns, Cleveland Indians, and Chicago White Sox, operated with the aim of delighting the paying customer, a mantra we'd attempt to duplicate. One of the game's great innovators, Veeck grew up around baseball. As a kid he worked the grounds crew that planted the ivy at Wrigley Field. Later, as an owner, he built and installed baseball's first exploding scoreboard, put in an outdoor shower in the centerfield bleachers at Comiskey Park, and began the tradition of having White Sox radio announcer Harry Caray sing "Take Me Out to the Ballgame" to the fans during the seventh-inning stretch, a tradition Caray famously carried over to his days with the Chicago Cubs.

Never afraid to push the envelope with the baseball establishment, Veeck is best remembered for sending 3-foot-7 Eddie Gaedel to the plate for the St. Louis Browns in 1951. When crouching in his baseball stance, Gaedel presented the pitcher with a two-inch strike zone, drawing both a walk and the immediate ire of baseball's commissioner Happy Chandler.

Veeck's most infamous promotion was 1979's "Disco Demolition Night," when an estimated 90,000 fans turned up in and around the 52,000-seat Comiskey Park to witness disco records being blown up by real sticks of dynamite. Though many fans were turned away at the gate, those that made it inside saw an event they would never forget. Known as "the night disco died," the promotion backfired and cost the White Sox a forfeit in the second game of the day's scheduled doubleheader after fans stormed the field and scattered debris everywhere, leaving it unplayable.

However, my personal Veeck favorite was "Grandstand Managers' Day," when he ceded control of the Brown's game strategy to the fans. Just five days after the Eddie Gaedel stunt, Veeck distributed large placards marked "YES" on one side and "NO" on the other, which the fans then used to make decisions in specific game situations, like whether or not to hit and run. The Browns won the game, 5–3, ending a four-game losing streak.

My friend and Terre Haute Schulte High School classmate Steve Schrohe suggested I read *Veeck—As in Wreck* when I was sixteen. Reading that book played a major role in setting me on my career path, as just a few years later I was off to study sports administration at Biscayne College (now St. Thomas University) in Miami, Florida.

What I learned in Miami was great, but my true influence was Veeck. With the Chill, we sought to emulate his risk-taking methods and fan-friendly style. Our approach was intended to stimulate specific audiences. To do so, we had to risk offending a few folks, which was a ballsy proposition in a city where professional hockey had tried and failed three times before. We sensed we had to go for broke to ensure our message would resonate with the younger crowd we wanted to attract.

Growing up in Indiana, I was a lifelong fan of Purdue University's sports teams. As Ohio State was (and still is) a fellow Big Ten school, I was aware of its popularity but less familiar with Columbus. It didn't take me long to feel the magnitude of the stranglehold that Buckeye fever had on the region, and it made me nervous that we would become yet another casualty unless we forced people to take notice of us.

That summer the *Columbus Dispatch* published a series of articles about OSU's men's basketball team's tour of Europe. The Buckeyes had a very good squad at the time, and even though the stories were mostly fluff and gossipy, they fed the insatiable appetite of Buckeye Nation at our expense. We just couldn't break through the endless cycle of hype for Jimmy Jackson, Chris Jent, and company.

Alan Karpick joined us from Purdue's athletic department and became my right-hand man. Larry Lane, an ex-Butler University basketball player who had been part of our front office team with the Indianapolis Ice, also joined our mini-staff, and together the three of us attended various events around Columbus to get a feel for the city.

On one such occasion we were at a major Buckeye dinner in which the featured speaker was a well-known, local Woody Hayes impersonator. Hayes, of course, was the legendary OSU football coach who died in 1987.

When the impersonator got up to speak he captivated the room. I scanned the faces in the audience and turned to Alan and said, "Oh my God, these people really think this guy is Woody." They hung on every word as he outlined his expectations for the upcoming season. It was spooky and somewhat pitiful that Ohio State fans were craving the good old days of Woody Hayes.

In the eyes of the OSU faithful, the Tennessee-born and Iowa State-bred John Cooper might as well have been the anti-Christ, as he was not a "true Buckeye" and had the audacity to do radio and TV commercials (one infamous one was for a hot tub company and ran ad nauseam the summer before his first season), things they felt Woody would never have done. In a way I felt bad for Cooper, as I had gotten to briefly know him some ten years earlier when I interned in the athletics department at the University of Tulsa, where he was then serving as athletic director and head football coach.

In the late days of summer in 1991, things got worse for Cooper, and his misfortune indirectly impacted our team's ability to get noticed. It gave us a first-hand introduction to the intense bond that exists between the city and the Buckeye football program. We learned that this bond ran far deeper than we had imagined, and I worried that any attention our team launch might garner that fall would get swallowed up by coverage of events beyond our control.

On August 19, 1991, members of the Soviet Union's government attempted to wrest control of the country from Soviet president Mikhail Gorbachev in a coup d'état (known as the "August Coup"). The leaders of the coup were Communist Party hard-liners who were opposed to Gorbachev's reform program. Boris Yeltsin, who had been appointed the first president of the Russian Federation only one month earlier, won international acclaim for casting himself as a democrat by defying the coup and dissolving the Communist Party. As the fate of the Big Red Nemesis teetered, the whole world waited in anticipation of its outcome. Well, the whole world *except* for the citizens of Columbus, Ohio, who had a more pertinent matter on their minds.

On August 23, less than seventy days from the Chill's season opener, star Buckeye running back Robert Smith (later a two-time NFL Pro Bowl selection with the Minnesota Vikings before becoming an analyst first for ESPN, then in 2016 for Fox Sports and the Big Ten Network) walked off the team and placed the blame squarely on Cooper and his staff, specifically, offensive coordinator Elliot Uzelac. Smith claimed that the coaches were less concerned with their athletes' educations than with keeping them eligible to play. Further, he charged that practices were interfering with his classes. Smith was a serious student-athlete who had his sights on medical school, and he felt football should take a back seat to his studies. While the story made headlines nationally, locally, Smith's comments set off a media firestorm and public fury unlike any sports story I had experienced to that point in my career.

In Columbus, the Smith story was front-page material and led the television news for nearly two weeks.

Cooper's popularity was as low as a thermometer reading during a Canadian winter and the *Dispatch's* letters-to-the-editor page provided the platform for seemingly every Cooper basher to vent their frustrations. Their writings were passionate, if not idiotic and unfair. The anti-Cooper forces saw the Smith incident as an opportunity to run the coach out of town on a rail. It provided an opening for his detractors to gather their pitchforks and galvanize the angry mob. The media joined in taking every opportunity to sensationalize the story.

Cooper was in a pinch and everyone knew it. Unfortunately for us, the story was the sole focus of the city's attention that late summer and fall, which made the mountain we had to climb that much higher. We had to be patient at a time when we wanted to charge full speed ahead. Weaned on college humor in films like *Animal House* and *Caddyshack*, we knew the value of a quick laugh and of making an immediate impact; yet this was a time when our maturity as a young staff would be tested, our perseverance challenged.

Smith didn't play football that fall but the discussion about whether or not he would return (he did for the 1992 season) remained a major story for months. Heading into our season opener, we were a complete non-factor as far as the mainstream media was concerned.

My anxiety level was rising. I was beginning to feel like the captain of a sinking ship. If we didn't do something dramatic, we'd continue to take on water until we joined Columbus' minor league sports graveyard. The team's launch, alone, was cause for angst because we were working on an extremely short timetable. I knew that if we didn't come out of the blocks quickly it might be over before we even got started; so I decided to call Mark LeClerc to discuss formulating a strategy for grabbing the public's and media's attentions.

I knew Concepts Marketing Group was the right place to start. They had been our advertising agency during my time with the Indianapolis Ice, the IHL affiliate of the NHL's Chicago Blackhawks, and I had developed strong relationships both with Mark and company president Larry Aull.

Mark and I worked together for years and were on the same wavelength. He was as creative as anyone I've ever been around, and the Chill was the perfect outlet for his wit. Mark is the kind of guy you'd picture writing jokes for *The Daily Show* or Stephen Colbert on a nightly basis. When I told him we had to take it up a notch because of what was happening in Columbus, he not only understood the challenge, but it made him giddy. Rarely, if ever, is an ad agency told to really push the envelope for a client, so for him, this was like Christmas.

Mark called back a few days later and started reading off some of the dramatic, in-your-face headlines he'd written:

I'll admit that I was a bit leery at first, but the Veeck in me said to go for it. I knew it was a calculated risk we had to take if we wanted to enter the public's consciousness. The headlines were meant to grab your attention, and they did. They were bold, dramatic and edgy. We were looking to get people talking and felt that this would ensure it. But we weren't looking to be like the World Wrestling Federation. We weren't cowboys or rebels; we just wanted to employ a brash delivery system to accomplish one goal: attract eyeballs to our product.

I told Mark that we needed to be prepared to counter critics of the ads. His copywriting skills were brilliant, and he found a way to walk the fine line in the subtext. As you read through the subsequent ad copy, it really softened (and explained) the headlines. The copy was creative, funny and served to remind everyone that the entire campaign was in good fun.

We were poking fun at people's perceived stereotypes about hockey. Columbus was not an established or sophisticated hockey market. By being different and entertaining, we had a chance to erode people's preconceptions about our sport and, we hoped, generate enough curiosity and intrigue to draw people to our games.

We believed that once we snared them, they'd come back over and over again.

Some just read the headlines and liked them but didn't dig deeper, and that was fine. We had at least made an impact. We knew that what we were doing wasn't right for everybody. Columbus is a midwestern, family-values type of city, but the strong influence of the collegiate and arts communities make it progressive in many ways. In our estimation, it hadn't had the proper venue in which to cut loose.

For $5, we can help you with all that unresolved anger you have for your mother.

She was overbearing. Controlling. Hypercritical. And deep down, when she was at her worst, didn't you want to check her real hard into the boards? Well, have we got a catharsis for you! At only $5 with a valid college I.D., Columbus Chill hockey is fun, exciting, and cheap therapy. And with home games played at the Ohio State Fairgrounds Coliseum, all the hard-hitting action is only minutes away from campus. Opening Night is Friday, November 1, at 8 pm. We're reserving a couch for you. But if you don't come, we won't be mad. Just very, very disappointed.

CHILL ®
C O L U M B U S
488

We had to be strategic about how to roll out our ad campaign. There were three primary targets: the 50,000 students enrolled at Ohio State, general sports fans, and the "night out" crowd, looking for entertainment.

The market wasn't totally void of hockey fans, we learned. There were still holdovers from the previous hockey failures (Checkers, Seals, and Owls) from the late 1960s and 1970s. There were also a fair amount of NHL fans—some from Detroit (three hours to the north), and many from Pittsburgh (three hours east), where the Penguins were in the midst of a Mario Lemieux-led renaissance at the time (their games could be seen on pay per view in Columbus in the 1990s). These were people who had moved to Columbus but found that their lone alternative for a hockey fix was visiting the antiquated OSU Ice Rink (1,600 capacity) to see the Buckeyes play. The Ohio State program reached its zenith in the 1983–84 season, when the Buckeyes opened with 13 straight wins to earn the school's first No. 1 ranking, but had five straight losing seasons by the time the Chill entered the market and interest in the program, in the community and on campus, was at an all-time low.

We believed that the students would eat up our marketing campaign, as would most male sports fans ages 35 and under. We weren't marketing to the old fogies. We were going after the young and hip crowd.

The Chill spent its first summer and early fall targeting the media and distributing the ads through those that we believed would "get it." The campaign never ran in the *Dispatch*. Admittedly, we didn't have the budget to afford a large campaign in such a large medium, but we also knew it wouldn't help us build the grassroots buzz we craved. Instead, we frequently placed ads in Ohio State's *Lantern,* the student-run daily newspaper that had a circulation of thirty-five thousand at the time, and *The Other Paper,* a weekly periodical that was an alternative voice to the *Dispatch*. These publications spoke directly to our target audience.

We also hand-delivered each new ad as they came out to selected morning and sports radio talk shows. We wanted to place the message in front of what we hoped would be a friendly audience and generate chatter. The ads struck a chord with the radio personalities and were often read verbatim and endorsed by the on-air talent. We were building momentum in key circles. Our unorthodox marketing caught the mainstream media by surprise but was a hit with those "outsiders" with whom we quickly built relationships. We received support in those early days from the *Columbus Guardian*—an alternative weekly; WLVQ's "Wags & Elliott"—the popular morning show team from the classic rock & roll format and their sports reporter Dave "the Rave" Johnson; WNCI's "Morning Zoo"—the No. 1 station in the market and the chief influencer of the "night out" crowd; and alternative radio WWCD 101.

Had we focused on trying to sell the mainstream media on our approach, we would have likely failed. The ads were edgy but in the wrong hands they could have been misconstrued as being negative, giving us another challenge in an already tough market.

Chapter Two

A FIRST-RATE SECOND CHOICE

"Fate laughs at probabilities."

—E. G. Bulwer-Lytton

The funny thing was that we weren't even supposed to be here. We landed in Columbus only after a failed attempt to place the franchise in Cleveland.

The Chill was owned by Horn Chen, a Chicagoan who had a variety of business interests, including real estate. Horn owned an office building on Chicago's Miracle Mile; The Pago Pago Chinese restaurants; the popular Sluggers sports bars (including the most famous, which was located directly across from Wrigley Field); and Eastern Star, the second largest importer of bamboo in the United States. As a lifelong Chicago sports fan, Horn became intrigued by sports ownership. After initially inquiring about the possibility of purchasing the Chicago Blackhawks, he soon realized that major league sports ownership was out of his financial reach. Instead, he began to explore minor league hockey and became convinced that the timing was right for a resurgence of interest in the sport.

Horn set his sights on Indianapolis. He had traveled with his son Chris on numerous youth hockey trips to Carmel (a suburb of Indianapolis) and became familiar with the city. Less than three hours from Chicago, Indianapolis had shown promise as a major league hockey city a decade earlier. The World Hockey Association's Indianapolis Racers had drawn significant fan interest. Unfortunately, Racers owner Nelson Skalbania mismanaged the franchise and ultimately liquidated his greatest asset, a gifted and hyped 17-year-old named Wayne Gretzky. Skalbania sold the future superstar (along with goaltender Eddie Mio and forward Peter Driscoll) to Peter Pocklington, the owner of the Edmonton Oilers, for a combined $700,000. In a classic "what if" tale, the Racers folded shortly after the sale, while a year later the Oilers were absorbed into the National Hockey League as part of 1979 NHL-WHA merger. Led by Gretzky and Mark Messier (who had also launched his professional career with the Racers), the Oilers became a dynasty, winning five Stanley Cup titles over a seven-year span.

The Indianapolis Checkers, of the Central Hockey League and, later, the International Hockey League (IHL), had most recently filled the city's hockey void, but folded in 1987. Horn purchased the rights to the market and he, Ray Compton, and I successfully launched the Ice in 1988–89, becoming the first hockey franchise in city history to turn a profit and winning the Turner Cup (IHL championship trophy) in only our second season. It would be the first of numerous sports ventures for Horn, which over time would include not only the Chill but the Central Hockey League, the Ottawa Rough Riders of the Canadian Football League, and, ultimately, a minority interest in the NHL's Columbus Blue Jackets.

Although a low-profile owner, Horn stayed in regular communication with me while providing his input to the operation. Those who worked for Horn found him to be an honest and fair person, but an extremely frugal owner.

In the spring of 1991, Horn purchased the sixteenth and (what was conveyed at the time to be the) final franchise in the East Coast Hockey League (ECHL) for $100,000. The league's developmental status was akin to the Double-A level in minor league baseball, but unlike baseball, its affiliation with the NHL clubs was far less structured. Most players were free agents and rules limited the number of veterans per team permitted to play in the league for more than three seasons.

I'd built a marvelous trust with Horn in my three years with the Ice, and he offered me the opportunity to run the new ECHL franchise. I happily accepted. We identified Cleveland—a city with strong hockey roots that had tepidly supported an NHL team, the Barons, in the late 1970s—as our primary target (The Barons later merged with the Minnesota North Stars, now the Dallas Stars). Cleveland was a major market and had a thriving youth hockey scene. The city had no minor league team at the time, making it more attractive. Plus, Cleveland State University was building a new 10,000-plus seat arena to host its basketball team and university events. However, it became apparent in our initial meeting with CSU officials that there was no plan to include an ice surface as part of its new facility. Making matters worse, there didn't seem to be anybody authorized at the university who could make decisions, especially in the short time-frame with which we were working.

Rumor had it that the Gund brothers, owners of the NBA's Cavaliers and, formerly, the Barons, had made a substantial donation to Cleveland State on the stipulation that the new arena not be equipped with ice. Supposedly, plans were already in the works for a Downtown arena, and they did not want to have any competition for ice events or hockey.

Before long, I had to be blunt with Horn on two fronts. First, it was clear to me that hockey wasn't happening at Cleveland State. Second, the other major facilities in the city were out of our league from a budgetary perspective. So I advised him that we should begin looking at alternatives.

Within a few days we reviewed a half dozen or so other possible locations. As we looked at and analyzed the pros and cons of each city, we kept coming back to Columbus. I had lived less than three hours away, in Indianapolis, for nine years and knew virtually nothing about the city. I perceived it to be a stepchild to Cleveland and Cincinnati and was astonished to learn the market was as big as it was. Also, Columbus' vibe seemed younger and fresher than either of those cities due to the presence of the university.

Columbus had a passion for the arts, undoubtedly influenced by billionaire Les Wexner, founder of The Limited, an apparel company best known for owning major brands like Victoria's Secret, Lane Bryant, Abercrombie & Fitch, and Bath & Body Works. The city was also the home of several national corporate headquarters, including Battelle Memorial Institute, Wendy's, Bank One (now JP Morgan Chase), and Nationwide Insurance. So why hadn't any minor-league hockey operator gobbled up the rights to Columbus yet? The reason was quite simple: there were no quality facilities.

If we were going to make hockey work in Columbus, we had only two venues to choose from (the convention center or the fairgrounds) because the OSU Ice Rink's capacity was impossibly small for our needs. The Columbus Convention Center had a rectangular hall that seated approximately 5,000. It hosted the occasional basketball game, concert, or trade show. While we liked its Downtown location, the facility had its drawbacks—no ice, for one—and after a couple of meetings with the general manager it became clear they had no serious interest in accommodating us. In other words, thanks, but no thanks.

A deal to play in the Coliseum wasn't a given by any means, either. The Coliseum was built at the end of World War I, in 1917, to be precise, making it the oldest professional hockey arena in North America. To be kind, it had seen better days and didn't exactly evoke images of fun. It was more of a place to bring your prized cow in hopes of winning a blue ribbon at the Ohio State Fair. It was not a venue in which we could effectively market ourselves as the local representatives of a cool new sport.

The Coliseum was a symbol of what made Columbus unremarkable in those days. For our younger audience it defined boring. Older, more affluent patrons deemed it beneath them. Still, we saw beauty in the Coliseum.[2] Okay, it's amazing what you will see when you have no other choice. Yes, the locker rooms and restrooms were inadequate, the hallways were way too narrow, there were no real amenities to speak of, and the parking situation was abysmal. But once you were in your seat, you were treated to perfect sightlines. With just over fifteen rows of seating, no fan was far from the action, a critical attribute for a sport that really resonates with fans the closer they get to the ice. The facility had a low, arching roof that amplified the sound. Plus there was ample space at the top of the seating sections and in the corners for standing room. Despite the many challenges the Coliseum presented, we

---

[2] In November 2019, the Ohio Expo Center would spend $5.4 million to upgrade Taft Coliseum, including a new ice system—the first renovations since 1985.

believed that if we could pull a few thousand fans into the barn, it would feel full. And if we could pack the place, it had the potential to rock.

A big problem, though, was that as one of the only decent-sized facilities in the market, the Coliseum was booked solid with events. With the Coliseum's dance card full, fairgrounds officials would have to be willing to shoehorn the dates we needed to play if we wanted to have anything resembling a home schedule.

Initially, fairgrounds officials were not only pleasant enough but were open to working out a deal. Still, it was clear that numerous steps had to be taken before we'd be able to secure a contract. First, the Coliseum had an ice system that hadn't been used in more than a dozen years. We offered to bring in a portable one, but they were skeptical. The dasher boards and glass, while meeting minimum standards, were rickety and inadequate. Neither Horn nor the fairgrounds were willing to invest in new boards for an upstart franchise, so we'd have to live with what we had. Also, due to conflicting events, there would be no ice availability for training camp, meaning we'd have to take it to Indianapolis.

The challenges continued from there. We'd have no home dates in October because of the nearly month-long All-American Quarter Horse Congress. We'd also play no home games in March during at least our first two seasons because of the Ohio High School Athletic Association boys basketball district and regional tournaments, and we would lose any potential April playoff dates due to the presence of the Aladdin Shrine Circus, a fixture at the Coliseum since 1950. Additionally, an existing tenant, the minor league Columbus Horizon of the Continental Basketball Association, had priority. Adding it all up, in year one we'd be forced to play four games elsewhere in the state just to be able to play our required number of 32 home games. This wasn't going to be easy, especially considering our short timetable to both launch the franchise and make our preparations for the upcoming season.

It was crazy to think we could pull this off but we were naïve (stupid?) enough to think that we could, and we moved to strike a deal. Alan Karpick, Larry Lane, and I set up shop in an extended-stay hotel in the northwest Columbus suburb of Dublin until we were able to secure an office. We spent May and most of June diligently doing our homework, trying to identify key media and potential sponsors. We prepared for an introductory press conference and the subsequent season ticket sales rollout.

Reports of hockey's return to Columbus were periodically showing up in the *Dispatch*. We agreed in principle to the contractual terms of the deal, but fairgrounds officials began to drag their feet, citing their continued concern over the viability of the portable ice system. Knowing we were running out of time, we took our first major calculated risk, and, without the blessing of the fairgrounds hierarchy, we called a press conference to introduce the franchise.

The team was officially announced on July 25, 1991, a little more than two months before training camp and three months prior to our home opener. To the surprise of all the invited guests in attendance at Damon's Clubhouse restaurant that day, the room was packed with more than 150 media, targeted sponsors, and ad agency executives. Our advance hard work had paid off in a big way, or maybe we were fortunate that it was a slow news day. The turnout surprised even us. We'd clearly created a curiosity factor and couldn't have been more thrilled.

There was one other group on hand—officials from the fairgrounds. We figured that if they saw all the support for and curiosity about us that they would be more inclined to close the deal.

The press conference was a straightforward event, without the stunts for which we'd later become known. The highlight was unveiling the Chill name. The team name, suggested by Amy Karpick and Gigi Kruza—Alan's wife and Larry's fiancée, respectively—could have been considered soft or trendy, in the vein of the NBA's Miami Heat and Orlando Magic, which had launched just three years prior. That was a concern, but in the end we found it to be the right choice to match the silver and black color scheme. Like Columbus, Chill started with the letter C. It easily rolled from the tongue and suggested winter sports.

After announcing the name, we unveiled a jersey mock-up, which, like the name, was well-received. The energy in the room gave a not-so-subtle hint to key community leaders that there might be something different about this minor league team. For now, we had those folks' attention, but we knew we would have to continue to earn their respect.

The interest from fairgrounds officials percolated shortly after our unveiling, and we arranged to roll out a demonstration of the portable ice-making equipment for their operational staff. Once they were satisfied, a deal to play in the Coliseum was at last finalized.

Our next public announcement, on August 1, was the hiring of Terry Ruskowski as our head coach. "Roscoe," as he was known, was the perfect fit. His infectious and charming personality included a unique talent for telling jokes that a fifth grader would find infantile. Yet he could make people laugh and instantly proved to be a person we could craft our message around. He loved the limelight and we pushed him to the forefront every chance we had.

Roscoe was a well-respected, fifteen-year WHA and NHL veteran, a tenacious player known for his grit and leadership, if not his scoring touch. He remains the only player in major professional history to captain four different clubs.[3] The team he would assemble in the next couple months would be built in his image.

More than a Coach

The lexicon of one Terry W. "Roscoe" Ruskowski, of Prince Albert, Saskatchewan, could be colorful, biting, direct, and rarely dull. In other words, he was the perfect choice to be the first coach of the Columbus Chill, even though the former NHL and WHA standout was a sub .500 coach in the previous two seasons—his first behind the bench—for the junior-level Western Hockey League's Saskatoon Blades.

"He doesn't know if the puck is stuffed or pumped," Roscoe once said, describing one player's intellect.

Roscoe, who as a player was known to drop the gloves occasionally and was a Houston Aeros teammate of Gordie Howe, had been a captain at all his stops and won admirers for his pugnacious play. He would bring that same attitude to Columbus, but his connections

---

[3] Ruskowski was the captain for the Chicago Blackhawks, Los Angeles Kings, Pittsburgh Penguins, and Minnesota North Stars.

throughout the hockey world and his infectious personality were exactly what were needed to draw attention to a new hockey team in a market dominated by Ohio State athletics.

"Sir, can I get a penalty for thinking?" he once said to a referee. "No? Good, because I think you stink tonight."

For newcomers to the game, Roscoe's irreverent demeanor marked a welcome departure from Columbus' stodgy, prevailing sports culture, and he did his part by being painstakingly patient in explaining the nuances of hockey to them.

Old-timers around town who had followed the city's previous pro hockey incarnations from the late 1960s and 1970s (Checkers, Seals, and Owls) saw a bit of Moe Bartoli in Roscoe.

Bartoli was a cigar-smoking, tough-as-nails player who later worked in the front offices of all three organizations and possessed a personality as rich and multi-hued as the sport coats typically worn by legendary Columbus NBC sports anchor Jimmy Crum, his longtime friend.

"Congratulations," Bartoli once said to a referee after a game. "I heard you were voted second-best ref in the league. Everyone else tied for first."

Roscoe was still raw as a coach, but he grew in the role with the Chill. He hated making training camp cuts, knowing he could be the one to end a player's dream. He demanded intensity and loyalty. He went to the mat for his players and he expected as much in return.

"Is he tough?" Roscoe once said when asked to evaluate a player. "He couldn't lick his [own] lips."

What made Roscoe so unique was his willingness to put up with a lot of unusual situations and promotional requests despite a small minor league salary. There were those 6 a.m. practices at the OSU Ice Rink the first two seasons, and the extra visits to TV and radio stations to plug the next promotion, and, oh, yes, the team. But Roscoe took it all in stride and dove headfirst into the community. His players followed his example—no hospital visit, classroom outing or hockey clinic was too small or unnecessary as long as Roscoe was in charge.

He devoted his life to hockey but he was a family man first to his wife and two daughters, though they, too, occasionally bore the brunt of his humor.

"My wife asked me if I loved her more than hockey," he quipped. "I said no, but I like you better than baseball."

You'd think Roscoe, the epitome of the western Canadian player who regularly engaged in fisticuffs, would be set in his ways but over time he evolved as a coach, welcoming skilled college players who never dropped the gloves and even Russian goalies at a time when athletes from over there were still a novelty in North American leagues.

His teams progressed from slow and prodding to skilled and skating and by his third season the Chill won 41 of its 68 games.

Roscoe was laughing most of the way. To avoid cussing he would say things like, "for suck's sake" or "son of a sea biscuit."

"He looks like he ran into a wall doing the 50-yard dash on a 40-yard track," Roscoe once said of a pug-nosed player from Dayton.

Maybe because the then-mustachioed Roscoe bore an uncanny resemblance to Cheech Marin, of the comedy act Cheech and Chong, he usually found humor the best method to make his point.

"He'd foul up a two-car funeral procession down a one-way street," he once joked about one of his mistake-prone charges.

That was Roscoe. Rarely subtle, but always entertaining.

One of Roscoe's early moves was to bring equipment manager/trainer Billy Brown to Columbus. Roscoe knew "Uptown" from his WHA days and the two had an immediate connection. They were fire and ice. Brown, from Birmingham, Alabama, had a laconic nature that tended to counter Roscoe's rabid intensity. When things got rough—as they often did during the start up of the franchise—it was Brown's southern drawl that calmed the situation, albeit, only temporarily. "Itl be aww rite" was his catch phrase, and he took it to heart. The thin framed chain smoker with a buzz cut had the ability to sleep through any commotion on the bus, a critical attribute for someone whose job required him to be the first one at the rink in the morning and the last to leave after a game.

Roscoe's first player signee was Jason "Smurf" Christie, who had played for him previously in major junior hockey at Saskatoon. A Ruskowski clone on the ice, with his aggressive, hard-nosed style, the 5-foot-8, 180-pounder with long, curly blonde hair would quickly become a marketer's dream.

Now we he had a coach and a player to serve as the faces of our franchise. Internally, the work continued to build our front office staff. We added Butler University graduate Brent Maurer, another of our Indiana sports marketing contingent, as public relations director, as well as four Ohioans—Ken Cohn, Dave Peck, Ron Rogers, and Sheryl Kolb—to complete the staff. Three of our staff were sports management graduates: Alan (graduate degree from West Virginia) Ken (Indiana) and Dave (Bowling Green). As a sports management graduate from Biscayne College, myself, I had a propensity to hire from that model.

Staffing correctly is essential to the success of any business. With the right people to develop, implement, and roll out our program, our organization had a chance to be successful, and while we were incredibly young we felt we had assembled a talented and committed group. Everyone was a promoter or salesman in one form or another. Other than Alan and I, who were both thirty-one, everyone was in their twenties and mirrored the audience we were trying to reach. This was a media-savvy group that grew up in the *Saturday Night Live* and David Letterman culture. My favorite book, *Veeck—as in*

Wreck, was required reading to establish the kind of push-the-envelope sports promotions mindset that I wanted.

Alan provided a critical counterbalance to that style. He was the rational one who prevented us from getting too carried away at times. "Thank God he was there to slow us down," said Maurer.

Who knows what might have happened if he wasn't? Maybe the Chill would have eventually vanished like so many of its predecessors.

Chapter Three

NAYSAYERS BE DAMNED

"I'm for the dreamers. The only really important things in history have been started by the dreamers. They never know what can't be done."

—Bill Veeck

As we moved toward Opening Night, we learned that not everyone was enamored with our marketing efforts.

A week or two before our first game in the Coliseum I received a call from a marketing professor at Ohio State, who proceeded to rip me for the print campaign we were running in its school newspaper, *The Lantern*. The professor was quick to explain that he was an expert on the subject and that not only was our approach classless, it would backfire. I tried to explain the tongue-in-cheek concept to him, but he wasn't hearing any of it. So, I decided to hear him out and try to take in his viewpoint. We knew our campaign was walking a fine line and needed to be aware of any potential backlash so that we could prepare ourselves to deal with it.

The professor then said something that nearly made me fall out of my chair. He said the ads had become a point of discussion and contention in his class and that "everyone on campus was talking about it." I perked up and countered by questioning his logic. "You're telling me that everyone is talking about it and that's a bad thing?" I said.

In the end we agreed to disagree. I jumped off the phone and grabbed the guys in the office and recounted the conversation to them. "Am I missing something?" I asked.

Perhaps even an expert marketer could be wrong. This was, to us, a clear sign that our message was getting through to the students.

My conversation with the OSU professor confirmed that our strategy to keep the print campaign more narrowly targeted was the right one. Yes, the Chill faced plenty of apathy, but we were confident that we could present a compelling product. Overcoming obstacles was nothing new for me. Earlier in my career, I helped rebuild the fan base for the Indiana Pacers—a franchise that, in the early 1980s, was on death's door. I had just graduated from the Sports Management program at Biscayne College (Miami, Florida) and was thrilled to be joining a favorite team of my youth—the former three-time champions of the American Basketball Association—only to feel like I had just walked into a disaster area. The Pacers were terrible and fan morale was at an all-time low. Worse than being hated, the fans just didn't care.

A few weeks after I arrived, absentee owner Frank Mariani conducted a fire sale, dealing three of the team's top players for cash to pay bills.[4] Ownership was in the process of dumping the franchise any way it could. The rumor circuit included daily stories of an impending move. The Pacers

---

[4] On September 22, 1982, the Pacers traded power forward Tom Owens (averaged 10.5 ppg and 5 rpg during the 1981–82 season) to the Detroit Pistons for a 1984 second-round pick (Greg Wiltjer), One month later (September 22), they traded small forward Louis Orr (11.5 ppg and 4.1 rpg) to the New York Knicks for a 1983 second-round pick (Scooter McCray). On December 31 (two months into the season), they traded shooting guard Johnny Davis (17 ppg, 4.2 apg) to the Atlanta Hawks for a 1983 second-round pick (Jim Thomas).

won 20 and lost 62 (including three 12-game losing streaks) my first season in Indianapolis (the 1982–83 season), and average attendance dwindled to fewer than 5,000 per game, a figure that included the team's 1,200 season ticket-holders.[5] The Pacers topped if off by losing the "Race for Ralph"—a coin flip in the NBA lottery between the league's two worst teams (the Pacers and Houston Rockets) for the right to draft 7'4" college superstar Ralph Sampson from the University of Virginia.

Yes, it's fair to say we had a few problems.

With a front office workforce of only a dozen or so people, the Pacers were staffed like a minor league team, not an NBA organization. Under the astute marketing leadership of Assistant GM and my mentor Ray Compton, we attempted to change the mood of the fan base by initially taking the focus off basketball. In Veeck's style, we pulled in paying customers anyway we could dream up and over the next few years attached ourselves to other still-popular entertainment acts of the day (postgame shows by the Beach Boys, the Temptations and the Four Tops, Three Dog Night etc.) to fill the building while we rebuilt the season-ticket base. We also sold hope for the future. We had accumulated a few high draft choices and pushed the idea that we were committed to building a good entertaining product that had a bit of a Barnum & Bailey feel, but were equally committed to repositioning the team for long-term success on the floor. The franchise was finally placed on firm financial footing when Pacers General Manager Bob Salyers brokered a deal to sell the team to Indianapolis-based shopping mall developers Mel and Herb Simon. With new ownership came additional staff and the resources to legitimately rebuild the franchise. Despite averaging 24 wins and 58 losses over my first four seasons, we were able to nearly triple our attendance numbers with a focus on quality

---

[5] The 1982–83 Pacers were second to last in attendance (188,642), just ahead of the Cleveland Cavaliers (160,537).

entertainment, creative marketing, and proactive sales initiatives. Years later, during the Reggie Miller era, the Pacers would rise to prominence and compete for an NBA title.

After the Chill's introductory press conference, the majority of the mainstream media still wasn't much interested or impressed. When we announced the team nickname, veteran local sportscasting icon Jimmy Crum, of WCMH-TV NBC 4, said to his viewers, "Chill?" with a quizzical look.

Though we had made an impact in certain circles, it was clear we had plenty of work to do to build brand awareness and secure cultural acceptance by the entire market. Our coverage on local television news remained sparse throughout the summer. After one interview with sports anchor Barry Katz, of WBNS-TV (CBS), he turned to me and said, "I got you some pub" in a condescending tone. He felt he had done us a favor and that was enough exposure for now. All of us would use moments like these as motivation.

Renowned Columbus sports personality George Lehner, of WTVN 610 AM, the top news and talk radio station in the market, dismissed hockey by saying, "if it doesn't have a ball, it's not a sport."

"To our core target, George symbolized the status quo, so we felt like comments like these were playing right into our hands," Karpick said in an interview for the book. "The audience we were going after ran counter to the mainstream. They saw us as a breath of fresh air."

Resisting the urge to fire back at Lehner right away, our group wisely showed restraint—an attribute that came in handy in the early days. We were patient and mature enough not to call him on it right away. Our response had to be well-timed, subtle, and with some humor. After all, it made no sense to make an enemy of someone we thought stood a chance to be an ally down the road. Our opportunity finally came when we placed his condescending quote in our game program with a giant "thumbs down" next to it. We took a shot across the bow from the media establishment and hockey fans were vocal in defending their sport, and Lehner quickly backed off from his dismissing position.

Because we never exposed the established media for being lukewarm in their initial response to us, Lehner, Katz, Crum, and the *Dispatch* soon became the biggest proponents of pro hockey in Columbus by giving the sport, and us specifically, extensive and serious coverage. After we enjoyed some early success, the choice to not berate them privately or publicly was crucial. We worked to win people over one at a time. However, with the old guard, many times it felt like an uphill battle.

Kinsley Nyce, a local attorney who later became the owner of the Columbus Xoggz of the United States Interregional Soccer League (USISL), invited Roscoe and Chill communications director Brent Maurer to speak at a Rotary-type dinner in German Village, just south of downtown Columbus. In the middle of Roscoe's presentation, one of the club members vocalized his complete loathing for hockey, describing the game as nothing but "glorified violence."

"Roscoe took the comments in stride and explained that fighting is an accepted tradition of the sport," said Maurer in an interview for the book. "The guy wouldn't have any part of it. He was so unrelenting that Nyce, embarrassed for the club, finally stood up and threatened to revoke the guy's membership. Then, at his own personal expense, Nyce reached in his own pocket and invited everyone else in the club to Opening Night because he 'believed in what the Chill was doing.'"

Even our partners at the fairgrounds had set the bar low.

A Brief History of Failed Franchises in Columbus

Columbus wasn't so much a graveyard as a minefield for pro franchises before and during the eight-year run of the Chill. That's why cynicism, even more so than apathy, greeted the news on July 25, 1991, that another minor league team was coming to town.

Oh, boy. Hadn't the owners studied history? And if they did, were they about to repeat it?

Forgive the few passionate hockey fans in the city for wondering if the ice was going to be pulled from under them a fourth time.

Even the *Dispatch* was cognizant of how difficult a task it was to make hockey work in a non-traditional hockey town. Exactly one month prior to the Chill's coming out party, the paper heralded an agreement between fairgrounds officials and the yet-unnamed franchise for games in the Coliseum by running a box on the front page of the sports section entitled "Franchise flops" and listed all the previous failed hockey ventures.

The first was the Checkers of the International Hockey League, a Chicago Blackhawks affiliate that lasted from the 1966–67 season through 1969–70.

Perhaps the initial sign of trouble came when the Blackhawks brought stars Bobby Hull and Stan Mikita to town for Columbus' first pro hockey game, an exhibition against the Checkers held in the Coliseum in September 1966. Moe Bartoli, who became legendary in Columbus as a player, coach and general manager while working for all three organizations prior to the Chill, remembered that the ice was barely playable and was down to the concrete in some spots because it didn't freeze. Hull, Mikita and their Blackhawks teammates wanted no part of the event but were convinced to play when the periods were shortened to 10 minutes—not that most in the sellout crowd knew the difference, Bartoli recalled.

The Checkers folded after only four seasons, but Columbus was without a team for only one year because mercurial Oakland A's (and the NHL's California Golden Seals) owner Charlie O. Finley bought the rights to the franchise and placed an IHL expansion team in the Coliseum, replete with white skates in the fashion of the footwear worn by his World Series champion baseball teams. To say the Golden Seals two years under Finley 's guidance were awful would be a gross injustice to the word awful.

He might have known baseball, but Finley did not stock the Golden Seals with talent for Bartoli to coach. They finished 15–55–2 in their first season.

"That's the longest year I ever put in, in my life," said Bartoli. Little did he know, it would get worse.

The next season the "Baby Seals" finished 10–62–2 and in one stretch won two of 49 games.

Attendance would hover around 1,200 for weekday games and double for weekend dates, except when Dayton or Toledo would come to town and with the help of their fans, the gate would be boosted even further. Fortunately, Indianapolis real estate developer and mortgage banker Al Savill rescued the franchise and the renamed Owls wore uniforms similar to the red and black of the Blackhawks for their run from 1973–74 to 1976–77.

The Owls became a winning franchise, hosted the IHL All-Star Game in 1974 and drew respectable crowds, but ultimately their fate was sealed in the spring of 1977 when the team, despite having home-ice advantage, was forced to play five of seven playoff games against Toledo on the road—including the series-clinching loss—because of scheduling conflicts at the Coliseum.

Savill, who was disappointed that the Franklin County Commissioners had spent millions to renovate a ballpark for a new International League baseball team (the Clippers) that year while no one seemed to want to help him, moved the Owls to Dayton in a dispute over the rental agreement and dates.

"We always drew well," Bartoli said later. "Even our last year, we had about 3,200 a game."

But it wasn't enough to save the franchise, and the Owls joined the list of failed Columbus pro ventures over the years, such as the Minks and Quest (women's basketball); Comets and Horizon (men's basketball); Magic and Xoggz (outdoor soccer); Invaders and Capitals (indoor soccer); All-Americans (men's softball); Redbirds and Jets (baseball); Hawks (roller hockey); Panhandles and Glory (football); Thunderbolts (arena football); and Landsharks (indoor lacrosse), among others.

Despite the Owls' demise, one must applaud the vision of Savill, who died in 1989. In a September 1973 interview with the *Dispatch*—a month before the Owls ever played a game—he said, "I've told Mayor (Tom) Moody that Columbus should be a major league town but we'll need a new arena. For me, I'd like to see the Owls as a steppingstone to an NHL franchise. I'm hopeful we can land a major league club here but it can't be done without the facilities."[6] The highs and lows of Columbus pro hockey pre-Chill were captured in International Incidents by Cincinnati writer, producer and director Eric Weltner (Twitter account is @eweltner), who was raised in the Columbus suburb of Gahanna during the IHL era.[7]

To ensure that the Coliseum was operationally as fan friendly as possible, we walked the facility about a month before the opener with Charlie Wilson, the facility's operational point person, and made several small suggestions for improvements.

While walking the back concourse, we noticed an area that was shut off to fans because it was adjacent to the team and referee locker rooms and served as the entryway for officials and players to the ice.

---

[6] The highs and lows of Columbus pro hockey pre-Chill were captured in the film *International Incidents* by Cincinnati writer, producer, and director Eric Weltner (@eweltner), who was raised in the Columbus suburb of Gahanna during the IHL era. The official *International Incidents* Facebook page is: www.facebook.com /Internationalincident

[7] *International Incidents* can also be found on their IMDb page.

I questioned Wilson about traffic flow by asking, "What happens when you have 5,000 or 6,000 people in the building? How will that work?"

Wilson's response was, "We don't expect you to ever have 5,000 or 6,000 people."

Wilson struck a nerve and I was hopping mad, which was a little out of character for me. I was growing tired of all the comparisons to the previous failures and all the doubters and said, "You better be prepared on November 1, because we're going to sell this building out."

My comments only served to piss him off and, of course, come Opening Night, the Coliseum was in no way prepared for a standing-room only crowd. In fact, they fell far short of even being ready to put on a hockey game. Our concessionaire, Becky Kaltenbach, was nicer about it. She delivered a standard line we'd heard all summer from potential corporate partners and city leaders—"good luck to you"—all the while thinking that what we were doing had no shot of working. It was no surprise, then, that they weren't ready for the crowd on Opening Night, either.

In the end we got the last laugh . . . kind of.

Chapter Four

IT'S NOT YOUR COMMON COLD

"The noblest art is that of making others happy."

— P. T. Barnum

The Chill intended to deliver fun and the unexpected, pure and simple. To get there and to silence the naysayers, we first had to hire a team of people who believed in our mission before we'd be able to consistently convey its message to the outside world. "I was a believer. As a baseball fan, I really 'got' the Veeck approach," said Brent Maurer, our key point person with the media.

Our basic formula was to combine two parts humor with one part shock and awe. Raising eyebrows once in a while and generating talk was a must. Traditions? Forget 'em. Nothing was sacred as far as we were concerned. We were looking for water cooler talk. In retrospect, if we did have a mantra it was to amuse, inspire, and delight the paying customer. Ultimately, we understood that the Chill brand was defined by the fan experience. Our goal was to exceed their expectations.

Our slogan that first season was "It's not your common cold." We were striving to be different. Our approach wasn't for traditionalists and we were well aware of that. We even considered naming the team the Knights of Columbus or the Lizard Kings—a tribute to rock star Jim Morrison—to make us stand out even more. But after seeing horror in Alan Karpick's and Larry Lane's eyes, I realized that those ideas were a little much (a few years later, though, when given the opportunity by Horn Chen to assist in setting up the Jacksonville, Florida, franchise in the ECHL, Larry, who had been my protégé in Indianapolis, worked up the nerve to use Lizard Kings).

"A handful of us were trying to form this piece of clay and make it work," said Karpick. "We could do whatever we wanted and were not afraid to try something new—nor did we even consider [the fact that] this could fail. That was key."

If we at the Chill could come out of the gates and prove that our event could live up to the hype created by our ad campaign, then we knew we'd produce the kind of word-of-mouth chatter that would help us to continue building momentum. While we were expending a tremendous amount of energy preparing for our home opener vs. the Erie Panthers, we also built a promotions plan that would take us through New Year's Eve. We had to get through the first six weeks of the season while simultaneously planning for January and February. That wasn't the usual way we liked to do business, but it was a necessity considering all that we were facing. For months our group was working twelve to fifteen hours a day to make up as much ground as possible, but none of us were sure if we we'd make it to Opening Night.

The promotional nights we planned were great and were an essential first step toward beginning to develop a solid fan base that would help carry us forward. Endorsements from those early adopters were critical to our ability to spread a positive vibe to the masses.

Considering our condensed time frame following the inception of the team in late July, we were thrilled to sell more than 1,200 season tickets that first year. It was a very good start and provided us with the crucial up-front operational revenue necessary to sustain our cash flow for at least a few months. Chen was vigilant with the purse strings, and I knew he'd pull funding for our sideshow antics if we weren't generating a profit. Nobody else was doing this style of promotion and advertising. We were breaking new ground. The edgy promotion and advertising campaign we employed bought us credibility with fans, media, and corporate partners. The promotions drew the fans in, but follow-up was the key. Once we collected their data, our account executives, Ken Cohn and Dave Peck, did everything they could to convert them into season ticket-holders. Ticket sales are the bread and butter of any minor league sports business and season-ticket holders form the backbone of any franchise. Building a season-ticket base was our number-one long-term priority.

Promotions

It wasn't enough to throw the doors open and expect the masses to walk through based on the product alone.

Unfortunately, that was still the mindset of many operators of professional sports teams in the early '90s as the Chill undertook the gigantic task of attracting fans to an aging building to view a sport unpopular to many.

Job No. 1 was to give them a reason to come and, more importantly, to return.

Just as the number of cable stations were expanding at the start of the decade, the consumer had an increasing number of options for entertainment, and the Chill contended with that new dynamic.

There was no better (or cheaper, mind you) advertisement for the Chill than word of mouth. "Did you see what they did at last night's game? What will they think of next?"

Mayhem and madness were at the core of a mindset permeated in the Chill's advertising, in-game experience, and game programming. Promotions were created to purposely generate talk and spark a jump at the turnstiles. Keeping the audience off-balance was a priority.

Dick Vitale Meets Hockey; Hanson Brothers (from *Slap Shot*, not the lame pop band); Jim Craig, the goalie for the 1980 "Miracle on

Ice" USA Olympic hockey team; Debbie Dunning, the *Tool Time* girl from ABC's *Home Improvement*; Larry "Bud" Mellman of *Late Show with David Letterman* fame; Dallas Cowboys Cheerleaders; Mr. T; and the Flock of Seagulls band highlighting an '80s New Year's Eve bash were just some of the special appearances that were fitting for the moment.

A few were designed to tug at the heart strings—Kimberly Clark baby races (to win a college scholarship) and Weddings on Ice (seven couples actually married on Valentine's Day).

Some were just flat out fun—Low Dough Carload Night (eleven people fitting in a Chevette for $10 admission was the most impressive) and using Rock 'Em Sock 'Em Robots to describe fights between periods on Chill television broadcasts.

Others pushed the envelope—Divorce Night; Leak on Blue (a tribute to the Michigan-OSU rivalry); Headlocks & Wedlocks (combining wrestling and marriage); and the Mr. Chill competition (winner stunning even us by wearing nothing but a jock strap). We'll leave the rest to your imagination.

The youthful promotional team had a feel for habitually catching magic in the bottle.

For instance, when David Letterman moved from NBC to CBS in 1993, Bangladesh-native shop operators Mujibar and Sirajul became regular characters and instant celebrities on the *Late Show*. The Chill paid tribute to their "cross country tour" and replicated their most well-known Letterman moment—trout fishing in Montana—by having Mujibar and Sirajul—while wearing their signature suit and tie—but this time in hip-waders, fish for and catch a live trout out of a kids' wading pool during an intermission. The duo later got the crowd going in a stirring performance of "YMCA," while wearing their "Storm Blows" t-shirts mocking our arch rival Toledo Storm.

The appearance paid further dividends when Sirajul was later spotted on the *Late Show* wearing his Chill jersey at Letterman's annual Christmas party and skate at Rockefeller Center.

Through it all, the front office was not above bait and switch tactics.

When the James Bond series returned to the screen after a six-year absence in 1995 with *GoldenEye*, fans were promised an appearance by Bond himself. Sean Connery, Roger Moore, or Pierce Brosnan, are you kidding? There was no chance. Instead, the Chill capitalized on the hype by digging up George Lazenby, the forgotten actor whose sole claim to fame was playing Bond in the 1969 film *On Her Majesty's Secret Service* before falling off the face of the earth. In a favorite theatre-of-the-absurd moment, Lazenby was paraded onto the ice in the character's famous Aston Martin DB5 while Bond-themed music played. It turns out that the Chill must have been on to something because a couple of nights later, Lazenby was on Letterman explaining what happened to his career in the twenty-five years that followed his most celebrated role.

Some promotions took on a life of their own, and audience participation was always encouraged.

When comedian/singer Heywood Banks performed after one game, a fan who didn't quite understand his act shouted out "Free Bird," trying to coax him into playing the famed Lynyrd Skynyrd song. Instead, Banks shot his middle finger to the stunned fan and said, "Here you go buddy, no charge."

The Chill had a seemingly endless vault of promotional ideas. Some were classic, some were funny, but others were just flat out embarrassing.

Case in point: After unsuccessfully trying to book a Blues Brothers tribute act for our third year home opener, their management sold the idea of a substitute—the Piano Guys—claiming "they knocked 'em dead in San Jose." However, while they may have been great for children's birthday parties, the Piano Guys were a little too "soft" for the Coliseum crowd. They were pulled after ten minutes to save their hides.

The Chill audience could be quite unforgiving when presented with a dud. On another occasion, WNCI's Morning Zoo producer Merlin unsuccessfully tried to duplicate one of his standard bar promotions, "Simon Says," with 99 on-ice contestants. When he failed to get the expected first-round exit of 90 percent of the participants, he was in deep trouble and within a minute was met with a heavy chant of "boring . . . boring . . . boring" until he sheepishly exited the ice.

Fortunately, flops were rare and there were several attention-getting promotions right from the start of the franchise to further build the Chill brand, which even included a kids' promotion by bringing in the popular Teenage Mutant Ninja Turtles.

On that gig, the Turtles' agency (yes, it sounds absurd) sent one actor and the Chill had to provide the other three people to wear the costumes. Struggling to find pseudo Ninjas, Brian Sullivan, the head of the security team, volunteered a few people to fill the roles.

The front office assumed he would get some of his staff, but that was not the case. Little did the kids enjoying the visit by their beloved TV characters realize, the three Turtles we provided were professional talent from a gentlemen's club. Yes, they were being hugged and embraced by . . . you guessed it . . . strippers.

The irony of the first kids' promotion being executed by some of Columbus' finest "talent" seemed to be right in step with the way things were going.

Expect the unexpected.

The lineup of promotions helped attract new fans and the in-game rituals formed a bond among regulars. The Chill were breaking through to new audiences on a grander scale and creating an emotional connection to the team. With a core audience in tow, it was now time to reach out to the entire city. To do that, we needed to extend an olive branch to Columbus' king of sports.

On Friday, November 20, 1992, the Chill was anointed from up on high when they secured the Ohio State University Alumni Pep Band for an impromptu, two-minute performance as they marched through the Coliseum in the middle of a Chill game the night before the annual, season-ending Ohio State vs. Michigan football game.

Their appearance caught fans off guard, as the band marched in from the east entrance, split into two groups covering both sides of the Coliseum, and then went out through the west doors. The Best Damn Band in the Land were gone almost as quickly as they arrived, but the fans erupted in a joyous moment that further cemented the fact that hockey was now becoming a fabric of the community.

Opening Night was designed to define and showcase our "alternative" approach. We tried a few things that ran counter to hockey tradition. We wanted to be different right out of the gate and that started with hiring jazz saxophonist Joel Johanson to play the National Anthem. We also planned an elaborate major league style player introduction that involved thundering music, smoke, and spotlights. We brought in our old friend "Bill the Beerman," the raucous Seattle-based vendor/cheerleader, who while not necessarily credited with inventing the wave certainly popularized the fad with his over-the-top exuberance. Also, to add a touch of class to the event, we secured Jeff LaBrake and Maradith Feinberg, the national figure-skating pairs champions, to perform between periods. This would help distinguish us from other minor league ventures, but we knew we had to add a "Chill style" promotion to top it all off.

Alan, Larry, and I visited with our ad agency, Concepts Marketing Group, and asked them for help in creating something even more offbeat for the Morning Zoo on WNCI (97.9 FM).

We made a continuous, conscious effort to distinguish ourselves from past, ill-fated Columbus franchises. We knew that most everyone we met probably figured that we were doomed for failure, so we did everything we could to let people know that our approach was not business as usual.

First, in our ad buys with radio stations, we didn't go in with our hands out. According to the media outlets we worked with, unlike those before us, we paid cash for an ad schedule with the stations we worked with promotionally. As simple and obvious as it sounds, those ad buys sent a clear message that we were truly partnering with the radio station. In the era prior to Clear Channel's (now iHeartMedia, Inc.) global radio domination, you'd be amazed by how much goodwill they engendered with everyone at the stations, from the account executives to the general managers. The buys signaled to them that we understood that they were in business, too. Secondly, we came into meetings with ideas that fit their personalities as much as ours. If we pushed their hot buttons on promotions, we knew they would be successful, both for us and the stations.

WNCI reached the trendy end of our demographic and it was critical that we get their buy-in. We met with the key station personnel and the morning show talent—Dave Kaelin, John Cline, and Shawn Ireland—and pitched them our entire Opening Night concept. The plan was for them to lead the "Chill style" promotion—three fans using giant sling shots to shoot frozen Cornish game hens at a goal during one of the breaks between periods, and for the winning fan to walk away with $5,000 in cash. Concepts' Mark LeClerc built a specific radio commercial around a fanbuilding and testing his slingshot for the opportunity to win the prize. The hilarious spot promoted the contest as "something to break the monotony between fights."

The promotion focused on fun, not hockey. The value of the prize and other Opening Night elements were significant by anyone's standards and took a big chunk of our marketing and promotions budget, but we knew we had to make a splash and leave an indelible mark right away.

The Morning Zoo ate it up.

Catch the Chill...
and win $5,000 at Opening Night!

Opening Night 1991 - Columbus Chill vs. Erie Panthers · Friday · Nov. 1 · 8 pm · Ohio State Fairgrounds Coliseum

Professional hockey comes to Columbus!
Winter starts Friday night. That's when the Chill make their Columbus debut. Exciting, hard-hitting professional hockey at the Fairgrounds Coliseum. And one thing's certain: It's not your common cold.

Why chickens? For $5,000, why not?
Here's something to break the monotony between fights. Twenty lucky fans will use a giant slingshot to shoot frozen chickens at the goal for a $5,000 grand prize. You want culture, try PBS.

The party before the party.
Come early for the 6 o'clock Pregame Party featuring food, drink, and live music from Men of Leisure.

Tickets are $9 for adults, $5 for kids 17 and under and college students with valid I.D.s. Tickets available at all TicketMaster Ticket Centers or charge by phone at ███████ The Rhodes Center box office located at the Ohio State Fairgrounds on the north side of 17th Avenue is open Monday - Friday, 11:30 am to 5:30 pm.

For more information, call 488-████

Wear white on Opening Night.
It's an Opening Night tradition. Okay, maybe not, but traditions have to start somewhere, right? Search your closet, scour your drawers, and find some white to wear. It'll be a tribal bonding kinda thing. And we'll all be a little bit better for it. Promise.

Yes, they'll do that spin-'til-you're-dizzy thing at the end of their routine.
World class figure skaters Jeff LaBrake and Maradith Feinberg will entertain during one of the period breaks.

CHILL ™
COLUMBUS

"The Chill came to us and pitched stuff because they were—and they didn't make any bones about it—barnstorming-type entertainment," said WNCI's Kaelin of those early meetings. "They didn't mind whatsoever to lead by promotion first, sports second. That was a good way to sum it up. I don't know if it came out of anybody's mouths but the vibe I got was: 'Hey, the circus is in town. This circus just happens to play hockey.'"

Our strategy with stations was simple: always design promotions that fit the format. This idea clearly did that. Sometimes we'd come into promotions meetings with one idea and then, after an hour of brainstorming that entertained and invited absurdity, we'd come out of it with something entirely different. But it wouldn't matter. As long as the station staff loved it and bought into the concept, that's all that mattered. It guaranteed that much more talk throughout the week. Nothing was more important to us than the endorsement of key voices who had command of and influence over their audience. Those voices would sell it for us.

"Morning shows were critical because in Columbus their personalities were the local celebrities. You had Jack Nicklaus, OSU athletes, and the media. That was it," said Maurer. "It was the hip thing to do because the morning show hosts said so. It was important to get their stamp of approval."

Having drawn our inspiration for the frozen Cornish hen shoot from the wisdom of *Animal House,* we felt what Columbus sports needed was "a really futile and stupid gesture to be done on somebody's part" and we were "just the guys to do it." Bluto would be proud.

The Opening Night stunt event helped us develop a special partnership and bond with WNCI. We scripted routines that John, Dave, Shawn, and our players would act out on the air. Together we created a series of promotions that would rival David Letterman's antics. In addition to the Morning Zoo, WLVQ (96.3 FM) with its "Wags & Elliott" (Mark Wagner and Jerry Elliott) a.m. drive-time show was also a market leader who helped us deliver our promotional message to our target audiences.

Our marketing efforts were clearly taking hold.

"As Opening Night grew closer, we were all constantly hitting the refresh button (on the ticket system) and eagerly watching the numbers go up and up and up: 2,000, 2,500, 3,000, and so on," recalled Cohn.

With our staff in place, we spent our remaining time soliciting corporate partners, season-ticket holders, and trying to build public interest in anticipation of what would be a momentous but chaotic opener. But before the first puck was dropped in Columbus, we found ourselves marred in a controversy that would shake us to our core and challenge our very viability as a franchise.

Chapter Five

A TAYLOR-MADE PROBLEM

"The Columbus Chill team will be one of the most successful minor league franchises in the history of the city."

—Psychic Ian Bliss sees the future in the *Columbus Dispatch* four weeks before the Chill's first-ever home game

With the Coliseum unavailable in early October because of the Quarter Horse Congress, we held training camp in Indianapolis. The players reported directly to Indy and, with an opening three-game road trip, they wouldn't see Columbus until just before Opening Night.

With an overwhelming amount of preparation still to be done—in an exceptionally short timeframe—I remained in Columbus and sent Brent Maurer, from the PR department, with the team to assist Roscoe.

Brent was young and lacked experience but was eager and hungry to do well. This was one of the key characteristics we looked for when hiring—smart, talented, driven, and a team player. Brent possessed all of these traits. Because of the low salaries we were offering, we hired nearly all of our folks straight out of college. Alan and I showed the guys the ropes, but out of pure necessity we entrusted them with a great deal of responsibility. That's the nature of minor league sports.

The Chill was Brent's first full time job, but I had plenty of confidence in him because he had interned with the Indiana Pacers during my time there. A native of Carmel, he stayed near home for college, graduating from Butler with a communications degree. Following his internship with the Pacers, Brent continued down the NBA path by interning in the public relations department of the Boston Celtics while completing his graduate studies at Emerson College. We crossed paths again when he returned home to Indianapolis after graduation and spent a summer selling tickets for the Indianapolis Ice. When I was tapped by Horn Chen to take the reins for the Chill, Brent immediately came to mind as someone who could fill an important communications role. Brent lived and breathed sports and certainly fit the profile we were building for our front office. As the conduit between the coaches, players and the media, he knew how to walk that careful line between protecting the team's interest and giving the media what it needed or wanted.

We called upon Brent's familiarity with Indianapolis and its media to facilitate sending TV footage back to the Columbus stations. But while Brent could get the tapes of training camp to Columbus television media, he couldn't make them run it. We were fully aware that it was the middle of Ohio State's football season and that the Buckeyes would dominate the local media.

Roscoe did his best to put a team together in sixty days or less. It was not an easy feat and at times, it showed. We were able to collect a few skilled players, but most of the squad was comprised of grinders and tough guys. We were stacked with fighters, so much so that the team's early DNA was more aggressive than we had counted on.

The most eventful moment of training camp was a donnybrook that broke out between future NHL enforcer Phil Crowe and former Ohio State player Al Novakowski.

It was early in the Chill's first training camp when the fight of all fights occurred. Epic in its proportions, the fight has since taken on legendary status. Yet, for those who witnessed this titanic match, the reality actually matched the rhetoric.

Roscoe was on a mission to build a tough team. When he played, he was well known as a grind-it-out, tough bugger in the corners and he wanted players cut from the same cloth. He also wanted enough guys who could throw punches in order to provide a little extra intimidation, and he'd begin the Chill's inaugural camp with no less than nine players on the roster who could legitimately be described as enforcers. Normally, a team might carry one or two.

Training camp at the Fairgrounds Coliseum in Indianapolis was a venue in which players could vie for one of the enforcer roles. It was a physical camp with plenty of fights, but nothing else matched the Crowe vs. Novakowski battle that happened during the afternoon session on the first day of camp.

Crowe, who would later gain notoriety as a teammate of Wayne Gretzky's with the 1993–94 Los Angeles Kings, was a legitimate heavyweight, ultimately tabbed by the fans in 1999 as the top enforcer on the Chill's All-Time team. Novakowski was a rookie out of Ohio State and a tough defenseman in his own right. He'd become an important part of the roster during the early part of the Chill's inaugural season.

Theirs was a no-holds barred duel conjuring up visions of Ali-Frazier. Roscoe, a 15-year NHL and World Hockey Association veteran who had amassed 2,117 penalty minutes in his pro career, called the fight "as intense as any I'd ever seen in my career."

The thundering sounds of fists pounding flesh and bone could be heard from the upper reaches of the stands, where Roscoe watched intently. Time, and all the players on the ice, stood still as the combatants eschewed any thoughts of "dancing" and immediately began throwing bombs: a right, then a right and another right.

Neither player backed down. Instead, they grabbed each other's jersey with their left hands and held on for dear life as the head shots connected, sending red splotches of blood down onto the pearly white ice. In a corner of the building, the Indianapolis Ice players stood with their mouths agape awaiting their afternoon training at the conclusion of the Chill's session.

It's hard to know what all of the other Chill hopefuls were thinking, but Don Granato suddenly had a revelation:

"Right then, I knew what Roscoe meant when he recruited me and said that he would make me the safest man in hockey. There's no question that Roscoe said something to Al between the morning and afternoon skates to watch my back."

As much as Roscoe loved the tough guys, he knew his skilled players such as Granato needed protection from bullying and intimidation.

But why that was necessary on that particular day is anybody's guess.

It was Granato, a mild-mannered standout from the University of Wisconsin, who was the genesis for the "Thrilla with the Chilla" after he took a stick to the mouth and ended up getting stitches while trying to check Crowe during the morning practice. Granato had no idea about Crowe's pugilistic background but vowed revenge later in the day and was about to extract it when, "Big Al knocks me from behind to get to Crowe. I didn't see him coming," Granato said.

"Novakowski tells Crowe, 'You want him [Granato]? You're going through me,' so those two guys go toe-to-toe for about a minute and a half and beat the living snot out of each other with no linesmen out there."

Granato reflected on his near-death experience: "That was almost me in the fight with Phil Crowe. I would have ended up with brain damage or dead. No doubt about it."

Neither Crowe nor Novakowski needed life support, but they did stuff their oversized bodies, still clad in bloodied gear, in Brent's car for a trip to the hospital to repair their broken noses and bruised hands.

You'd think the combatants would have wanted separate vehicles but that was not the case, as evidenced by the scene immediately after the fight when Crowe and Novakowski gathered their wits and equipment and sat side-by-side on a bench awaiting their ride. There, with enough ice bags between them to cool a keg, the pair exchanged compliments and compared notes on their bout as if they were best buddies from Moose Jaw.

The final tally from the tilt was a broken right knuckle and two stitches to the lip for Novakowski. Crowe sustained a broken nose and five stitches to close a wound on his head.

They honored the fighter's code of not taking the skirmish personally. Novakowski and Crowe were just two young, eager players trying to make the team anyway they could. And sure enough, they both would.

This was going to be one tough team. "It was an amazing fight and kind of set the tone for what our team was going to be about under Terry's tutelage and the cast of characters we had as a team," Chill defenseman and heavyweight enforcer Barry Dreger recalled.

Despite the team's pluck, there wasn't much talent on the ice, particularly at goaltender, and in the preseason games we were giving up an ungodly amount of goals. It was embarrassing. The goalies were so dreadful that Roscoe cut all of them in training camp and was left to find another solution on the waiver wire as the season approached.

To Roscoe's credit, he worked the phones and used every hockey contact he knew in an attempt to form a competitive team for the season opener in Roanoke, Virginia. The Chill lost all three preseason games, being outscored 21–8, and in the two days leading to the first regular-season game on October 24, 1991, he brought in four players—a defenseman, two forwards, and a goalie—to complete the 17-man roster.

While Roscoe was gearing up for the inaugural game, those of us on the staff back in Columbus were greeted the morning of the opener with an article in the *Dispatch* next to a Chill preview that stated the NFL-backed World League of American Football (WLAF) was about to grant Columbus a franchise for the 1992 spring season, with its games played in Ohio Stadium, home of the Buckeyes.

I didn't view the WLAF franchise as direct competition, but certainly it could potentially be another challenge as we sought attention, sponsors, and ad dollars in this football-crazed city.

What was even more interesting, in retrospect, was the rejection by the team's owners of a nickname and colors suggested by the league office: the Blue Jackets, in Columbia blue and magenta uniforms.

Yes, the same Blue Jackets moniker that would be chosen seven years later by the NHL expansion franchise.

Blue Jacket (1743–1810) was a Shawnee Indian chief known for the defense of his people's lands in Ohio and was the forerunner to the more famous Shawnee leader Tecumseh. Many Ohioans learned of them through the several annual outdoor dramas throughout the state.

"Magenta is pink to me and Blue Jacket was an Indian name. We don't need that," the football team's general managing partner Jerry Saperstein told *Dispatch* sports editor George Strode. "Those are decisions we're going to make, not what somebody on Madison Avenue wants."[8]

Eventually, the WLAF franchise was called the Ohio Glory and went 1–9 in its first and only season in Columbus in 1992 before the NFL owners decided to suspend league operations, which was restarted in 1995 as NFL Europe with all six teams based on the continent.

With the hockey season fast approaching, I was convinced we'd be awful, based on the early reports from camp, but I was praying Roscoe's makeover would prove me wrong. If we could just win one game so we didn't come home from season-opening road trip 0–3, we would all be thrilled. We got our wish by somehow taking the first game in franchise history, 8–7 in overtime, against the Roanoke Valley Rebels. Tough guy Mark Cipriano scored the winner and all of us who stayed in Columbus working toward the home opener in eight days exhaled. At least we'd win one more than the Arena Football League's Columbus Thunderbolts had won (0–10) earlier that summer in the Coliseum. The Thunderbolts moved to Cleveland the next year, another

---

[8] The NHL team, by the way, said "Blue Jackets," for their purposes, honors Ohio's Civil War contributions when many of the Union soldiers' blue coats were made in the area.

casualty among Columbus' pro sports franchises. Their lack of success was always in the back of our minds.

In 1991, sports radio had yet to take off in Columbus. There were only a couple of viable options for stations to carry our games, but we had no takers in the first season. We wanted the publicity that live broadcasts could bring, but only if we could make the right deal. We knew our lack of a broadcast partner would cause some gnashing of teeth from our more ardent fans, but it meant little to the people we needed to attract to be successful. Eventually, we would cut a deal with WBNS-AM to cover a major portion of our schedule for the 1992–93 season. We aired only 20 games (17 on Friday nights) but, hey, we were on the flagship home of the Ohio State football team, so that brought us much-needed publicity and credibility.

Butler University graduate Jim Talamonti would be our play-by-play man for the next seven seasons. Everybody loved "Talo." He had the respect of the players and handled the uneasy task of criticizing the team or a player—and then having to ride four hours on the bus with them—adroitly and professionally.

Talamonti truly was the voice of the Chill and engaged the fans from the moment he did his first broadcast for us in Erie, Pennsylvania. Over the years he endured the tribulations that came with covering a minor league team: the patchy phone lines, futile searches for electrical outlets, sketchy information on the opposition (pre-Internet days), but I'm sure very few others had to deal with something as crazy as having to help construct our own broadcast and press row table in the top rows of the Knoxville Coliseum.

Without a radio broadcast that first season, Brent, the only front office member to make the trip, would call me between periods of each road game so I could stay updated on what was happening on the ice. Our second game was at Hampton Roads, one of the "glamour" franchises of the league, owned and operated by Blake Cullen, formerly a Major League Baseball executive as the administrator to the president of the National League. Under Cullen's leadership, the Hampton Roads Admirals were considered to be the best-run and most-respected franchise in the league. We lost the game, but it was an incident that happened away from the play during the game that caught our attention.

The episode involved our team captain, Jason Taylor. "JT," whose father, Ted, was a teammate of Roscoe's with the WHA's Houston Aeros, got into a dispute near the Chill bench. Players from both teams were pushing, shoving, and engaging in some serious trash talking. Hampton Roads player Harry Mews and several of his teammates parked themselves in front of the Chill bench and continued their chatter. In the heat of the moment and in his haste to stand up for his teammates, Taylor swung his stick wildly in the direction of the Hampton Roads players in an attempt to clear them away from the bench.

Whether intentional or inadvertent, Taylor struck Mews squarely in the jaw, shattering it. It had to be wired shut and prevented Mews from playing for several months. Taylor would become public enemy No. 1 in hockey circles. It was clear that he had crossed the line.

Cullen and the Admirals were justifiably up in arms. They wanted Taylor's head on a platter and ECHL Commissioner Pat Kelly delivered it with swift justice. Within days, Taylor received a season-long suspension. Initially, we agreed that the punishment fit the crime, although we later challenged the sanction because we felt Taylor wasn't given due process.

This marked the first of several incidents we had with the league's administrative office, which had the effect of putting on us on the commissioner's shit list from the onset.

The first time I laid eyes on Taylor, I delivered the news to him that his career with the Chill was over before he ever set a skate on the ice in Columbus. Losing our team captain wasn't exactly the way we wanted to get started. It was an additional distraction that we didn't need and only increased the pressure we were all feeling as we readied for Opening Night.

Also, the league forced us to play that game vs. Erie and the next two games with 15 players—one under the limit (you could carry 17 on the roster but dress 16 for games)—because of Taylor's actions. He created a void in leadership, but what was forgotten was that he was a darn good player before the incident, having scored the first goal in franchise history at Roanoke and another goal later in the game.

In the ensuing days, I gathered Alan Karpick, Larry Lane, and Brent to specifically discuss pulling the plug on our most recent marketing campaign in wake of the incident. We had just put out a slick but ominous looking TV ad that showed numerous tough images of hockey with menacing music playing in the background. We ran it on cable for about two weeks to set the stage for Opening Night. We also ran the ad on every AMC Theatre movie screen in the Columbus metro area, a first for minor league sports, directly engaging the entertainment seeker.

The Taylor incident had really rattled us. It was serious and we knew it. We were facing a "lose-lose" situation: if we stayed the course, we'd be subject to criticism and become easy targets for a lawsuit, but if we softened our campaign, we'd lose the edge that had begun to define the franchise.

After extended and serious internal debate, including input from Chill owner Horn Chen, we decided to keep the ads. We believed in what we were doing and in our minds, separated the ad campaign from what was happening on the ice. We may have been in denial a bit, but we were marching forward come hell or high water. In our estimation we had no other choice.

"This was a pivotal moment," said Maurer. "In the end we decided 'we are who we are' and didn't change our approach. In hindsight it was the right call. If we would have gotten gun shy and gone too politically correct we may not have had the same results. To me it would have seemed horrible to have forsaken our vision."

The unfortunate stick swinging by Taylor, coupled with our aggressive play and rough and tumble ad, cemented the Chill brand that first season. It wasn't exactly how we drew it up, but it was becoming our reality.

As awful as the Taylor incident was, it was only the first in a series of tests that would threaten everything we believed in and had worked for.

Chapter Six

OPENING NIGHT MELTDOWN

"Most big cities have an alternative newspaper, an alternative radio station, and an alternative theatre. Columbus, Ohio, now has alternative athletics—or, more specifically, Hockey for the Hip."

————*Wall Street Journal,* December 31, 1991

We fired out a heavy dose of print, television, and radio advertising in the days leading into the home opener. As a result, the phones at our 1460 West Lane Avenue office were ringing off the hook. Tickets were being gobbled up quickly and it was apparent early in the week of the game that we were headed for a sellout. What was not clear, however, was if the game would actually be played.

The season was rushing toward us like a freight train. We barely had enough days to set up a business, let alone market and sell it while dealing with a major on-ice problem.

My biggest concern was the Coliseum itself. We were running out of time to get it ready for the opener and the fairgrounds staff's lollygagging was killing us. We'd been in fifth gear for weeks but our landlords were stuck in first. Something was about to give.

To make matters worse, opening week would start badly when, unbeknownst to us, our contact for the fairgrounds operations, Charlie Wilson, delayed the delivery of our Zamboni (the ice resurfacing machine all hockey facilities require). Did he not know how to make ice? Actually, no he didn't. Apparently, Wilson didn't completely understand the gravity of the situation.

The fairgrounds management had not yet hired or trained anyone on staff to oversee the day-to-day ice operation, nor had they given it any serious thought as far as I could tell. The complete lack of ice expertise, coupled with Horn's frugal budget practices, was about to show up in a major way.

A (very) used (and cheap) machine we had recently purchased was to arrive Monday, allowing us time to get it in shape before the home opener four days later.

The Quarter Horse Congress had ended over the weekend and Wilson apparently was concerned that the delivery would interfere with the cleanup of the event, or vice versa. Without consulting us, Wilson changed delivery of the Zamboni to the end of the week. His move inadvertently created further chaos in an already frenzied ice-making process. To make matters worse, we were having major problems with the portable ice system we had purchased from Burley Equipment. The plan called for the system's piping to be hooked up to the existing Coliseum chillers. The chillers, however, had not been operational since the Jimmy Carter administration, having only been turned on for a brief trial run earlier that summer. This time things were not going so smoothly. It was clear John Burley, one of the portable ice company owners who was on site to supervise installation, was literally on thin ice.

The problems would only escalate as the week went on, in large part because the fairgrounds' operation was understaffed and those who did work had no sense of urgency. It quickly became clear to us that if we wanted to have playable ice for Opening Night we were going to have to figure it out ourselves.

By Tuesday, three days before the home opener, when the Coliseum staff proved yet again to be of little help, we were forced to send over several members of our office staff to assist in any way they could. These were marketing and ticket sales people, not ice experts, but they did their best.

And Ron Rogers, our ticket operations director, worked around the clock to build the home and visiting benches that, for whatever reason, were not part of the Coliseum's existing dasher board system. Meanwhile, our aggressive marketing push was paying dividends and the buzz around Columbus was building. There was a sense that there was something different about the Chill and people were curious. We were prepared to sell our souls if we could just get through the opening weekend slate of two games. Then, I figured, we would at least have a few days to regroup.

Meanwhile, the players were just trying to figure out how to get around Columbus. The Chill had played two games in Virginia before setting foot in the city early on the morning of October 26, having spent the preseason based in Indianapolis for a week and another five days in Louisville, Kentucky, before the season opener.

For some players, their journey began even earlier at NHL tryout camps. Phil Crowe, for example, left Calgary at the beginning of September for Chicago to practice with the Blackhawks. After a month there, he was assigned to the Blackhawks' affiliate in Indianapolis and stayed there when he was reassigned to the Chill.

Crowe saw Columbus for the first time after the game against Hampton Roads and finally emptied his suitcases the next day in his new apartment and made a home-cooked meal, as it were. "I hadn't unpacked in two months," he told the *Dispatch* at the time. "It's a good feeling to put some macaroni on the stove. Macaroni and hamburger, it's great."

There was little time to kick back, though, because the Chill headed out again on October 30, albeit for a bus trip of a little more than two hours, for the first meeting against its northwest Ohio rival, the Toledo Storm. Returning from a 9–2 loss at the Toledo Sports Arena, the team—at long last—arrived at its new home to unpack gear in the Coliseum, as the practices prior to the Toledo game were at the OSU Ice Rink.

Even at 2 a.m. on that Thursday there was activity in the building as the players and Roscoe got off the bus and got their first look at the Coliseum. It was hard to believe at that point that a game would be played there in 42 hours, but that wasn't a concern of theirs. They just wanted to hang their wet gear, go back to their apartments and get some sleep.

The foul odor of the horse show was still lingering in the air as the players got their first glimpse of the dressing room. "It really smelled bad. It was tight, cramped," defenseman Barry Dreger said. "Needless to say, it was not ideal."

Inside the Coliseum, the tension continued to build as Burley struggled to get the ice made. On Thursday evening, just twenty-four hours before the scheduled opening faceoff, and with our full staff practically holding vigil on site, things appeared to be unraveling at an alarming rate. I did my best to assure our group that everything would be fine but I knew that any new dramatic turn of events meant we were cooked.

I'd witnessed a similar disaster during my time with the Pacers. It occurred nearly a decade earlier at a highly anticipated preseason game at the Fort Wayne Coliseum—home of the IHL's Fort Wayne Komets. We faced the up-and-coming Detroit Pistons and their young superstar Isaiah Thomas. Thomas was wildly popular in the Hoosier state, as just a few years earlier he had led Indiana to the 1981 NCAA National Championship. The promoters expected a full house. What they had not anticipated, however, were warm and humid weather conditions. The Coliseum was not fitted with a proper ventilation system and the thin piece of plywood separating the basketball court and the ice did little to prevent heavy condensation from developing on the court. Futile attempts were made to wipe it away, but it was point-less. Without the proper ventilation system the indoor conditions remained humid and condensation continued to rise to the floor. The players slipped and slid during pregame warm ups. After consulting with the coaches and team management, NBA officials correctly made the decision to cancel the contest in order to ensure the safety of the players. The announcement made at the scheduled tip-off time was met with thunderous disapproval. The near-capacity crowd let the local promoters, and anyone within earshot, have it. It was a very unpleasant scene. As that painful memory flashed through my mind, I realized that this one was entirely on me. With the potential fate of the franchise on the line, we had to find a way to play.

Desperate times called for desperate measures, so we called the OSU Ice Rink and asked them to send anyone who might be willing to help. The cavalry came in the form of about a dozen adult hockey league players, including Toronto native Greg Cheesewright. Cheesewright, whose parents were from England, carried a heavy English accent and referred to everyone around him as "mate." He was joined by several others who would become part of our minor official's crew. Alongside Burley and our staff, the cavalry pitched in for the next several hours. We worked well past midnight, which gave us an outside shot of creating a sheet of ice that might be passable enough to get through our first game.

Because the ice lacked thickness, however, Burley decided to flood the surface with a fire hose at about 2 a.m. It was a risky proposition because several in the group, including Cheesewright, argued that the water needed to be layered more carefully in order to have it freeze properly. Cheesewright and company meant well, but Burley determined that at this pace there was no other option. We went for broke. We'd know by morning whether Burley was right or wrong. We all crossed our fingers and agreed to meet back at the Coliseum no later than 8 a.m.

The Chill were scheduled to have their first-ever morning skate on the Coliseum ice at 11 a.m. It didn't happen. At that time, the surface was more like a pond than a sheet of ice. We were having trouble inserting our in-ice advertising logos and ultimately would have to scrap them for the opening weekend. I visited with players Don Granato and Kurt Semandel, each of whom was convinced the game would be cancelled.

"We wondered if we would be skating or swimming," Semandel said. They were not alone in that notion. Craig Merz, who was the Chill beat writer for the *Dispatch*, asked his bosses to hold a spot on the front page of the paper for a possible meltdown (no pun intended). I told him the same thing I told the staff: "We are playing."

I was not sure it was possible to will a game to happen, but at this point it was worth a try. Still, we spent the entire day in limbo. The unseasonably warm weather in Columbus wasn't helping matters, as the mid-day ice temperature stood at 24 degrees, about six degrees above normal.

"There is simply no denying that the last few days were absolute bedlam," said Chill staffer Ken Cohn.

The ice wasn't the only thing we were sweating, either. The Zamboni still had not made its way to the Coliseum and the delivery company was unable to guarantee that it would arrive before game time. It was almost getting comical now, but no one was laughing.

Without the benefit of a preseason game or two, our staff had no dress rehearsal from a game-operations standpoint. With the exception of Larry Lane and me, our staff had never put an event together before. The stakes were enormous and this high-wire act was working without a net.

Whether it was sleep deprivation or off-the-charts stress, the rest of the day was a blur. A few members of our staff stayed in the office as late as possible to deal with the constant barrage of ticket calls, but most of our group headed to the Coliseum early in the afternoon in order to set up.

We were assisted by reinforcements who had been there before, which had a calming effect on our staff. Members of the Indianapolis Ice, Concepts Marketing Group and even owner Horn Chen's family were on hand for the big night. Horn's son, Chris, who handled the financial aspect of his father's sports businesses, was there to assist us in tagging our merchandise for sale at the game. The problem was that Ken, one of our ticket sales guys who doubled as our lead on merchandise, was nowhere to be found an hour before the doors opened. He was given the role just a month or so before the home opener, and with the monumental under-taking of launching the franchise, merchandise sales had become almost an afterthought.

"One day I mentioned [to David] that I had worked in a sporting goods store in high school," Cohn said. "So he said, 'Great, you're in charge of merchandise.' I had no contacts in the team merchandising business, no experience in creative design, but all Columbus Chill fans were about to have no choice but to buy what I came up with."

By default, Ken was our most experienced retailer. Trouble was, this facet of the operation was coming down to the wire and because of the short time frame, none of our products were ready until game day. Ken had packed up all the merchandise earlier in the afternoon, but time was not on our side. "I only had a few hours to load dozens and dozens of boxes, deliver them over to the Fairgrounds, unpack and get set up," said Cohn.

Later that afternoon he got caught up in the heavy traffic that was beginning to make its way onto the Fairgrounds' parking lots and a five-minute drive turned into a two-hour ordeal, jeopardizing our sale of merchandise.

Ron Rogers, from our front office, had told me Ken went home to "freshen up" and I was ready to berate him if this was the reason he was running late, only to find out later that wasn't the case. When he finally arrived, Ken, Chris Chen, Indianapolis Ice GM Ray Compton, and a few of his crew scrambled to quickly tag as much merchandise as possible.

"This was my first job and I was in pure panic," Cohn said. "I arrived just as the building was opening. Then it was pure adrenaline, trying to lug box after box through the fans. I felt like I was bringing water to a city in the midst of a six-month drought. I was absolutely swarmed by fans wanting to buy something . . . anything . . . with a Chill logo on it!"

About the same time that Ken arrived at the Coliseum, so did the Zamboni. We had waited all week, and it showed up at 6 p.m., two hours before the scheduled start.

Naturally, there was a problem. There was no ramp to get the Zamboni off the back of the truck. So several wooden planks were commandeered from who knows where and we prayed that they would hold long enough to push the bulky piece of equipment from the bed to the ground.

Luck was on our side and, after seventy-five minutes, the Zamboni had landed.

I was carrying a few company checks in my pocket and met the delivery folks in the parking lot, where I signed a check for the remaining $10,000 balance on my knee. I breathed a temporary sigh of relief, only to see the machine needed about a week's worth of work before it would be ready. It certainly wasn't in shape for a game that was scheduled to start shortly. Our guys began diligently tinkering on the machine but it wasn't operable for the pre-game skate. We had to use a hose and shovels to make the ice playable and hope the Zamboni would function for the first intermission.

While all this was going on, the fans just kept coming. The game sold out by 3 p.m., but word obviously had not reached everyone. On I-71, the freeway accessing traffic to the Coliseum was backed up several miles to the north. We also blew through the remaining standing-room-only tickets. Hundreds of fans were ultimately turned away at the box office or in their attempt to get there. The Ohio State Highway Patrol had only two troopers on duty for the game but quickly realized that was insufficient to handle the throng.

In order to allow the crowd to usher in leisurely, we planned on opening the doors ninety minutes before the 8 p.m. game. We delayed it until closer to 7 p.m. so the merchandise team could have as much time as possible to get themselves organized.

The fairgrounds workers, who all week had lacked any sense of urgency, were still setting up the facility when the doors finally opened. Some of the Plexiglas in the dasher boards was still being secured in place and the workers had to carry the remaining sections through the stands to complete the work. The last piece was finally put in place as the teams took the ice for their pre-game skate.

Delaying the opening proved useless. The system that Chris and Ken had devised for merchandise sales couldn't keep up with the furious demand. After about fifteen minutes, the normally reserved Chris turned to Ken, said "fuck it" and scrapped the plan on the spot. We handed over the merchandise to the fans as fast as we could collect the cash. "We weren't set up to take credit cards yet, so it's an all-cash sale. Chris is piling up wads and wads of cash in his shirt, thousands upon thousands of dollars in bills. No box. No cash register. No Brinks Security. It was scary, but we were making a killing," said Cohn.

I didn't have time to even think about overlooking the obvious, so it was not surprising when we had. Burley had forgotten to bring the pegs that hold the goals in place, known in hockey parlance as moorings. The teams skated during the pre-game, shooting at goals that were not fixed to the ice. Over the sound system, Albert Collins's "I ain't drunk, I'm just drinkin'" appropriately set the party mood as the crowd continued to pour into the Coliseum. I grabbed another one of our ticket salesmen, Dave Peck, and hurried him out the door to run to Ohio State's rink, which was just over two miles away, to see if we could borrow theirs. Never mind the traffic jam.

Due to the circumstances, we delayed the game's starting time to 8:45 p.m. The ice was still a mess, but somehow it had survived the pregame skate. Maybe we'd make it after all.

Dave somehow made it back and we were able to get the goal pegs moored.

The place was now packed, the energy was electric, and the anticipation for team introductions was reaching its peak. Larry Lane, who also doubled as our game presentation director, got the show underway. The lights went out and the fog began to roll. Music pounded through the Coliseum's ancient speakers and the spotlights hit their marks.

About this time, down by the players' tunnel, I ran into the emcees from WNCI. I'll never forget that over the roar of the crowd, Zoo morning show host Dave Kaelin turned to me and said, "David, you've really pulled it off."

I was thinking, *Are you kidding? This is the biggest disaster I've ever seen.* But in front of me, I could see that the opening ceremonies were spectacular. Against all odds, we were off and running.

The entire day was a series of near misses. "John Burley screwed in the goal lights during the national anthem," Peck said. "We were hanging by a thread."

That's how close we cut it. Yet after a fourteen-year absence, professional hockey had finally returned to Columbus. The date was November 1, 1991, but it felt like an early Christmas present. Operating in a combined state of panic and euphoria, I was functioning on pure adrenaline. We all were.

The team, feeding off the energy of the home fans, came out swinging, quickly living up to its advanced billing as a tough team by getting into five fights in the first 22 minutes. The two teams would eventually combine for 140 penalty minutes for the game. The busiest people that night might have been identical twins Joe and Ron Mongolier, who ran the respective penalty boxes and had to keep track of all the infractions to make sure the players exited the sin bin at the appropriate time, all the while avoiding pools of blood from the many combatants.

"We focused on abusing one of their veteran tough guys," said Chill defenseman Barry Dreger. "We kept calling him the 'old guy.' He wasn't old, but to us—we were twenty-one, twenty-two—he was."

The record Coliseum crowd of 6,298—almost 600 above seating capacity—loved every second of it.

Amidst the throng that night was our owner, the unassuming and far from meddlesome Horn Chen. As would be the case on numerous occasions in the future, he showed up unannounced and settled among the hundreds of standing-room fans because he did not want to occupy a ticketed seat that could be sold. Once we heard he was there, it took two periods for the staff to locate him.

During the first intermission, the on-ice contest featuring the Cornish game hen shoot became an instant classic (our apologies to PETA). The Morning Zoo did a great job of setting it up for the fans and the impact of the birds skimming across the ice at warp speed and slamming into the dasher boards made a thunderous sound. The place was really rocking and fans were dancing in the aisles. It was quite a sight.

Half of the twenty contestants survived the first round. Just four made the shot on their second attempt. In the end, Shawn Kelly, from Louisville, walked away with the $5,000 prize—and that's no chicken feed.

But behind-the-scenes, the drama had not ceased. With a quarter of the twenty-minute intermission already gone, it was time to debut the Zamboni, now outfitted with yellow caution tape to keep the propane tanks strapped to its side. Its first effort turned into a comedy of errors. The late delivery of the machine really set us back. Apparently, to get the Zamboni operational, Cheesewright had "borrowed" a propane tank from a midway tent that smoked barbecued ribs.

Through no fault of his own, our driver, Brian, a student who had worked at the OSU Ice Rink, had no ability to steer the machine. I think it took him fourteen or fifteen minutes to do just a poor resurfacing job that normally takes half the time. Hockey crowds are known to be a bit unforgiving, and the Chill fans didn't disappoint. Brian was booed unmercifully off the ice and then quit on the spot.

I turned to the group from Ohio State that had shown up the night before to find the next Zamboni driver. A student named Tim Allwein stepped up. He was really good-natured, playing to the crowd, and somehow managed to get through the second intermission unscathed. The fans roared with approval and gave him a standing ovation. It was a party and they were having a blast! Tim would drive for us the remainder of the season.

Before the second intermission, a few of our team of newly appointed ice experts from Ohio State's adult hockey league—whom the front office affectionately nicknamed "the prophets of doom"—warned of impending disaster if we allowed the figure skating team of LaBrake and Feinberg to dig the toe picks of their skates into the ice. They counseled that the ice was too thin and they might hit one of the portable pipes. Then all hell would break loose and we'd be forced to cancel the game.

They might have been making a reasonable point, but by this time I was fed up and said flat out that I didn't care. I screamed into my walkie-talkie—which I used to communicate with our staff during game nights—that we weren't paying them $5,000 to sit on the sidelines. Much like everything else that evening, it somehow worked out. LaBrake and Feinberg did a terrific job and, luckily, we encountered no issues.

If all the craziness of the day and night weren't enough, the Chill's Cipriano and Erie's John Batten made their way onto the ice in order to settle a score from earlier in the game, just before the two teams took to the ice to begin the third period. Reminiscent of a scene right out of *Slap Shot*, they went at each other toe-to-toe while the referees were still ensconced in their locker room. The Coliseum crowd went absolutely wild. I guess these guys didn't realize our ad campaign wasn't to be taken *that* seriously.[9] Despite all the chaos going around it, our team played great and we rallied from a two-goal deficit for a 7–5 win that evened our record at 2–2.

---

[9] It was certainly no laughing matter to Commissioner Kelly, who suspended Cipriano for a few games and vowed to Brent Maurer that he would "run that kid out of the league."

As the crowd counted down to victory, dozens of fans were climbing on the boards and reaching over the glass to congratulate the players. It was a spectacular display of emotion, but I was cringing all the while. The boards were rickety and were swaying all night and I had no idea if the glass would hold. All we needed was to have some serious injury or major incident to end the night. But the boards and glass stood strong as the players skated over to accept the accolades from their newfound well-wishers. Thank God the night was over. We not only survived, but we appeared to have a hit on our hands.

We were all completely spent. Down to the last minute, the organization faced what could have been the biggest professional sports disaster that this city had ever seen. Instead, however, it became our finest hour. I could not have been more proud of our staff and our team. It was our own little miracle on ice.

"It was all coming apart at the seams [and David] kept telling us to not worry about the ice-related stuff," said Karpick. "Just get your job done and it will be okay. Somehow, I knew it was going to work out, and about four-and-a-half hours later, it did."

The Ohio State football team played at home the next day and word of the Chill opener spread through the crowd at Ohio Stadium. Everyone said the same thing: A Chill game was something you had to see.

Chapter Seven

MAGIC AND MAYHEM

"Show me a hero and I will write you a *tragedy*."

—F. Scott Fitzgerald

Attendance for the next two home dates after Opening Night was only 2,600 and 1,800 respectively, the lowest in the team's eventual eight-year history, but those numbers were a welcome sight to us. While the opener had been a tremendous success, we still had a lot of bugs to work out. The smaller crowds at home games two and three gave us the chance to work on our event presentation in a less stressful atmosphere.

We needed the break, too, because what we had planned next would demand the complete attention of our entire staff.

We knew that we needed to follow the home opener with another major promotion and decided to secure an appearance by the Los Angeles Laker Girls for our second home weekend. It was a "can't miss" idea that we felt would solidify us with the college students and younger male sports fans in Columbus. Selling young guys on the sex appeal of the Laker Girls was a layup. It was a recipe we'd used before to great success and a well we would draw from time and time again.

Two years earlier, while working with the Indianapolis Ice, I'd happened to read a profile of Art Berke, the Vice President of Communications for *Sports Illustrated*, on the inside cover of the magazine. I decided to reach out to Berke and see what it would take to book an appearance by one of *SI*'s swimsuit models. I initially inquired about Elle Macpherson or Rachel Hunter, each of whom were world famous by that time, but, instead, Berke recommended the lesser-known but rising star Kathy Ireland. We knew interest would be huge, so we were thrilled to get any of the models. Somehow, I was able to convince Berke to secure an early February date for the appearance, coinciding with the release of the swimsuit issue's twenty-fifth anniversary edition. It was the ultimate example of luck occurring when preparation meets opportunity, to paraphrase the Roman philosopher Seneca. When the magazine was released with Ireland on the cover, we'd struck gold. With copies of the special edition flying off the shelves (it is still the bestselling *Sports Illustrated* issue of all-time) and all eyes now fixed on its gorgeous cover model, the only place she could be found was at an Indianapolis Ice game. Needless to say, we sold out the building.

By booking the Laker Girls we were hoping to strike gold again, but, instead, what we got was pandemonium. There was no greater show in professional sports during the 1980s and into the 1990s than the Los Angeles Lakers. Superstars like Earvin "Magic" Johnson, Kareem Abdul-Jabbar, and James Worthy helped bring notoriety to the entire Lakers organization, including its dance team the Laker Girls. On a level with the Dallas Cowboys Cheerleaders, the Laker Girls were at the top in terms of visibility, and we felt that getting them to perform for us would help us reach our goal of making an immediate impact on the first two Friday nights of the home schedule. The event was a bull's eye for our target audience of college kids, young male sports fans, and the on-the-town crowd in their twenties and thirties who had disposable income and were looking for something different. This was to be a distinctive event, but, as it turned out, it was, for reasons we could not have imagined earlier in the week. As part of the deal to drive advance ticket sales we brought in two of the squad's dancers—Teresa Tuazon and Dana Cuartero—on Thursday afternoon, prior to Friday's game, to create some pre-event press coverage and partake in a couple of public appearances, including one on the Ohio State campus.

Unfortunately for us, Brent Maurer had been unsuccessful in his attempts that week to lobby the television stations for press coverage of our event. "We pitched live shots to television, but there were no takers," said Maurer. "It was a tough sell."

It was also frustrating. Despite the success of Opening Night, we knew we needed all the publicity we could get because the local TV coverage had slipped back into its usual routine of endless Ohio State football coverage, while we competed with prep football for the miniscule media leftovers. If we couldn't convince the local TV stations to do an advance story on the Laker Girls, then what would it take to entice them?

Radio presented its own challenge. Since most radio stations typically don't like to promote an event being presented by a competing station, the only morning radio coverage we knew we could count on was a bit with our radio promotional partner WMGG-FM (99.7) and its personality Perry Stone.

Stone was one of our early champions and he hit the appearances hard all week. He had embraced our approach from the beginning and literally spent entire morning show segments talking about our print ads and marketing campaigns. His audience was stoked for the Laker Girls, even if Columbus television couldn't have cared less.

Despite the lack of media interest, we were well on our way to another sellout. But that wasn't the point. The objective was to create more coverage and maximize the momentum generated by the success of Opening Night. With the television stations, we were begging for exposure a little more than I would have liked. But as fate would have it, the tables turned dramatically with a single announcement.

Early on the afternoon of Thursday, November 7, 1991, Brent grabbed me as I was leaving for the airport to go pick up the first two Laker Girls.

He was on the phone with his best friend, Brad Beery. Brad and I were also friends, having worked together with the Indiana Pacers and most recently for our sister organization, the Indianapolis Ice. Through one of his NBA contacts, Brad had been tipped off that some major news was about to break out of Los Angeles. Brad provided us a small jump on the information that within the hour shook all of America: Magic Johnson announced that he had the HIV virus and would be retiring from basketball.

I was stunned. We all were. This was an era in which AIDS was still thought of as an imminent death sentence, and one of the biggest sports icons on the planet just announced that he had the virus that causes it.

I was also a little concerned that we had hadn't heard the news from a reliable media source. I knew Brad well enough to know that it was possible he was playing some kind of sick joke on Brent. "I thought Brad was full of it," said Maurer. "Keep in mind, we always had this tit-for-tat Lakers-Celtics thing going. Years earlier, he called me with the news Len Bias died." (Bias, the projected future Celtic superstar and heir apparent to Larry Bird, died tragically of a cocaine overdose just two days after being selected No. 2, overall, in the in 1986 NBA draft.) "I told Brad, 'I didn't believe you then and I don't believe you now.' Finally, though, he convinced me he was serious," said Maurer. "Still, we continued to check radio reports to confirm the story."

The timing seemed too coincidental, and I thought there was a good chance that Brad was setting Brent up for some kind of gag. Nevertheless, we had to get to the airport and I did not have time to investigate further. Instead, I told Brent to monitor the radio stations for any information while I went to the airport and that I would call him from a pay phone once I was able to. I scanned the radio to find a report on my half-hour ride to Port Columbus International Airport but had no luck. Brent did not have an update when I finally reached the airport and was able to call. Once the plane landed and I was about to meet the Laker Girls I thought to myself, *Well, this is going to be an awkward conversation.*

I decided to broach the subject a few minutes after Teresa and Dana arrived and we'd had a chance to introduce ourselves. It was a bit uncomfortable, to say the least, but I relayed the news, adding that I had no way of confirming the story. After a short pause, their reaction said it all. Their faces dropped and one of them said, "That explains all the rumors of closed-door meetings at the Lakers' offices." They both knew something big was up but didn't know what it was. As it turned out, Magic had not believed the initial test results and had gone for a second test, and then a third, before finally accepting the diagnosis. What had been thought of as a disease that exclusively the gay community had now infiltrated the heterosexual world. This was earth-shattering news, and everyone—including the most plugged-in national media types—was caught off-guard, although one week earlier there was an eerie foreshadowing nobody seemed to pick up; I certainly didn't as I was preoccupied with getting through Opening Night.

Previously, the day of our home opener, the *Dispatch* ran an Associated Press story about Johnson not playing the Lakers' season opener that night against the Houston Rockets because of fatigue after a bout with the flu. "I'm not aching or hurting," he said. "I just don't feel like myself."

Everyone was now in hot pursuit of what was one of the most significant breaking-news stories in years.

Next, I relayed to the girls that we didn't have any evening appearances booked, as we had originally hoped for, but we knew the interest would increase in the immediate wake of the Magic Johnson announcement. I said it was their choice: we would do interviews if they approved, but we'd understand if they decided to wait until their scheduled radio appearance the next morning. Respectfully, the girls opted not to speak publicly that night.

News of Johnson's announcement transcended the sports world, captivating the entire nation. It was classic tabloid material and was covered insatiably by all of the biggest news outlets in the world. In Columbus it was no different. Suddenly, the interview we struggled to book all week became the biggest "get" in town. The television media all wanted their piece of the story. We were about to get first-hand experience in how to deal with a "paparazzi" style media frenzy.

I headed straight back to the office and spoke with Brent and Alan Karpick to set our strategy. Under no circumstances were the women to be bothered that night. We would respect their privacy and allow them a little time to determine how they wanted to handle questions. In a way this was counter-intuitive to our style, considering how we pushed so hard all week to get the Laker Girls in the spotlight, but we all knew it was the right thing to do.

The rest of the evening was crazy. "The phone rang off the hook," said Maurer. "Barry Katz (WBNS TV sports anchor) called to immediately set a live shot for the next day." Other outlets were relentless, particularly WBNS's Bob Orr, who a few years later catapulted his coverage of the Lucasville (Ohio) State Prison riots into a reporter position with the CBS Evening News. "Orr told me 'I have to speak to the girls tonight,'" Maurer recalled. "'This is a major national news story and the interview will lead our newscast.' I told him no, but he called several times, begging for the interview. I wasn't familiar enough yet with Columbus media establishment to be fazed by the presence of the local personalities. Again, we said no."

Brent dealt with the growing heat from the media and touched base with me several times throughout the evening, but we did not relent. Oddly, it was like we were the doormen at the hot new club in town—the more we said no, the more the media wanted in. We had something the press really wanted, and we were not going to give it to them. Through no planning or intention of our own, we had turned the tables on what had been, for the most part, a disinterested media and forced them to acknowledge our presence and influence.

As it turned out, game day was just as crazy as it had been the previous week. It started in the morning at Tee Jaye's Restaurant near Downtown, where our scheduled, live morning show appearance with Perry Stone turned into a media circus. The place was packed, and one of our players, Jason Christie, showed up on his own, not as Stone's guest but with an eye toward meeting the star attractions. He wasn't the only one.

"No sooner than we arrived at Tee Jaye's, out the window I see a TV van jump the curb and fly into the parking lot," said Maurer. "They were on a mission. A reporter and camera person pushed their way into the event.

The girls were live on the air with Perry [at the time], but they insisted on an interview immediately." The restaurant was packed full of an odd mix of an audience—Perry Stone's followers, Chill fans, breakfast regulars and all the TV camera crews. It was a circus. The bedlam continued all day. Later, to top it off, a reporter asked the girls if they had any reason to be concerned by Johnson's announcement.

If things weren't already crazy enough, early that afternoon I received a call from Leo Hunstiger, the general manager of the Louisville team we were scheduled to face that night. He warned me that they were unable to get the team bus started and that they might have to reschedule the game. Leo and I had interacted several times over the years because the Louisville IceHawks were also owned by Horn, but he was not one of my favorite people to deal with. I found him to be a know-it-all.

Knowing that Horn wasn't about to squander another sellout, I told Leo, after a bit of a contentious back and forth, that his team better get to Columbus because we were playing the game that night no matter what.

"I don't care if you have to pack everyone in cars," I said. "You will be here."

They did eventually manage to get their bus started, but it was clear that Louisville wasn't going to make it in time for the scheduled 7:30 p.m. faceoff. There was a buzz when we opened the doors at 6 p.m. It was only the second Friday home game and there was a tremendous curiosity building among the fans. They showed up early and made pregame skate a big part of the event, interacting with the players. Unfortunately, Louisville was so severely behind schedule that their bus got caught in the traffic jam on their approach to the fairgrounds, delaying the game by nearly an hour. That was not good because it gave fans added drinking time before the first puck was dropped. At the time our concessionaire placed no limit on beer sales, and fans were permitted to take whole trays of beers back to their seats.

Laker Girls. Unlimited alcohol. You get the picture.

The alcohol policy, or lack thereof, caught us off-guard, especially given the circumstances. After the game, we insisted on immediately implementing a two-beer-per-person limit, but we had to make it through *this* game first. The combination of the overserved fans, Laker Girls, and delayed start made this the ugliest and scariest crowd I have ever been part of at a sporting event, as the throng was not only bloodthirsty but lustful. The Laker Girls danced during both intermissions. We secured rubber mats that were heavy enough to hold to the ice when they performed. It was not only their first appearance at a sporting event outside of California, but it was likely also the first time they had been asked to dance on top of ice at a hockey game. Nevertheless, the Laker Girls were professionals and impressive in how they handled the situation. Alan and I walked down to the tunnel area from which the Girls had emerged and heard a little bit of what some of our low-brow fans were shouting at them. It made me feel like we were feeding the girls to the wolves. The hooting, hollering, and stupidity emerging from those drunken fools was truly embarrassing. We wanted to have an edge, but this was way, way over the line. To their credit, the Laker Girls went on and executed their dance routines brilliantly during both intermissions. They handled the cat-calling with professionalism and aplomb and helped us to once again we make the big splash we had hoped for.

Fortunately, the event proved to be an anomaly, too. Typically our crowds were rowdy but not nasty, especially after we instituted the new two-beer-per-customer policy.

It is funny how sometimes things have a way of working out. Our first two weekends almost ended in disaster, but, somehow, we pulled a rabbit out of the hat each night. We had five Friday-night games that November, sold out all of them and went 4–0–1. Our overall record was only 8–9–2, but, heck, we played well in front of the biggest crowds at the most important moments.

We couldn't have written a better script. Outside of the hockey diehards that followed us and knew better, everyone thought we were a good team. It didn't matter that most of our fans didn't know the truth about our skill level, because everyone was having such a good time. Eventually, though, we knew it would be important to field a competitive team.

After several weeks, we began to find our groove. Our presentation was improving and the fans kept coming back. A core of enthusiastic fans would begin to make up our foundation. The roots for hockey in Columbus were beginning to take hold.

While the fans immediately took to Christie for his rambunctious play and nickname, there were other characters such as defenseman Brad Treliving, a media favorite for his quips and stories.

Before becoming a charter member of the Chill, Treliving got his professional start in the hockey hell known as Winston-Salem, North Carolina, in 1990. Despite the nice weather in the heart of tobacco country, playing for the Thunderbirds had its drawbacks.

"They didn't know anything about hockey," Treliving said in a 1991 interview. "The rink was bad. No one knew us around town. We had to fend off our own fans. They used to hang over the boards and yell at the coach. It was the only place you went into the crowd in your home rink."

There were other challenges, as well, such as the running joke that that the Winston-Salem Memorial Coliseum was the only sports venue in which people were fined for *not* smoking, due to the dominance of cigarette manufacturing in the area.

"They would turn on the lights after the national anthem and there would be this big cloud of smoke," Treliving said. "We had a saying, 'Stay in it the first two periods; [by] the third, the other team would be smoked out.'"

Overall, Treliving's first impression of how the young ECHL operated wasn't favorable. "I thought, 'If I die down here, my parents will never find out,'" he said.[10]

---

[10] Treliving was named the general manager of the Calgary Flames on April 28, 2014.

Chapter Eight

THE LAND OF MISFIT TOYS

"With the marketing savvy of a slick corporation, the cohesion of a family business, and the juvenile charm of the Hanson Brothers, the Chill melted the hearts of central Ohioans."

—David Martin, *Columbus Guardian*, November 3, 1993

Have you ever wondered what makes people so crazy about sports? Why fans form lifelong emotional attachments and live and die with the results of their favorite teams?

Psychologists will tell you that it's our instinct for tribal affiliation, our desire to participate in tradition, and our hunger for compelling characters and dramatic storylines that's at the root of it. I guess that explanation helps me understand why some people are so enamored with professional wrestling or the brutal, sanctioned violence of mixed martial arts. Personally, I don't get either one, but those leagues have their legions of die-hards and, as a promoter, I admire them for it.

Some fans are so obsessive that they devour every morsel of information about their team they can find and their self esteem rises and falls with their team's fortunes. Others are able to step back and enjoy the skills of a particular player or the game itself while being no less devoted to their favorite team.

Then there are those who enjoy the event equally as much but are less passionate about the result and see the games as social outings with friends, family, or others in their community.

The bottom line is that as fans we seek experiences that enrich our lives in some way. We feel a need to connect to other people, cultures, and experiences to navigate to that sense of who we are. Not everyone has the same motivation, and the trick of sports marketing is to find ways to appeal to each of these groups without alienating the others. I believe that the Chill struck a nerve that tapped into those more complex desires.

I can relate to this because I'm a fan, too. I have a foot in all three buckets: as a casual fan of minor league baseball, I love to go to the games and socialize. As a devoted fan of Purdue football and basketball, my moods can sometimes be dictated by a win or a loss. Some might also call me a borderline obsessive fan of Bruce Springsteen, whom I've seen perform live more than sixty times. "The Boss" once described his shows as part circus, part political rally, part spiritual meeting, and part dance party. We wanted to create that same kind of vibe in the Coliseum.

We intuitively set out to make Chill games the centerpiece around which our fans felt connected to a larger community. We provided a venue in which fans could feel free to tear off their masks and pour out their hearts without any feeling of awkwardness or fear of ridicule. In essence, we were the collection of misfit toys that found a home together.

We also set out to prove that, contrary to popular opinion, minor league sports marketing didn't always have to be about "affordable family entertainment." Instead, we lampooned our opponents and the events of our times with rapid-fire satire. It was all part of the formula that made hockey at the Coliseum special.

We never varied from our irreverent method, which enabled us to remain relevant right through Last Call, when we shut the doors for good. Everything we did during our games, from the audio clips, music, and promotions, to the contests we held, was selected with the purpose of attracting a youthful and modish audience. A Chill game was an experience in perpetual motion from the moment the doors gates opened until the last fan left the building.

The on-ice product was a bit unpolished, of course, because the ECHL was two steps below the NHL, but there was nothing phony about the zeal of the players or coaches. They were professionals who played their hearts out while maintaining the dream of one day making it to the big leagues, as several of them did. The emotional connection, loyalty and respect that Chill fans had for the team were beyond explanation. The passion and energy the players and fans brought to each game was central to the team's success.

In year two, the fans took an immediate liking to goalie Sergei Khramtsov in an era when Russian players were not often found playing in North America and were looked upon warily, a byproduct of the still-lingering Cold War. Even though he spoke little English, he had an engaging smile highlighted by a few gold-capped teeth. It didn't hurt that Khramtsov was the best goalie in our young history and the fans responded with signs of encouragement in Russian to make him feel at home.

With hockey as the centerpiece, Larry Lane—from his perch in the top corner of the Coliseum—did a magnificent job of engineering the game presentation with precise timing. As script writer, director, and deejay, Larry effectively coordinated the behind-the-scenes staff, all while pumping out the appropriate music and sound bites to fit the situation, a la David Letterman's long-time musical director Paul Shaffer.

We used music as a psychological trigger. By touching their senses and raising their heart rates, we felt that we could shape the fans' emotional states. We used the rhythm and tempo of the individual songs to put people in good moods, move them to laughter, or encourage them to celebrate. If we needed a little more aggressiveness from the fans, we'd drop in a hardcore, hard rock, punk, or alternative song that had some edge to it. Done correctly, it allowed us to take the fans on a wild roller-coaster ride of emotional highs and lows.

We were in sync with the college music scene, which had a tremendous impact on our young staff. The Newport Music Hall, known as "America's Longest Continually Running Rock Club," showcased many national acts in the early stages of their careers, as well as emerging local talent. Our staff became fixtures at the Newport and later the now-defunct Polaris Amphitheatre, and this had a profound impact on shaping our musical approach.

Another influencer was WWCD 101 (now CD 102.5), a ground-breaking local radio station that was a forerunner to the alternative rock format that exploded a few years later when Seattle's grunge scene hit it big. We loved the station for what it represented and who it reached. Much like Chill fans, the CD 101 audience could best be described as disenfranchised prior to the station's arrival. It wasn't the biggest, but it hit the sweet spot for a younger and smarter audience, chiefly college students and individuals in their twenties. It also represented those who rejected a mainstream presentation of any kind. Their listeners wouldn't be caught dead tuning in to the silly chatter of a Morning Zoo or the aging classic rock format of a WLVQ. The news and talk format of WTVN? Forget it. As radio stations evolved into cookie-cutter formats, CD 101 was like an oasis. Their audience was searching for something deeper. The station found a niche in Columbus, which, like many college towns, prided itself as being progressive. While the station was more of a complimentary promotional tool for us, symbolically and musically, it matched the Chill perfectly because of its style and demographics.

Once again, we found ourselves in the right place at the right time. The popular musical landscape in the early 1990s was undergoing dramatic changes. We gravitated instantaneously to the subversive sound and angst of grunge artists. "It was made very clear to me that we were to push the envelope," said Lane. "We were getting a hold of local stuff that wasn't even released yet and throwing it into our mix." While we featured all styles of music, our bread and butter was alternative rock.

Our inaugural season coincided with the release of Nirvana's *Nevermind* and Pearl Jam's *Ten*, two of the most impactful and bestselling alternative albums ever. Not surprisingly, songs like "Smells like Teen Spirit" and "Jeremy" became instant anthems in the Coliseum.

"Our music presentation made us credible with the Gen-X audience, obviously playing well in a college town," said Lane. "On the other hand, most of our rotation was retired very quickly. If we were true to our style, we had to stay ahead of the curve."

Chill games often featured the sounds of the Smashing Pumpkins, Soundgarden, Alice in Chains, Rage Against the Machine and Stone Temple Pilots, among others. As the musical festival Lollapalooza—also inaugurated in 1991—began to bring alternative music into the mainstream, the style became more widely accepted.

We just happened to be at the front end of that wave. With that in mind, we'd admit our presentation wasn't for everyone. For instance, I'm not sure it would have "played in Peoria," so to speak. On the other hand, for the 50,000 college students located just a few miles down the road, it made us en vogue.

The Chill's game presentation style was evident from the moment our fans stepped into the Coliseum. Joel Johanson commenced each game by playing the national anthem on a tenor saxophone, which was my subtle tribute to Clarence Clemons, of Bruce Springsteen's E Street Band. "Joel was uniquely cool," said Lane. "It was an opening statement that said the Chill was not your father's sporting event."

That stirring rendition was followed by the moment that made visiting teams cringe but delighted our fans—the player introductions. As our modern-day gladiators prepared for battle, the player introductions gave us an opportunity to feed the Christians (our opponents) to the Lions (our fans), Chill style. It wasn't good enough to just announce the opponent's starting six. Instead, each name was followed by a sound bite: "In goal for Toledo, No. 30, Sammy Smith. . . . That boy is a p-i-g *PIG* (from *Animal House*)." Our diehards would take the cue and join in the deriding of the other teams, and we, naturally, enjoyed feeding our fans' carnivorous appetites.

The sound bites came mostly from contemporary pop culture sources like *The Simpsons* ("I've seen teams suck before, but they were the suckiest bunch of sucks who ever sucked"), the aforementioned *Animal House* ("Fat, dumb, and stupid is no way to go through life, son") or from songs like Right Said Fred's "I'm Too Sexy."

These sorts of antics might be commonplace in the minors today but what we did back then was considered edgy, or even blasphemous, to traditionalists.

We didn't care, though. We weren't catering to traditionalists as much as trying to amuse, inspire, and delight a younger, progressive audience.

After the opposition was properly grilled during their introductions, the next sounds to blare out of the Coliseum's speakers were the haunting instrumentals of *Sirius* by the Alan Parsons Project, a song that became famous at Chicago Stadium and later the United Center during the Chicago Bulls championship years (though it was originally recorded a decade earlier). Specially designed gobo spot-lighting projected multiple Chill logos upon the ice in rapid motion during the song for added effect.

In-game rituals were plentiful, including the playing of Gary Glitter's rollicking "Rock & Roll, Part 2" after we scored. Chill fans inserted their own chant into the middle of the song, adding "we're gonna beat the (fill in your favorite expletive) out of you!" And whenever an opposing player was escorted to the penalty box, they were also greeted by MTV's cartoon duo, Beavis and Butthead: "I hearby sentence the defendant to . . . huhh, uhhh, hhhuuuh, saw off his tweener" (followed by chainsaw sound effects).

Naturally, our fans embraced the rebel attitude. Columbus firefighter Mike "The Sign Guy" O'Harra regularly razzed opposing players by carrying a flimsy cardboard sign with "let's harass the goalie" written on one side and the target's name spelled phonetically on the other. His hell-raising let the visitors know that the Coliseum was one tough barn to play in. Other fans in various corners of the Coliseum hurled their own organized insults at the opposition, adding more flavor to the game.

Bill DeMora, one of the leaders of the Democratic Party in central Ohio, got so wound up during games, waving his arms during bad calls, that a couple dozen fans in his section would playfully mimic him. It was amazing seeing everyone flailing in unison. We even highlighted the image on the cover of one of our game programs, *Chill Illustrated*.

Never afraid to go for a laugh, Chill games also featured plenty of tongue-in-cheek moments. Riffing off of the idea of boxing round card girls, we featured an attractive but-not-so-talented female skater between periods who carried a sign denoting whether it was the first or second intermission (as if fans couldn't figure it out) on one side and "Meet me at Bumpers," a message to drive fans and players to the popular north side bar after each game, on the other. Not only was it funny, but we sold it as a sponsorship for a few grand each year.

We kept the momentum going at the start of the third period by having Brian Sullivan's security crew race the oval walkway behind the dasher boards past crazed fans to pitch Donatos Pizza boxes with coupons attached into the stands. We had originally assigned our first season intern, Bruce "The Javelin" Javitz to the role, but after being tackled during his debut on Opening Night by overzealous fans, he requested and received an immediate reassignment.

If that wasn't enough, fans could also walk away with certificates for free Whoppers if the Chill scored during the designated Burger King Power Play.

The Chill experience even inspired a board game, "A Night at the Chill," created by our first season-ticket-holder, Steve Miller. What a joker.

Possibly the Chill's most well-known in-game tradition began during the 1992–93 season by closing each home win with the Fat Lady singing "God Bless America." WLVQ morning show hosts Wags and Elliott solicited their audience for appropriate-sized women to contend for the prestigious title and thus become part of our in-game ritual. The Fat Lady appeared late in the game whenever a Chill victory was in hand.

The bit was inspired by the Philadelphia Flyers who, in the late 1960s, chose legendary singer Kate Smith's version of Irving Berlin's "God Bless America" instead of "The Star Spangled Banner" to play before important home games in the hope of bringing good luck to the Flyers. The pre-game ritual reached a crescendo when Smith overwhelmed Flyers fans by appearing at The Spectrum to sing it in person before Game 6 of the 1974 Stanley Cup Finals. Philadelphia defeated the Boston Bruins that night on their way to the first of back-to-back championships, the franchise's only titles. Her legend was immortalized shortly after her death in 1987, when the Flyers erected a statue of Smith outside The Spectrum.

Legend has it that back in the 1950s in Philadelphia, Smith's popular TV show was the last program of the evening on its station before it went dark for the night. She would end each telecast with a song, thus inspiring the axiom "It ain't over until the fat lady sings."

Of the dozen or so women who registered for the Chill contest only four actually had the nerve to face the audience for the competition. Perhaps the others were deterred by the official "weigh in" as part of their formal introductions, or the thought of auditioning in front of 6,000 fans. During the fan judging, "Large Marge" stole victory from the jaws of defeat, winning over the crowd by lifting her shirt to reveal a WLVQ bumper sticker on her exposed midsection.

Annie Vian, WLVQ promotions director, sensed Large Marge was a little unstable and potentially incapable of fulfilling her end of game duties. Alan Karpick assigned intern Andrew Jahant to track Large Marge's every move but within ten minutes a frantic call came over the walkie-talkie as Andrew horrifyingly relayed to Alan, "I just turned my head for one second and she was gone."

About thirty seconds passed before screams emanated from one of the women's restrooms. Large Marge, who was of the transgender community, was apparently freaking out the less liberal-minded patrons inside the restroom as our contest winner's appearance seemed a bit inappropriate to them. Within seconds, two uniformed officers on security detail had Large Marge in handcuffs. The postgame appearance was not to be.

After talking the officers out of arresting Large Marge, we decided to part ways with the colorful but unpredictable contestant, paying her the $1,000 prize money to avoid any potential disputes.

The Chill instead turned to first runner up Judith Kielkopf, who became the Fat Lady in full costume, replete with Viking horns and long blonde braids, taunting opposing teams near the end of every win over the next several seasons. Judith and the Fat Lady would go on to receive major acclaim in established hockey circles when Larry Millson wrote a feature about her for the Toronto *Globe and Mail* in November 1993.

Chapter Nine

MARDI GRAS MEETS HIGH STICKING

"The Columbus Chill has no right to be soooo hot. It's the deep minor leagues, twice removed from the flash and bash of the NHL. No Gretzkys skate here. Worse, the Chill chose a city in which Ohio State football is king and basketball is the crown prince. It is no coincidence three times hockey has failed there. Paitson and his young (24 to 32 yrs old) hustling staff weren't going to sell hockey as much as they were going to have fun and share it."

—Steve Love, *Akron Beacon Journal*, March 8, 1992

The first season moved at such a furious pace that we felt as though our hair was on fire. It was truly a remarkable chain of events. In just over two weeks we endured a league smackdown of epic proportions caused by the Jason Taylor incident; narrowly survived the disastrous ice system issues that threatened Opening Night; and carefully managed our way through the media tumult surrounding the Laker Girls' appearance after Magic Johnson's HIV announcement.

There was more craziness the next month. It seemed both like destiny and a good promotion when journeyman goaltender Steve "Bubbles" Wachter was forced into a starting role on December 13, 1991, the same night the Chill gave away 2,000 replica goalie masks like the one worn by Jason Voorhees in the *Friday the 13th* slasher films. With the regular netminders hurt, the Chill had little choice but to turn to the ironworker/cement finisher and bouncer at a nudie bar in Weirton, West Virginia. As fate would have it, he still wore the old-style fiberglass mask, a la Jason, instead of the increasingly popular cage and helmet.

"I think there's only one other goalie who still uses this type," Wachter proudly said prior to the game.

Unfortunately, Wachter—whose previous pro experience was two brief outings with the Chill—allowed two goals in the first four minutes and was pulled for Doug Brown, who had just been signed to a contract after coming off a hamstring injury. Brown didn't fare any better in the 9–3 loss to Toledo before another Friday sellout of 6,145.

Although Wachter never again played for the Chill, he stuck around as a fill-in in several leagues and finished his career by totaling 19 games across seven seasons, the last with the Fort Worth Fire of the Central Hockey League in 1998–99.

The loss to Toledo came during a stretch of seven losses in eight games that dropped the Chill to 9–14–5 and had the players looking forward to a few league-mandated days off for Christmas. No one was more eager for the holiday break than Phil Crowe. He was always respected as an enforcer but was considered somewhat of a rube when he joined the Chill in 1991.

In that vein, Chill forward Don Granato recalled how anxious Crowe, his linemate, was not to miss an evening flight home to western Canada for Christmas after a Sunday matinee in the Coliseum vs. Erie on December 22. Convinced he wouldn't make it to the airport in time, Crowe schemed to get himself thrown out of the game as quickly as possible.

"It couldn't have been more than the third shift," Granato said. "He pitchforks a defenseman in the balls. The kid doesn't want to fight him, so he latches on. Then Crowe drops his gloves. The other guy is scared shitless. [Crowe] grabs him by the shoulder pads with both hands. The kid is backing up and trying to get out of there. Phil looks at me, looks at the ref. All he's got is two minutes right now, roughing, maybe four minutes. He pulls the player in and head butts him. The ref goes, 'That's it. You're out of here!'

"I had a flight to Chicago that night about 8:30," Granato continued. "The [airport] is packed. I'm walking down to my gate and who do I see? Phil. His flight was delayed like four hours."

The good news was that, despite our record, we were able to grab the attention of the local media, which was remarkable in itself at that juncture, considering the continued heat on Ohio State football coach John Cooper. A 31–3 loss at Michigan on November 23 was his fourth defeat in as many games against the Wolverines and gave the Buckeyes an 8–3 record.[11] Critics were in full force calling for Cooper's head in the five weeks leading to a bowl game; yet the spotlight was beginning to shine on the Chill nonetheless as our franchise's brand was beginning to take shape.

We were known off the ice for our creative marketing and promotions and on the ice for being an entertaining and ruffian team in an era when fighting was still considered an integral part of the game, as well as a selling point.

Our players were doing their part. We weren't great, but we had enough wins to earn attention, and that's all we needed to sell our product. But we got much more than we initially thought possible, as Roscoe and the players perfectly fit the bill from a public relations standpoint.

Roscoe brought an authenticity that elevated our organization. We loved his aggressive style of play and he had gained just enough coaching experience at the junior level as head coach of the Saskatoon Blades of the junior Western Hockey League to know what he was doing, but not so much so that we couldn't afford him, considering our budget.

But Roscoe's real appeal was his personality, humor, and running string of bad jokes, i.e., "My office is so small, I have to walk outside to change my mind."

He was charming, good natured, and engaging with the media. We were looking for a salesman as much as a coach and he fit the bill perfectly. We'd put him in front of a camera and he'd would do the rest. "If there were two

---

[11] The Buckeyes would also lose to Syracuse, 24–17, in the Hall of Fame Bowl in Tampa, Florida, on January 1.

people standing together, he was ready to talk hockey," said Brent Maurer. "Roscoe was two parts hockey coach and one part salesman. He was the perfect guy at the perfect time."

Our strategy was to lead with Roscoe and the players in the media, letting their personalities shine in the public's eyes. Hockey players are known to be media-friendly and we found the characters we had to work with an ideal match for our script that first season. Our leader was Jason Christie, who was named captain as a result of Jason Taylor's suspension. Smurf's small stature but big heart and willingness to mix it up with anybody made him an instant fan favorite.

College players Don Granato (Wisconsin) and Jim Ballantine (Michigan) were terrific skaters, playmakers, and intelligent athletes who provided the team a different element of skill and finesse.

They were part of the oil and water that needed to be mixed. Roscoe favored the rough-and-tumble guys from his native western Canada, but they didn't always see eye-to-eye with the more collegial types.

But the core of the first Chill team was its enforcers. After all, we were promoting hockey, and it didn't require a bunch of Boy Scouts.

The Chill's in-your-face attitude was present from the onset of the franchise and it sometime led to comical moments.

In one pathetic episode, defenseman Rob Lewis was so enraptured by the first-year team's aggressive attitude that he punched the Louisville mascot, Tommy the Hawk, because he was mocking Chill goalie Alain Harvey. Most observers called the skirmish a draw.

Most of our players' No. 1 skill was dropping the gloves. Our games tilted more toward the chaotic style of a pro wrestling than the finesse of *Swan Lake*.

We racked up 2,751 penalty minutes in 64 games for a then-pro record average of 43 penalties in minutes (PIMs) per game. When we selected the team's colors of black and silver, it was with the intent of creating a bold, fierce image. The team didn't disappoint, and we made sure to promote it in our ad copy: "Go to the ballet if you can't stand the heat, wimp."

The fans ate it up. Only a few weeks after dropping the puck, *The Other Paper* (an alternate weekly paper that ran from 1990–2013) ran a cover story proclaiming the Chill as "the hottest game in town." Another publication said Chill games were where "Mardi Gras meets high sticking."

"We enjoyed instant credibility in the business community," said marketing director Alan Karpick. "All of a sudden were looked at as marketing experts."

With our newfound status, advertisers, who months before ignored us, were eagerly jumping onto the Chill bandwagon. Unlike the general public, we kept a few seats open for the latecomers.

But with all the publicity we were getting, the fact that college kids were hooked on our team gave us the greatest satisfaction. We averaged nearly a thousand students per night that first year. We struck a chord with them and they brought a youthful vigor that raised the energy in the Coliseum.

The print advertising campaign was spot-on for those young minds being shaped through their psychology classes. We joined in:

For $5, we can help you with all that unresolved anger you have for your mother. She was overbearing. Controlling. Hypercritical. And deep down, when she was at her worst, didn't you want to check her real hard into the boards?

We reached out to the editorial side of OSU's student newspaper as well. We treated *The Lantern* with the same respect as any daily newspaper. "(The *Lantern*) was tickled to death that we not only bought the ads but paid attention to them," Maurer said.

Brent worked their writers hard, including sports editor Mike Citro. His efforts paid dividends as Chill stories ran in virtually every issue. It was attention the students weren't quite used to receiving.

"Their own athletic department didn't give them the time of day, but in our case we made it easy to report on the team and they had fun doing it," said Maurer. "Even when we were the hottest ticket in town we went out of our way to treat them with respect. That went a long way in earning their coverage."

Even *Columbus Monthly* credited us for having reached the students, saying Chill games were "the world's largest dorm party."

What we're doing for college students this season is discriminatory, prejudicial, and borderline illegal. But, hey, this is hockey, the rules are different.

Let the animal rights people squeal like a possum in a leg-hold trap. Let the feminists pout like a housewife with a broken dishwasher. And let the enviromentalists whine like a chainsaw felling a 2,000-year-old redwood.

Let them bitch, moan and gripe. We don't care. Because the Columbus Chill recognizes only one special interest group: college students. That's why we're reserving 200 seats per game, every game, strictly for those privileged denizens of the halls of higher education.

These very special seats are on sale at Wexner/Mershon Box Office at 15th and High. Tickets are only $7, and there's even a reduced service charge exclusively for college students.

Our lawyers claim we're treading on very thin legal ice. And we say let them howl like the siren of the ambulance they so eagerly chase. 'Cause if loving you is wrong, we don't wanna be right.

791-■■■

In late November 1991, we capitalized on our business goodwill in a different way. Local attorney Greg Kirstein had arranged a meeting with officials from the northwestern Columbus suburb of Dublin to discuss building an ice rink in their community. Although we were less than six months old as a franchise, and had our home debut only a few weeks earlier, we felt as though it was imperative that we address our facility issues sooner rather than later. We knew the 6 a.m. practices at the OSU Ice Rink would soon become a major disadvantage in recruiting players.

I had met Greg in the summer of 1991. A Pittsburgh native and a life-long hockey fan, he was high energy and focused, embracing our efforts from the beginning. In the ensuing months we outlined the possibility of building the rink as a practice home for the team, but also as a solid business that could lead the Chill franchise and hockey, in general, to bigger things.

With Greg's help, we had visited with Columbus officials but instantly realized that any opportunity through the city was going to be a slow process. Greg was a Dublin resident and had strong connections with the town's leaders. He felt their progressive nature equaled ours, making for a greater possibility of the two sides coming to an agreement.

It was a Saturday morning—the day of the Ohio State–Michigan football game—when Greg, Alan, Horn Chen, and I met with Dublin City Manager Tim Hansley and his right-hand man for economic development, Terry Foegler.

We visited with their staff, toured the area, and even went as far as to view a couple of possible rink sites. From the get-go we clicked and left the meeting agreeing to chat about the project with Dublin throughout the winter months.

Back at the Coliseum, the party continued. Despite the gains with the students, our audience was a great cross-section of the Columbus public. It was also made up of families, couples on dates, young professionals, and blue-collar workers. It was a younger and progressive crowd that just needed the chance to break out and get a little crazy. And in the city of Columbus, Chill games became that platform.

Chapter Ten

AMERICA DISCOVERS COLUMBUS

"The Chill is hot."

—Ray Gandolf, ABC's *World News Tonight*

We had one more gimmick in mind to draw attention to our team before the start of the New Year.

Knowing that the time around Christmas was typically slower for news and sports, we decided to help the television stations fill the void by providing our brashest gag thus far: a whimsical holiday-flavored video starring our players and head coach Terry Ruskowski.

We worked with our friends Mark LeClerc and Larry Aull from Concepts Marketing Group to create "Home for the Holidays." As with all of our marketing to that point, the video was tongue-in-cheek and played upon the stereotypes that the public had of hockey, its players, and fans. Laughing all the way, Aull said it best when describing our video holiday greeting card: "It was something we wanted to give back to the community." God help us.

Roscoe opened the video by noting that the holidays can be a lonely time as players are far away from their families and urged fans to take Chill players into their homes. The ensuing scenes showed players Jason "Smurf" Christie, Alain Harvey, Kurt Semandel, and Brad Treliving at Christmas dinner shoving food into their mouths and belching as the horrified hosts looked on. The players continued with a few non-traditional carols, including "Louie, Louie," by the Kingsmen.

Then Semandel introduced his "friend" Muffie—a gum-chewing, blonde groupie in a short skirt—while Harvey showed a young boy how to rake an opponent's face with a hockey stick.

Finally, in the closing scene, Roscoe asked Christie what he's looking for in a host, to which he replied, "Just a warm, loving family . . . with an attractive teenage daughter."

If we weren't pushing the envelope far enough, the announcer concluded his voiceover by inviting those interested in hosting a Chill player to send inquiries to "100 Charlie Bauman Drive, Columbus, Ohio."

As anyone familiar with Buckeye folklore knows, Charlie Bauman is the Clemson football player that Woody Hayes punched in the 1978 Gator Bowl. It immediately ended Hayes's coaching career and tarnished his reputation forever. It was like we were dancing directly on top of his grave. (Hayes died on March 12, 1987, at the age of 74.) We were cruising for a bruising, but somehow got away with it.

No one called us on the Bauman thing or the teenage girl reference. It was a testament to the power of people laughing with you instead of at you.

The video was a tremendous success. We delivered it to television stations on or around Christmas Eve, one of the slowest sports nights of the year. If stations were ever going to air something like this, tonight would be the night.

After the first run all of the television stations were slammed with calls requesting the commercial be replayed. It ran for three consecutive days and had the effect of pouring gasoline over a raging fire. A Chill game was already a hot ticket with our target audience, but the video was huge in helping us make an impression on the rest of Columbus. In just eight weeks, we blanketed the city in black and silver.

"The print campaign really woke people up, and the 'Home for the Holidays' and *Friday the 13th* videos set the tone for gaining national attention," said Alan Karpick. The video helped us drum up interest in our plans for December 31, 1991.

With a 6 p.m. start, we were an entertainment choice for families and the "bar crowd" who were just beginning their party for the night. We happily served both audiences.

Hockey and New Year's Eve would become a Columbus tradition from that point forward. We created some fun promotions each year for the event, with our first being a sold-out Coliseum watching 2,000 Frisbees being flung simultaneously at a target on the ice as part of a pre-game contest to win a prize. We dismissed the naysayers who thought it would be an operational nightmare and just went for it. It was one of the coolest pictures I've ever seen at a sporting event and was shown by all the TV stations.

But the Frisbee toss was not the only thing that made the night memorable. During the first intermission, our "shock jock" friend Perry Stone, who emceed the Frisbee toss, started setting up the next contest.

"He was one of the first on-air personalities to latch onto our ads," Brent said. "He understood hockey and loved our approach."

The promotion took on a life of its own when Stone went off-script and began leading one side of the Coliseum to chant "The Storm" while the other screamed "blows," to taunt the rival Toledo Storm.

"Perry picked up on a few fans chanting 'The Storm Blows' and laughed a little too heartily," Maurer said. "I instinctively picked up a vibe that he might use the line between periods and addressed my concern, but he assured me he wouldn't. It was like feeding red meat to the animals and the crowd picked up on the chant. The fans' hatred for Toledo ran deep. To them, it was a magical moment."

Toledo coach Chris McSorley, the brother of former NHL enforcer Marty McSorley, rushed over to Brent and demanded that Stone stop insulting his team.

"McSorley approached me and was clearly pissed off. 'This Storm blows chant is crap,'" Brent recalled. "He knew our core group was from the Indianapolis Ice, where he had played a few years earlier. He appealed to us to lay off. I told him, 'We'll make sure it doesn't happen again.'"

Brent asked Stone to ease up, but in the second intermission, Stone relayed McSorley's pleas to the Coliseum fandom and said of the coach, "He can eat me raw."

Well, maybe New Year's Eve ended up playing better to the bar crowd than the young fans. Stone would later be banned from the building by ECHL commissioner Pat Kelly, who would later question me about the incident by asking, "What kind of circus are you running in Columbus?"

To cap a perfect night from a Columbus standpoint, the Chill scored two controversial goals in the final nine minutes to win the game 3–2.

The winner came in the closing minutes when Phil Crowe took a point blank shot that broke his stick. The black-taped blade—not the puck—crossed the goal line, but goal judge Lester Lyle flipped on the red light and referee Bob Henry signaled a score.

Legend has it that after the game McSorley got off the Storm bus and tried to stop Henry from leaving the parking lot by leaping on the hood of his car and pounding on it.

While we were antagonizing the Storm, about five hundred miles to the east, friends gathered at a New Year's Eve party in New York City. The theme of the bash was for invited guests to wear their favorite sports apparel.

A fashion faux pas occurred when two of the attendees who had never met wore identical jerseys—that of the Columbus Chill. There were maybe only a few hundred of our replicas sold at that point.

The odds of this coincidence were astronomical but confirmed that something magical was obviously happening with professional hockey in Columbus because that New Year's Eve morning the Chill went national, thanks to a story in the *Wall Street Journal* headlined "Hockey for the Hip." The article was unbelievable recognition for a franchise that had played its first home game just two months earlier, and it reinforced our plan to be edgy and provocative.

We were in the center of an incredible buzz, but what came next overwhelmed us all.

On January 16, 1992, ABC's *World News Tonight* sent in a crew to see what all the fuss was about. We spent significant time with their reporters and producers over the next couple of days.

They interviewed our staff, players, fans, and members of the community. They attended one of our sellout games that weekend against Dayton and chronicled the way we interacted with the fans.

The ABC crew was friendly, but we were far from sure how the story was going to be portrayed. We did not want to come off as a national joke.

Keep in mind that not everyone was enamored with our approach. Allan Harvie Jr., the Richmond Renegades owner, said, "I think it's despicable what they've done," referring to our non-traditional approach to marketing. We hoped the focus of the story would not be on our detractors.

The following weekend, Ray Gandolf, the host of ABC's *World News Sunday*, introduced the piece. From the moment that Gandolf labeled us the "Chill's Merry Marketeers," the story gained momentum. It's not often that you get a three-and-a-half minute feature on national television. We gathered as a staff to watch the piece at Alan Karpick's house, not knowing for certain if it was going to air. At the end, we all sat there a little stunned, left to watch it again and again on the VCR to make sense of what we just witnessed.

We knew right then and there that the ABC piece had the effect of putting our franchise on the national stage, even if only for one Sunday evening. Yet it sparked dreams of even bigger things to come for hockey in Columbus.

It was unbelievable recognition for a franchise that had only dropped the puck two months earlier. *Sports Illustrated* followed shortly thereafter (January 20, 1992) with a blurb about our print ad campaign and recent holiday video. *The Hockey News*, the bible of the sport, declared: "Columbus discovers Chill is not so cold after all."

I knew at that moment the Chill would never be hotter, so I decided to take advantage of all the extra momentum that the press had created.

"We were selling out games in advance—in fact, the final seven of the season sold out to start our record streak of 83—so we looked to leverage that scarcity of tickets into season-ticket purchases," said Karpick. "The demand to see the Chill was a scalper's delight, with tickets going for four and five times the face value, a phenomenon probably equal to a minor league franchise being featured by a national network."

At the same time, hockey was getting more exposure through the 1992 Winter Olympics, and we had secured four of our games to be produced by Coaxial Communications and shown on both Coaxial Cable and Time Warner Cable, further confirmation that it was time to strike and build off the momentum of our first season and prepare for year two.

We made the decision to go on sale with the next year's season tickets on Saturday, February 1, 1992, at 10 a.m., with six weeks still remaining in our season and a full nine months until the 1992–93 home opener. We placed a few print ads and pounded the date in radio buys, our TV game broadcasts, and at every home game.

When I walked into work at 8 a.m., there was a line of 25–30 people waiting outside the office sitting on the worn carpet that was a daily reminder to our staff that we were still in the minors. I was a little caught off guard at first by not immediately processing why they were there.

The response was incredible. In three days we sold 750 new season tickets. "We couldn't keep up with the demand, it was so crazy," said ticket sales staffer Ken Cohn. "It was the best decision we ever made." With a full spring and summer sales campaign ahead, executed by the entire organization, and specifically Ken and Dave Peck, we were on our way to more than 5,000 full and partial season tickets for our second season.

The small capacity of the Coliseum put us in a position to sell out every home game and showcased the need for a better facility.

Our Coliseum home finale was on February 22, 1992, against Cincinnati, even though there were still 10 games left in the season, including three "home" games around the state (we had already played in Troy, Ohio, on January 29, when the Coliseum was being used for another event, and we knew we were going to be four games short of a complete 32-game home schedule) because the Coliseum was booked with Ohio High School Athletic Association boys basketball tournaments for much of March.

We were forced on the road because of those games and the fact that the Coliseum, to that point, did not have insulated flooring used by many facilities, which allowed for a court to be placed over the ice without condensation forming. Fair officials deemed it impractical and unsafe to do the necessary changeovers from basketball to hockey and back and had the ice taken out after our final home game, even though there were three weeks left in the ECHL regular season.

Two days before the home finale, we ran into a problem after starting goalie Alain Harvey sustained a season-ending knee injury, leaving Doug Brown as our only netminder.

A jewelry salesman, Kevin Sawchuk (no relation to hall of fame goaltender Terry Sawchuk), heard on the radio the next morning that Harvey was out. Sawchuk had been a backup for us for a game earlier in the year but had not heard from the Chill coach Terry Ruskowski since. Sawchuk placed a call to Roscoe, who had tried to reach Sawchuk, but had misplaced the jewelry salesman/goaltender's phone number. Sawchuk got off work early and hopped on the bus to Louisville, never expecting to play. But when Brown pulled his groin on the IceHawks' go-ahead goal with 7:46 remaining in regulation, guess who made his pro debut?

Sawchuk, who had played two years in the amateur South Central Senior League in Saskatchewan, stopped three of the four shots he faced in the game's final minutes, but it was clear that he wasn't starter material.

Fortunately for us, Horn Chen's other team in the ECHL—the same Louisville club that just beat us—wasn't playing the next night, so we got one of their goaltenders on a one-game loan.

Only in the Coast.

Lance Madsen was spectacular on our final home game of the season, making 42 saves, and we thrilled the 6,450 fans in attendance with a 5–2 win over the Cincinnati Cyclones. That was the "official" crowd, but it was pushing 7,000, despite the game being televised on local cable. Ticket director Ron Rogers just kept letting the fans in. It was a madhouse, and I kept thinking, *thank goodness the fire marshal was not there to close us down.*

Madsen, our tenth goalie used that season, returned to Louisville the next day and retired after the season, but in that one shining moment for us, he helped send the fans into the summer begging for more, at least for those who couldn't make it for our traveling home games in Cleveland, Athens, and Bowling Green.

We duplicated our Low Dough promotion in Cleveland, drawing 6,000 in Richfield Coliseum (at the time, home of the NBA's Cavaliers) on March 9, sparking a renewed interest in pro hockey in northeast Ohio.

The game in Athens on March 1 was notable for our opponent the Hampton Roads Admirals and who was in our lineup for the Sunday matinee in Bird Arena, on the campus of Ohio University.

Jason Taylor sat out 41 games because of the stick attack on the Admirals' Harry Mews, but he received a court injunction on January 30, allowing him to play for us pending an appeal for the lack of due process on the October suspension. His first game back was the next night, at Cincinnati.

He continued to play thereafter, although for the game at Hampton Roads on February 7, we wisely did not dress him, at the request of Admirals and league officials.

However, Taylor faced the Admirals in Athens, although Mews, who was eventually able to resume playing after his jaw was broken (and even had a stint in the AHL), was on the Hampton Roads roster but did not play.

Taylor's return lit the fuse of Hampton Roads head coach John Brophy, one of the ECHL's most colorful characters. The grizzled Brophy, a Ric Flair (of professional wrestling fame) look-alike, was reported to be the model for the character Reggie Dunlop in *Slap Shot* (played by Paul Newman), and his teams played in the film's image.

Brophy, who reached his professional peak with a two-year stint as head coach of the Toronto Maple Leafs from 1986–88, was the quintessential career minor leaguer. As a player he racked up nearly 4,000 career penalty minutes during his 18 years in the Eastern Hockey League. He had also had 13 successful seasons as the head coach of the Hampton Roads Admirals, winning three championships (1991, '92, and '98).

Brophy was one tough customer. When Roanoke Valley twice cancelled games at Hampton Roads—their reasons were that the bus company refused to travel through a major winter storm that hit the East Coast and that its equipment was stuck under the roof that collapsed at their home, Lancerlot Arena, during the same storm—Brophy was right there with his supportive voice: "They're a joke anyway and don't belong in this league. It's always the piss-poor franchises dragging down the good ones. That's the way it always is in minor league hockey."

Tensions were unbelievably high between the teams, but the game was surprisingly tame considering the amount of enforcers on both sides. It was sort of a super-power stare down, but the presence of ECHL Commissioner Pat Kelly at the game and the determination of the referees not to let any skirmishes break out frustrated the sellout crowd of 1,500, and both teams.

There were 18 minor penalties and two misconducts, but Taylor had his one shining moment by scoring the winning goal at 7:13 of the third period for a 4–3 lead after the Chill had been trailing by two. (Cam Brown added an insurance goal with under two minutes to play for the 5–3 final.)

Taylor told the team between the second and third periods that he would score.

"I don't know why I said it," he said to reporters after the game. "I was just pumped up. It was one of those feelings."

Brophy was less ebullient: "I have nothing to say. What I say or think doesn't matter. The league makes a decision and someone turns it around in court."

The win kept the Chill in the playoff hunt but it was only matter of time before the wear and tear of traveling contributed to a tough stretch, as we played the final 10 games away from the Coliseum.

A "highlight" of the Chill's final stretch occurred when a shapely young lady got a little too excited at a game against the Dayton Bombers at Dayton's Hara Arena on March 11, 1992. She had been thrown out once already that night for dancing suggestively on the end zone seats near the Chill bench, but, for some reason, the inebriated lady was allowed back in for the third period. In the final two minutes of what was a close game, all eyes were upon her as she did more swaying. This time, she lifted her shirt above her shoulders to reveal, shall we say, her ample bare essentials.

Back on the ice, Len Soccio was in the process of scoring an empty-net goal to wrap up an important Chill victory. To this day, you can't find anyone who was on the Chill bench that night who can recall the goal.

Despite a win in that game, we would go on to finish the season with a 25–30–9 record and finish seventh of eight teams in the ECHL West Division, missing the playoffs by 11 points.

Jason Christie led the team with 84 points (28 goals and 56 assists) and had 218 penalty minutes—one of 10 Chill players with at least 100 minutes. Kevin Alexander was second, with 81 points (29–52); followed by Jim Ballantine's 76 (30–46). Frank LaScala had a team-high 34 goals in 59 games, while Barry Dreger was tops with 362 penalty minutes. Harvey, before his injury, was 13–16–5, with 4.51 goals against average.

Although the season ended early, the accolades continued for the franchise when the Chill was named the "Best Sporting Event in Columbus" and the "Best New Addition to Columbus" by *Columbus Monthly.*

Also, *Columbus Alive* chose Chill players to represent the "Athlete you'd most want to drink a beer with." It was a year of being able to leap over every obstacle, and at times we felt as though we were on top of the world. But that did not last long, as a born-again used-car salesman named Billy Inmon was about to place the future of our franchise in peril.

Chapter Eleven

A BORN-AGAIN USED-CAR SALESMAN

"[Inmon] knows no more about running a fair than a hog does about ice cream."

—Ohio Expositions Commission member Roland St. John to the
Columbus Dispatch (December 1991)

With the overwhelming success of the inaugural season and strong winds of public support at our backs, we sprinted into the spring of 1992 confident we had something special on our hands.

There was other good news. The CBA's Columbus Horizon decided to move their basketball team to the downtown convention center, freeing more quality dates for us in the 1992–93 ECHL season . . . or so we thought.

As would become our practice each year, I assembled our staff for a couple of days for an offsite retreat. The first location was at Miami University in Oxford, Ohio, and the idyllic college town served as the perfect place to review the previous season and formulate our marketing, business, and operational plans for the following year.

The gathering was the first chance since the start of the franchise to catch our breath, and we bonded as a staff over a few beers at Oxford's downtown bar scene.

We had a young and terrific group of dedicated talent who were eager to learn the business. As their leader, my philosophy was to share a vision and strategy, then work with the staff to outline the specifics. We also left enough room in our promotional plans for the ever-changing cultural environment, so that we could be ready to pounce on the next big wave or tabloid sensation.

My philosophy was pretty simple: I empowered those who were responsible to execute the initiatives. My role was to link tactical planning to implementation and follow up relentlessly. Experience taught me that cultivating creative ideas is the easy part; carrying out those ideas is much harder. My most important responsibility as their leader was to instill a discipline of execution.

I am a believer that coaching is the single-most important part of expanding others' capabilities. Alan Karpick and I were in our early thirties and had credibility with our group due to our relative age and experience. We were the mentors and encouraged the younger staffers Ken Cohn, David Peck, and Sheryl Kolb to speak up, ask questions, share their thoughts, or draw upon previous experiences. We were also seen as genuine because we encouraged differing points of view, including those opposite of ours. The fact that Larry Lane and Brent Maurer had worked with me in Indianapolis also provided two more people in our group who had seen how to operate an organization over several years, as opposed to several months.

We refused to kick issues under the rug. Yes, the staff was capable of fighting like Canadiens vs. Bruins, but the accountability we placed on each other was central to our success. It made for an amazingly open and candid dialogue that served us well. In the end, we built a great trust between the entire staff.

The NHL was in growing mode with plans to add five teams between 1991 and 1994 to bring the number of franchises to 26, and there were murmurs in *The Hockey News* and other media that more expansion would come before the decade was over.

Nobody outside of our circle ever brought up Columbus as a potential expansion city but it became a recurring part of our discussion that summer: *Why not Columbus?*

- We were the largest city in the US without a major league franchise.
- Ohio, the seventh largest state, had no NHL team, and a franchise wouldn't compete directly with Ohio State's primary sports of football and basketball.
- With Columbus' relative proximity to Cleveland and Cincinnati, hockey was Columbus' only real shot at a major league franchise. We just had to make the case.

I had also kicked the idea around with our attorney Greg Kirstein and Alan over beers at the Blackhorse Inn in Upper Arlington. Greg was quickly becoming a confidant in all major legal and financial decisions, and I knew he had strong ties with the city, an unwavering passion for hockey, and believed the possibilities for sports in Columbus were unlimited. While we were in dream-big mode, any serious public talk of the NHL was premature. Columbus was not remotely on the minds of the league and big-time pro sports were not part of our city leaders' near-term agenda.

But there was a far bigger hurdle looming—one that was quickly on the horizon. Columbus didn't have a major league facility, a fact that simply doomed any discussion when talk of a major league franchise would begin. It was not for lack of trying by some of the town fathers, but several arena and stadium referendums fell way short when put to the voters.

People felt burned by many of those previous efforts; four were on the ballot from 1978 to '87, but none came with a major league team attached to a positive outcome. Any public talk of a new effort, at least at this point in time, would have been seen as a joke.

What we talked about as a staff was doing what we could to *position* Columbus for potential NHL expansion discussions. We knew the best thing we could do was hold any discussions about it for now and just do our jobs.

Brent had researched what the consecutive minor league hockey sellout record was, and we were shocked to find out that it was only 24, by the Cape Breton (Nova Scotia) Oilers of the American Hockey League. We felt as though we were in a spot to smash that mark and made it our mission to sell out every game in 1992–93 and to start building a streak that would be impossible to top.

If we could break the sellout record, it might give us some ammunition to go to the community leaders and media to show them that Columbus can sustain a more prominent stage for hockey. While it was enjoyable to envision the NHL coming to town someday, we still had to focus on the work at hand, or else we could fall in with the other one-hit wonders.

While we worked on selling tickets for the 1992–93 ECHL season, we had to deal with the recent regime change at the Fairgrounds.

Ohio Governor George Voinovich had appointed Billy Inmon as the State Fair Manager in December 1991, seen as a political favor for help in raising money for the Voinovich's successful gubernatorial race the previous year.

While Inmon was approved in a 6–0 vote by the Ohio Expositions Commission, three members abstained, in a harbinger of potential trouble ahead.

"I didn't think they had the right guy," Commissioner Roland St. John said to the *Columbus Dispatch*.

Naturally, we were eager to meet with Inmon. From our initial encounter, a red flag went up. I found him to be suspect, intuitively had a bad feeling about the guy—how he handled himself in a less than professional manner—and was concerned about whether I could trust him.

It did not take long to find out why some of the folks on the Fairgrounds selection committee questioned his qualifications. He didn't have a background in event management and was now in charge of running one of the biggest exposition facilities and state fairs in the country.

Our first meeting with him gave confirmation that Inmon was way out of his league.

I almost burst out laughing when he proclaimed almost immediately that he was signing both Bruce Springsteen and Eric Clapton to play at the next State Fair. Never mind that these artists were still in their prime and demanded at least fifty times what a State Fair gig could offer, nor were they going to play second fiddle, so to speak, to corn dogs and tractor pulls on a horse racing track where the proposed concerts would be staged.

Alan was also astonished at the proclamations Inmon was making. From that point on, I always brought Alan to be a witness, in case of any possible disputes.

But Inmon did not stop there. In his early days at the helm, he also told the *Dayton Daily News* on April 2, 1992, that he envisioned a 22,000-seat arena on the Fairgrounds. He said he had "been told by certain people in this city that they can come up with the money for it" and stated that no public money would be used.

His shoot-from-the-hip style would later catch up with him, and we were one of those who got caught in the crossfire. Inmon was the poster child for the good-ol'-boy network in play. In the end, however, it would be an appointment that Voinovich and the Chill would come to regret.

Our battle with Inmon began in May of 1992 with a major concern over playing dates at the Coliseum. The fans and media may have been showering the Chill with love and support after the success of our inaugural season, but it was a different story with the Fairgrounds officials.

They offered far fewer opportunities to fit the 32-game home schedule than were necessary. Here, the league was trying to accommodate all of the team's wishes for prime dates as best as possible, but the Coliseum's other bookings left us with little or no alternatives.

As one of the city's few large facility options, the Coliseum was loaded with events, and opening a few more dates for the Chill wasn't a priority. In fact, some Ohio Expo Board members were convinced that the Chill was a fluke that would fail in a few years, leaving an opening for what they hoped would be more profitable suitors.

"I think the dates [for the Chill] are worse this year than last year," ECHL Commissioner Pat Kelly told the *Dispatch*.

Attractive home dates were critical to our very livelihood, as we were already pinched at both ends of the season. We lost the month of October to the annual All-American Quarter Horse Congress and late February through March to high school basketball, as Coliseum officials rejected the idea of putting a basketball court over the ice.

For that reason, the Fairgrounds had given us only four open dates in February (17–20) and zero in March of 1993. We mistakenly thought from our success in filling the building that the Fairgrounds would be our ally in trying to secure more dates for more sellout crowds. In reality, it could not have been any further from the truth.

April wasn't any better, as the Coliseum had a long-term commitment to the Aladdin Shrine Circus to make any potential playoff dates challenging as well.

Playing games around the Ohio countryside each year was not a viable option from an operations or financial standpoint. We lost about $100,000 in opportunity costs because of the four "neutral" site games during the inaugural season and were not about to transplant our team, staff, and fans again.

We had to take a stand. We knew when we came to Columbus that we would need to cram our home schedule each season, but this was getting ridiculous. Though it had only been nine months, it was time to leverage some of the equity we had already built.

I simply was not going to lose the fight with Inmon. It was essential that we play all of our home games at the Coliseum in Columbus. Yes, there were anxious moments, but we absolutely could not afford to become gypsies for another year, or ever again, for that matter. I was bound and determined not to allow that to happen, even if I had to play a little hard ball, something that

I was not accustomed to doing. The financial losses would have mounted and Horn Chen would not have had the patience to run an operation in the red. Without a solution, there is no doubt we would have been on track to become just another footnote in the minor league sports graveyard, going the way of the Checkers, Seals, and Owls.

I met with Alan and Brent Maurer and we set our strategy—entering into a game of high stakes poker. Our only agent for change was popularity. But the question was: would all of the goodwill built up from year one be enough to allow us to have an effective appeal with fans and media for the future?

I called Commissioner Kelly to review our dilemma and solicit his help. After battling with the league over the Jason Taylor incident and clashing with the commissioner on several occasions over the Chill's bold and aggressive marketing style, I was more than a little concerned that he might not be willing to help.

My worries were unfounded, as Kelly considered Columbus one of the gems of the ECHL. He was more than eager to help us through the crisis, asking "What do you need me to do?"

We had just one request, but it was fraught with peril. We wanted to ask the league to provide a letter addressed to the Chill's ownership threatening to pull the franchise if we were not able to secure the required dates to fulfill the season.

Kelly allowed us to write the letter, under his signature, an unprecedented move that allowed us to get our key points mentioned and subsequently communicating the gravity of the situation. Our plan was to bluff Inmon via the media by hanging the threat of pulling the franchise over his head in hopes that it would be enough to strong arm the Fairgrounds general manager into getting the dates changed.

"Totally unacceptable" is how Commissioner Kelly described the situation in the letter that we penned on his behalf. "We are running out of patience."

In an attempt to drive home the direness of the situation (while hopefully also getting maximum newspaper coverage) we offered the letter exclusively to the *Dispatch*. Fortunately, the story on May 16 and public outcry got Inmon's attention. In short order, we were provided the green light to turn in additional dates in the second half of the season.

"We could not help but think that all that publicity is what changed Billy's mind so quickly," said Karpick. "We were very relieved this firestorm was, at least for the most part, solved."

We gave the league a schedule with six home games in January and eight straight games in the Coliseum in February, including four Fridays and three Saturdays. We would still have a long stretch on the road to end the season in March, but this was palatable resolution . . . at least for now.

We were not the only ones having our issues with Inmon. In the ensuing months he would become the ringleader in a circus act that grew bigger every day. He was infamous for his daily exaggerations of the number of visitors to the upcoming State Fair, which irked a lot of people.

Using what he called a "secret formula," he proclaimed that 3.4 million people attended the 1992 Ohio State Fair. It was later reported to be more like 500,000. The figures most likely had been padded in a vain attempt to compete with Texas for the title of the country's largest state fair.

He was also a political lightning rod. In a classic case of violating First Amendment rights, the ultra-conservative Inmon imposed his personal religious beliefs by trying to ban the Stonewall Union. After fourteen years of leasing a booth at the State Fair, the organization—whose mission was increasing the visibility and acceptance of the gay, lesbian, bisexual, and transgender community—was prohibited from being on the premises.

Inmon pulled Stonewall Union's space because they were distributing *Gaybeat*, a Columbus-based newspaper that focused on gay and lesbian rights. Inmon accused it of "actively recruiting Ohio's young citizens at the State Fair."

It sparked a media backlash and embarrassed Governor Voinovich to the point of seriously scrutinizing why he had appointed Inmon.

Not surprisingly, things went from bad to worse for Inmon. The 1992 Ohio State Fair was about to lose $3.8 million under his watch, and Ohio House Finance Chairman Patrick Sweeney had requested an investigation of what he called the "erratic management" practices of Inmon.

It was only a matter of time before Inmon was dismissed, especially after one of his top assistants was accused of sexual harassment of a secretary in late August. The woman happened to be married to the son of former Governor James Rhodes, a.k.a. "Mr. Ohio State Fair."

Inmon was combative to the end, holding two press conferences the day prior to a hearing on his dismissal. During one of them, he vowed it would be the "second week of never" before he resigned.

His feistiness was matched only by his delusion. He implored people to call Voinovich's office to show support for him and even provided the office phone number.

They responded all right. The Associated Press reported the next day that there were 222 calls—145 (65 percent) saying he should resign or be fired.

Inmon was canned on August 28, 1992.

He was gone—but certainly not forgotten—and the chaos he left for interim director Mark List would have a profound effect on the Chill and ultimately the entire city.

Chapter Twelve

A GAME-CHANGING MOMENT

"The difficulty the Columbus Chill had in nailing down dates for their coming season was one of the main reasons we've decided to appoint a citizens commission to study how and where a sports/civic arena might be built in Columbus."
—Columbus Mayor Greg Lashutka, *Columbus Dispatch*,
September 11, 1992

We may have bid farewell to Billy Inmon, but, unfortunately, his legacy would live on just a bit longer. Long enough, that is, to cause us some serious pain.

We assumed that after the letter from the league's office went out, everything concerning our homes dates had been resolved. So when the official ECHL schedule was released on July 30, we had the eight consecutive home games from February 5–20 as was agreed upon with Inmon earlier that summer. This allowed us three full months to sell tickets before the home opener and plan our promotional schedule well in advance, or so we thought.

The amount of sales lag time seemed like an eternity compared to the year before. With Inmon out of the way, we could concentrate on building trust with Mark List as he assumed running the Fairgrounds on an interim basis, as of August 31. With Labor Day a week away, it was the last quiet period for our staff. Post-holiday meant it was hockey season in the Chill camp. The respite never came, as Inmon had one more blindside check that dropped the Chill franchise to its knees.

Inmon had somehow managed to cause a scheduling snafu of monumental proportions by double-booking three other events in two buildings over the same time period for February of 1993. The conflicting dates in the Coliseum were with the *Dispatch* Sports, Vacation, and Travel Show, but also impacted the Red Roof Inn's Buckeye Classic gymnastic meet and the Scott Antique Show, scheduled for the nearby Celeste Center. We went from the eight games as verbally agreed upon to having two, possibly three, home games in February.

Fair rental manager Russ Rauch told the *Dispatch* that the Chill sent its home schedule to the league based on his commitment to open up more dates.

It was as if our previous conversations with Inmon when the scheduling issues first surfaced in May never happened. Rauch, who attended our meetings with Inmon, was sympathetic but could offer no relief.

"We are going to see what we can do," he said. "We would like to work together and not hurt our relationship with the Chill."

The ECHL schedule was completed and if the issue could not be resolved it meant that nearly a quarter of our home games would be played out of the Coliseum. It was too late to change the schedule, as 90 to 150 of the league's games would have to be moved to accommodate the Chill's revisions.

I told the *Dispatch*, "It puts the season in jeopardy," because the league had the right to revoke a franchise if it couldn't meet its obligations.

This was a potential disaster of epic proportion. We knew we had to do something . . . and quick.

We learned of this potentially crippling scheduling snafu just as Mark List was taking over. And rather than hearing this directly from them, we got the news from WCMH NBC 4 news anchor Doug Adair.

You had to wonder at what point they were going to tell us. Through a Christmas card? *Season's Greetings and, oh yes, no ho-ho-home games in February.*

We were fuming but, initially, held our tongues. We had been through crises before (Jason Taylor, Opening Night, and the scheduling problems in May with Inmon), so we were prepared to battle.

I decided that patience was the best plan at the time, so we waited for the precise moment to go public and then hit them between the eyes with our most recent scheduling dilemma. Our strategy was to take advantage of the chaos caused by Fairgrounds leadership transition in late August by unleashing a media fury supported by the outrage of our fans.

We had scheduled a meeting with List for Friday, September 4, but we met the day before with Craig Merz from the *Dispatch* to update him on the situation.

I felt the future viability of our franchise was truly at risk and wanted that point to come across in his story. We reviewed details of the scheduling dilemma and revisited the threat posed by the Pat Kelly letter published months earlier.

We believed that when the *Dispatch* story came out the following morning that it would cause a firestorm and be covered by every news outlet. Of course, if that strategy didn't work, we were dead in the unfrozen water.

Once again we called upon fans for help. They would read the article and be livid. By the time we were to meet with List, the press *and* public would be all over him.

To emphasize the seriousness of the situation, I wrote a letter to our season-ticket-holders with a very simple opening line: "We need your help."

The letter outlined the quandary and asked for the fans' immediate and direct assistance. We provided the names and phone numbers of the mayor's office and all the key sports and news media contacts and asked that they flood them with calls and letters on behalf of the Chill.

We also organized a town hall-style meeting the night of the *Dispatch* story at the Parke Hotel, home of Damon's Clubhouse, the site of the original press conference announcing the Chill just thirteen months earlier.

With the breaking news literally hours away from being on the door-steps of unsuspecting fans, not to mention Fairground officials, we took the calculated risk of mailing the letters Thursday evening—actually driving them to the mailbox of the Downtown branch of the post office to ensure timely delivery. We knew many of the fans would receive the letters shortly after Merz's article appeared in Friday morning's paper.

"It was a dangerous game of chicken because, in reality, we had no genuine options," said Brent Maurer. "We had the fan base in our pocket but we had to be strategic as to when to play our ace card."

The reaction of the *Dispatch* story appearing on the front page of the sports section and the personal letter to Chill fans was received as we expected it would be. The television and radio media flooded the Fairgrounds that morning, tagging List with questions about the scheduling issue.

He was new on the job but understood the gravity of the situation.

"It's among the very few top priorities I have," List said. "I have to see what commitments were made by Mr. Inmon."

While we had built up a relationship with the sports reporters, those covering the story were primarily news reporters who, at that point, were still unfamiliar with us. We were all too happy to supply them with the Pat Kelly letter from May and the necessary details. When we saw an opportunity to control the story and steer it in our favor, we quickly took advantage.

One TV reporter showed up late and approached Alan Karpick and me to ask who he should talk to about the story. He didn't know who we were. We pointed to List. "That's the guy," I said. We got the attention we wanted; the plan worked like a charm.

That evening Alan, Brent, Larry Lane, and I met with the fans at a meeting room at the Parke Hotel. We had a few hundred people show up and they were furious. We reiterated the importance of contacting the media through phone calls and letters to keep the Chill's problems at the forefront of the news.

And our fans did not disappoint. The response was overwhelming, with hundreds of calls and letters to each of the media outlets. From the moment our supporters received word of the scheduling problems to the time the issue was solved, they stayed after it. They loved their hockey team and they were not going to let it get bullied out of existence.

"The fans went ballistic," recalled Maurer. "With only a little prodding needed, the vocal contingent had been revved up. It was a calculated gamble and we got it right."

I later learned that a member of the *Dispatch*'s senior management team had reacted to the fans' onslaught by asking, "Who is David Paitson and why is he shutting down my newspaper (with calls and stacks of letters)?"

Labor Day came and went and we were still riding a series of emotional highs and lows. We not only had the passion of our fans but the general public, as they also saw how we had been wronged. The only problem was we still did not have the issue resolved. Once the media got ahold of the story, we were able to open up a dialogue between the Chill and List, who seemed genuinely distressed by the whole matter. I delivered a conciliatory, but cautionary, note to the *Dispatch* after our first meeting with him:

> Mr. List is the fourth manager we've worked with, and we've just been here just over a year.
>
> We left things in such a way that we can continue to look at the situation. I really don't envy Mark's position. He is, in many ways, deciding the future of this team. I can guarantee that there are 4,300 people who bought tickets already who are not going to be happy if things don't work out.

If there's anything that gets the attention of politicians, it's disgruntled constituents.

Columbus Mayor Greg Lashutka was no different. Feeling the heat from the community, he called me on the afternoon of September 4, after Alan and I had met with List. As it turned out, Lashutka brokered a deal over the next ten days that ensured we would have all the dates promised to us on the original ECHL schedule. It was a monumental heavy lift, but the mayor came through.

Under the plan, the *Dispatch* Sports Vacation and Travel Show moved from the Coliseum to the Celeste Center from February 2–14 and the Buckeye Classic gymnastics meet was delayed a week to February 19–21 at the Celeste Center. The Scott Antique Market agreed to move out of the Celeste Center for the gymnastics competition and use other buildings on the Fairgrounds. Playoff dates in late March and early April would continue to be a problem (possible postseason dates had to be turned into the league office before the season so a team making the playoffs would not be blocked out because it didn't reserve them).

We held a press conference on September 14 to announce the agreement and to publicly thank Mayor Lashutka, List, and the show operators who made the arrangements possible.

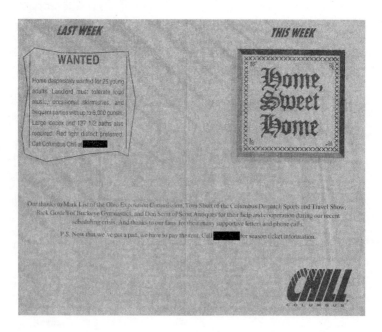

Another crisis was averted and the unintended benefit of added exposure during the start of the college and pro football seasons were welcomed by us as well.

Actually, what happened four days before our press conference would have an even more profound influence on the future of the city.

We did not it know at the time, but the whole scheduling crisis was *the game-changing moment* that triggered discussions on building an arena to attract a major league franchise to Columbus.

How could we be so sure? Because on September 10—just six days after our predicament became public—Lashutka announced that he would appoint a public commission "in the near future" to study the location, financing, and building of an arena for Columbus, in conjunction with the convention center that was to open in 1993.

He cited the Chill's troubles at the Fairgrounds as an example of why such a venue was warranted.

"There is a major facility need in central Ohio," Lashutka told the *Dispatch*. "We can ill-afford to lose sports entertainment, which is a vital part of what makes Columbus feel good and is available for people when they come in for conventions."

The timing could not have been a coincidence.

In 1989, Downtown Columbus, Inc., made a recommendation for a $78 million, 20,000-seat arena at the old state penitentiary site to be built with a combination of tax dollars and private money, but the plan had sat idle for three years. *Yes, three years!*

Now, all of a sudden, after one of the major players in town—the *Dispatch*—unwittingly got snared in the Chill's facility trouble, here comes the first step toward an arena.

The two events were intertwined.

It was the initial point of engagement for Mayor Lashutka and other city leaders and brought into the process the pair who would eventually become Columbus Blue Jackets' owners—John F. Wolfe of The Dispatch Media Group and publisher of the *Dispatch*, and developer Ron Pizzuti.

The whole scheduling incident was sordid, but it did elevate our profile and, while not yet putting us at the table with the city's big shots, we were at least in the same room. It would serve as the unofficial beginning to the city's efforts to build a downtown arena, with the ultimate goal being an NHL franchise. This incident was the tipping point that forever changed the sports landscape in Columbus.

My philosophy is if you want to keep a secret, don't tell anyone. If that is not possible keep the circle as tight as possible. Through the entire fairgrounds scheduling fiasco I kept the details of our no holds barred counter strategy—including the letter we penned on behalf of ECHL Commissioner Pat Kelly—to a handful of Chill staff (Alan, Brent, Larry). That is, until now.

We used that platform to lead Columbus in believing that we could indeed become a major league city, and the NHL would be our pathway. I built a strong rapport with the mayor and as an organization, we diligently stayed after the issue until action was taken.

Nearly a year after Lashutka's initial announcement in September of 1992—and with our continued, but subtle prodding—he did appoint a citizens commission to determine if there was merit in a more in-depth study for an arena.

The three members were:

- Ron Pizzuti, who had once taken a run at purchasing the NBA's Orlando Magic;
- Bill Hosket, former Ohio State basketball star and broadcast personality;
- Guy Cole, a leader in the African-American community, and later, a federal judge on the US Court of Appeals for the Sixth Circuit.

Another year passed before the Multi Facility Sports and Facilities Task Force was formed with ten community members. I would be one of two private business people on the group and the sole voice for hockey and professional sports.

The push for an arena got another boost in 1994, when Lamar Hunt was awarded a franchise in the fledgling Major League Soccer (the Columbus Crew began play two years later in Ohio Stadium on the OSU campus). In due course, a soccer stadium would be added to the wish list of downtown sports facilities.

With the help of Mayor Lashutka and Mark List, we were on our way . . . but what would become of the man who caused the fiasco in the first place?

Undaunted, Billy Inmon opposed George Voinovich in the 1994 governor's race. After being excluded from debates, Inmon staged a hunger strike while living in a tent on the lawn of the Statehouse in downtown Columbus.

On the 18th day of his demonstration, a man protesting Inmon's anti-gay policies urinated on the tent, provoking Inmon to point a gun at him. The episode cemented Inmon's image as someone not playing with a full deck. Nine days later, Inmon collapsed and was hospitalized. Gandhi, he was not.

Those of us in the Chill office watched each passing day of the hunger strike with more amusement, although we were not the least bit surprised by his latest stunt.

We could not help but think it was the perfect karma for Voinovich— having to deal with his former appointee on his front lawn.

Ultimately, the "Inmon Incident" was the best thing to happen to the Chill organization and professional sports in Columbus.

Without the precise timing of his monumental scheduling screw up, we would never have gotten the arena issue on the table in time for Columbus to be considered for one of the four NHL expansion franchises.

I guess we all should be thanking him.

BILLY INMON'S TOP 10 CAMPAIGN SLOGANS

10. Vote for me and I'll get you a really good deal on a '72 Dodge.

9. Hey, I didn't eat for 26 days. That outta be worth something.

8. Vote Inmon before he runs for something really important.

7. Inmon. 'Cause the Governor thing's a great gig.

6. I'm the man for the job and that's debatable.

5. Vote Inmon. Working to preserve your right to wave a pistol at passing cars in front of the Capitol Building at three o'clock in the morning.

4. Inmon. Like Perot, but without all that soul-corrupting cash.

3. I've governed livestock. Now I'm ready to try people.

2. The time is right. Because when's the last time you voted for someone named Billy?

1. Be young; have fun, vote Inmon.

Chapter Thirteen

PIPELINE TO THE SHOW

"Hockey belongs to the Cartoon Network, where a person can be pancaked by an ACME anvil, then expanded—accordion-style—back to full stature, without any lasting side effect."

—Steve Rushin, sportswriter and author

Minor league hockey was resurging in the 1990s, and the Chill was fortunate enough to ride that wave at its peak. Timing was clearly another factor in contributing to the team's improbable success and, like many American cities, Columbus caught hockey fever.

The East Coast Hockey League, founded by John Baker, Henry Brabham, and Bill Coffey, opened play in 1988 by combining five teams (Carolina Thunderbirds, Erie Panthers, Johnstown Chiefs, Knoxville Cherokees, and Virginia Lancers) from the defunct Atlantic Coast Hockey League and All-American Hockey League. A quarter of a century later, it now stands alone as the top Double-A league, a rung below the American Hockey League.

When the Chill joined in 1991, the league was still years away from being able to legitimately earn that distinction.

The ECHL started as an old-school bus league. Teams would play three or more times per week and almost always had combination games on Fridays and Saturdays, as weekends had the most profitable gates. To keep expenses down, clubs often traded tickets and advertising for apartments to house players. Teams usually had their equipment men doubling as trainers in most cases, which is pretty scary when you think about it. We became the first franchise in the league to hire a certified trainer, Chris Mizer, and later successfully petitioned to make it a league requirement.

As we quickly learned during our inaugural season, if you lost a goalie to a last-minute call up (promotion to a higher league) or injury, you had the option of replacing him with an "emergency backup" for just $75 per game. It was a common occurrence in the minor leagues and usually the spot was filled by a local amateur league or former collegiate player. In a pinch, we once secured a local police officer and Chiller men's league player Kenneth "K. C." Jones. Another time, being a bit overly frugal, I paid our intern Jason Rothwell, a former Ohio State walk-on goalie, only $50. In both cases (and no offense, but thankfully) we didn't need to use them in a game.

In 1997, the brother of Chill defenseman Corey Bricknell expected to watch the game from the seats, but Brad Bricknell was made the emergency back-up goalie when starter Jeff Salajko was recalled to Indianapolis just hours before the game. Inspired, Corey Bricknell scored only his third goal in three seasons to help the Chill defeat Toledo, 5–4, at the Toledo Sports Arena.

It was the first time the Bricknells had played together. Brad Bricknell, 26, was five years older than Corey and a senior-league (amateur) goalie in Port Perry, Ontario. He drove from Canada and arrived 50 minutes before the game, only to learn that the desperate Chill was going to use equipment manager Jason Stypinski as the backup until he showed up.

"I paid nine bucks for a ticket to be the backup goalie," Brad Bricknell said at the time.

In many ways, during those early years, the ECHL was just a step up from *Slap Shot*. We even had a real Hanson brother coaching in Johnstown, Pennsylvania, where much of the classic flick was filmed.

The ECHL aspired to be a true developmental league, but also a profitable one. With that in mind, cost containment was the key.

The ECHL put in place a number of well-thought-out business strategies that provided teams with the foundation for a sound fiscal operation.

The ECHL had one simple strategy: Cap the number of teams at 16 and drive up the value of each franchise. It was basic supply and demand. This was a good plan and, in my opinion, the ECHL should have stuck with it. Instead of doing so, when concerns were raised over losing quality cities to rival leagues, the ECHL adopted a "manifest destiny" approach. It was an easy sell amongst the owners who couldn't resist the short-term temptation of receiving the next big check from expansion money. Ultimately, all bets were off and "The Coast" would eventually expand "coast-to-coast" by absorbing seven teams from the defunct Western Hockey League and, in May 2003, officially moved from being called the East Coast Hockey League to just ECHL, with no further meaning behind it, much in the way the Big Ten remains despite having 14 conference schools.

The ECHL fielded 27 teams in the Chill's final season (1998–99) and at its peak reached 30 franchises. The league stood at 26 teams for the 2019–20 season, with all but Norfolk having NHL affiliations.

"These additions strengthen our base in the center of the country and give the ECHL, for the first time, a true national presence," then ECHL commissioner Brian McKenna said of the merger. "It expands our ability to act as a development league and more closely aligns our number of teams with both the American Hockey League and the National Hockey League."

Back in my time with the Chill, there was a hard salary cap of $5,000 per week (now $13,300) for a roster of up to 20 players to contain operational costs. Teams were allowed one exception for a "franchise" player or player/coach, for whom half of their salary would not be counted against the cap. Players were provided housing and per diem to limit out-of-pocket expenses. But, in all honesty, these guys were not incentivized by money as much as the chance to chase their dreams. In the ECHL, it was either "move up, or move on."

To ensure this process, the ECHL instituted a "three-year-and-out" rule, again with a loophole or two. The thinking was that if you weren't prepared to advance to the AHL or IHL by that point, you would never be ready. It was a sound idea but also had another benefit the owners cherished. The rules would draw young players who, for the most part, were just happy to be playing professionally. Yes, they'd haggle over nickels and dimes, but, for the most part, the cap would theoretically keep payrolls in check.

Another terrific rule on the surface was that each team had to have six Americans on its roster. It allowed the franchises a great selling point and promoted our relationship with the national governing board (USA Hockey).

The reality was, however, that while many of the owners were touting pro-American ideals, the league could only secure enough visas from the Department of Immigration to cover up to a dozen or so players per team. This meant we had to have at least six Americans to fill out the roster. Once the league secured more visas, the American player roster requirement was reduced to four.

Most teams secured affiliations with the NHL and either an AHL or IHL team. These teams might supply only two or three players, but it looked good to have that connection. That's how it was in our relationship with the Vancouver Canucks and, later, the Chicago Blackhawks. We saw a couple of players per season sent our way, but the affiliations also enabled us to more easily move players up to the AHL or IHL, an incentive for players that helped us in recruiting.

From an administrative standpoint, there were plenty of good people in the league when the Chill entered, but for each quality owner, there was at least one knucklehead or shyster who would lie to your face or stick a knife in your back. The most boisterous, rather than the most principled, ruled the league in those early years.

Despite all the rules, cheating allegedly ran rampant in the ECHL. To win recruiting battles, teams would regularly find ways to pay players under the table. One of the more blatant examples took place in South Carolina in the summer of 1997.

Commissioner Pat Kelly took action after a two-month investigation, which uncovered that the South Carolina Stingrays paid its players an average of $1,400 per week extra in checks issued by the city of North Charleston. The money was first paid by the Stingrays to the city as a donation to its youth hockey program. South Carolina coach Rick Vaive was suspended all of six games for his role in the deliberate salary cap violations. Forget about actually putting teeth in the rules!

In another blatant violation, after a 10–1 start to their 1996–97 season, the Louisiana IceGators went from the best record in the ECHL to the worst in one day after the team was forced to forfeit its first nine games—all of which were victories. League officials said Louisiana played one more "veteran" than allowed. A veteran is an individual who has played at least 200 regular season games of professional hockey. Taking no accountability, the IceGators said they relied upon information provided by the player's former team as the reason for not listing him as a veteran. Their research department must have been sick that day, as the information was widely inaccurate.

We never fell into the trap of paying players under the table. It made it tougher for recruiting and I was in a constant battle with our coaches because I insisted in staying within the rules but by doing so, they were at a clear disadvantage to teams that bent or broke the rules. But I couldn't do it. It was an integrity issue. Either that, or I just didn't have the nerve. Too much Catholic guilt, I guess. It was something we couldn't dodge, as we later learned when to open our third season, we faced a major showdown with our players over the issue.

During the early days of the ECHL, it was not very difficult to become an owner and form a team; that was part of the price of a new start-up league. But as a result, it led to attracting some of unstable operators and retreads. By almost any definition, the ECHL has had a tumultuous run in its quest for its niche in the hockey world.

There are a lot more variables involved in a team's success than many aspiring operators care to admit. It's not solely about ambition and hard work. It involves resources, research, analytics, community support, timing, and a little bit of luck. There was a clear shortage of sports marketing business experience in the ECHL when the Chill joined the league in 1991. As a result, many teams had no business plan, were underfunded, had unreasonable revenue expectations, and no conception of containing costs.

The effect was that, while the ECHL was becoming a rising force in minor league hockey, its uneven development made for some colorful characters and outrageously entertaining storylines.

While the first two letters in ECHL stood for "East Coast," the early years of the league were more similar to the "Wild West," with rules being broken or unenforceable and zany situations portraying a not-so-professional image.

As our Alternate Governor, I attended all league meetings at the request of Chill owner and Governor Horn Chen. It could be enlightening, but at times the meetings were mostly just a circus. I remember one incident where Allan Harvie Jr., owner of the Richmond Renegades, who despised our marketing strategy, was secretly taping a Board of Governors meeting. That is until Henry Brabham, a good ol' boy and owner of the Roanoke Valley Rampage, caught him. The two nearly came to blows right there in the middle of the meeting, demonstrating that the mayhem was not limited to the ice.[12]

Similar to the California gold rush of 1849, there was a misconception among interested minor league franchise buyers that this was easy money. Consequently, there was a mad dash in the 1990s to either buy or start a franchise, only for them to discover it was fool's gold.

Owning a minor league hockey franchise was either boom or bust, or, as with the dotcom bubble of the late 1990s and 2000, boom, followed by bust.

---

[12] Brabham passed away at the age of ninety, on March 30, 2020.

Case in point: Of the 33 ECHL franchises awarded from 1988 to 2001, only two—the South Carolina Stingrays (1993) and Florida Everblades (1998)—as of September 2020, continue to operate in their current markets without interruption. The rest have either moved on to new cities or folded completely. The Toledo Walleye stayed in the same city as their predecessors—the Storm—but there was a two-season ('07–08 and '08–09) gap between the separately-run franchises.

The "boom" led the race to expand into the "Deep South" in the mid-to-late 1990s. "The Coast" added 13 teams[13]:

Alabama - Mobile Mystics (1995–2002)

Louisiana – Louisiana IceGators (1995–2005), New Orleans Brass (1997–2002), Baton Rouge Kingfish (1996–2003, previously the Erie Panthers)

Mississippi – Mississippi Sea Wolves (1996–2009), Jackson Bandits (1999–2003)

South Carolina – Pee Dee Pride (1997–2005), Greenville Grrrowl (1998–2006)

Arkansas – Arkansas RiverBlades (1999–2003)

Florida – Jacksonville Lizard Kings (1995–2000, previously the Louisville IceHawks), Pensacola Ice Pilots (1996–2008, previously the Nashville Knights), Tallahassee Tiger Sharks (1994–2001, previously played in four other cities under five different names, starting in 1981)

Georgia – Augusta Lynx (1998–2008, previously the Raleigh IceCaps)

Most franchises started out like a house on fire, drawing big crowds and ticket revenue, only to see a sharp decline after the novelty wore off. With either a lack of vision, financial depth, or plans to counter a downturn, nearly all of these franchises simply dissolved.

To demonstrate this example, the Greenville Grrrowl folded after running a one million-dollar deficit during the 2004–05 season, leaving the

---

[13] List does not include the South Carolina Stingrays (established in 1993) or the Columbia Inferno (established in 2001), which were either established before this wave or after.

team unable to attract new investors. The Grrrowl began losing money after attendance slid from 7,000 per game in their first season (1998–99) to just 2,100 in 2004–05.

The Louisiana (Lafayette) IceGators were another franchise that enjoyed a meteoric rise, followed by a dramatic fall. In their first season (1995–96), they averaged 9,775 for 36 games. In year two, they became the first and only ECHL team to draw more than 400,000 fans during the regular season, with an average of 11,433 per game, for a league record that still stands as of 2020. They led the league in attendance their first four seasons, but after a sharp downturn in interest, the team ceased operations after the 2004–05 season. So much for sustainability.

Despite all the issues, the ECHL did manage to improve in quality over the years. Rick Adams was named President and CEO replacing Pat Kelly as the leader of the ECHL in 1995–96 and continued to break new ground. Kelly, who continued on as commissioner emeritus (the "Kelly Cup," awarded to the ECHL Championship team, was named in his honor in 1997), had been instrumental in establishing affiliations with teams in the NHL, as well as creating opportunities for players, on-ice officials, and front office personnel to develop and move up the hockey ladder. Kelly had done an admirable job in getting the league launched—particularly from a hockey operations viewpoint—but Adams gave the ECHL a serious business-first approach.

Under Adams's leadership, the league executed its first collective bargaining agreement with the Professional Hockey Players' Association, launched ECHL Properties—the licensing and apparel arm of the league (I was appointed president), unveiled a new logo, and launched the official league website, ECHL.com.

By its tenth season in 1997–98, the league drew 4.7 million fans. An expansion franchise that cost $25,000 in 1989 was going for more than $1.5 million a decade later. Minor league hockey was at its peak.

Nevertheless, owning a minor league hockey franchise is still a risky proposition. Of the 33 ECHL franchises granted (excluding league mergers), only 12 still exist today (including the Chill franchise, which was sold to Spectacor

Management Group in 1998 and relocated to Pennsylvania, starting play as the Reading Royals in 2001–02).

As the quality of ownership and team management personnel improved, so did the quality on the ice, as more and more players were advancing to the AHL and IHL.

The ECHL evolved into a proven development league and became the only Double-A league accepted into the collective bargaining agreement between the NHL and the NHL Players' Association. That meant a player signed to an entry-level NHL contract and designated for assignment had to report to either an AHL or ECHL club.

Today, the ECHL is widely respected as a breeding ground for future NHL talent and can legitimately claim its status as "The Premier AA League."

Since 2002–03, when it changed its focus and became the primary developmental league for the NHL and AHL, there have been 483 ECHL players who have reached the NHL and "the Coast" have had more call-ups to the AHL than all other professional leagues combined. All-time, 675 players have gone from the ECHL to the NHL through the end of the 2019–20 season. Among them were former Washington Capitals goalie Olaf Kolzig (Hampton Roads Admirals), forward Rich Peverley (South Carolina Stingrays/Dallas Stars), defenseman Francois Beauchemin (Mississippi Sea Wolves/Anaheim Ducks), Jay Beagle (Idaho Steelheads/Washington Capitals—only person to win Kelly Cup, Calder Cup, and Stanley Cup titles during their career), Jordan Binnington (Kalamazoo Wings—2019 Stanley Cup champion with St. Louis Blues), and forward Jody Shelley, who played for the Johnstown Chiefs before taking his pugilistic skills to the Columbus Blue Jackets in 2001. He later became a member of the Blue Jackets' TV broadcast team.

And there looks to be no slowing down for the league in sight. There were 13 more ECHL players who debuted in the NHL during the 2019–20 season. Also, a record 93 former ECHL players were on NHL opening-day rosters that season, as well as five coaches, 32 assistant coaches, and 33 on-ice officials. Prominent head coaching names include Nashville Predators' Peter Laviolette (Wheeling Nailers), Anaheim Ducks' Bruce Boudreau (Mississippi

Sea Wolves), Bruce Cassidy (Jacksonville Lizard Kings/Trenton Titans—head coach of 2019 Eastern Conference champion Boston Bruins), and Jared Bednar (Huntington Blizzard/South Carolina Stingrays—head coach of Colorado Avalanche, one of only two coaches to lead teams to both an ECHL and AHL championship).

We did our part. The Chill proudly promoted its first three coaches (Terry Ruskowski, Moe Mantha, and Brian McCutcheon) directly to the Triple-A level.[14]

Our team contributed five players to the NHL: Phil Crowe (Los Angeles, Philadelphia, Ottawa, and Nashville), Sasha Lakovic (Calgary, New Jersey), Eric Manlow (Boston, New York Islanders), and Peter Vandermeer (Phoenix). All were promoted after their time in Columbus. Blair Atcheynum (Ottawa, St. Louis, Nashville, Chicago), Cam Brown (Vancouver), Trent Kaese (Buffalo), and Andre Racicot (Montreal) played in the NHL before they joined the Chill, although Atcheynum appeared in 192 of his 196 NHL games after being with the Chill in 1993–94. Brown would be named to the ECHL Hall of Fame in 2010.[15] The Chill also promoted coaches Brian McCutcheon (Buffalo) and Don Granato (St. Louis, Buffalo) as NHL assistants.

The ECHL is good, solid entertaining hockey, a rising commodity and, if managed properly, its franchises have the makings of a sound business investment. Still, some owners never understood that the wave of popularity that minor league hockey enjoyed in the 1990s would cycle back down at some point. Most were not prepared for that eventuality. Even with all the safeguards in place, many would foolishly spend themselves out of business within a few years. While the Chill was riding high at the moment, we realized the intensity of our following would eventually give way to the routine. With the clock ticking, we set our sights on capitalizing on our success and to generate a public dialogue to make the case that Columbus, Ohio, was indeed a major league city.

---

[14] Don Granato also was promoted to the AHL, but spent one season in Peoria first.

[15] The other Chill players enshrined are Marc Magliarditi, in 2013, and Derek Clancey, in 2020.

PIPELINE TO THE SHOW

Minor Officials

Players, coaches, front office personnel, and even franchises come and go, but the anchors of any team are the volunteer support staff that makes a game possible.

Those who worked Chill games as statisticians, scoreboard operators, penalty box attendants, and goal judges were referred to as minor officials—but there was nothing minor about them.

And no one represented the spirit of Columbus hockey better than Richie Shepard, whose unpaid jobs in hockey spanned the very first professional game in September 1966, through the first decade of the Blue Jackets.

Shepard was doing custodial work at the state fairgrounds in Columbus when he was asked to care of the equipment for a new minor-league team, the Checkers, playing there at the Coliseum as a member of the International Hockey League.

"I'd never seen a game before," he would say later. But he was immediately smitten. Shepard vowed to never miss a home game at the Coliseum and he didn't, spanning the Checkers (1966–69), Golden Seals (1971–73), Owls (1973–77), and into Chill's final season in 1999.

When Columbus was without hockey for fourteen years after the Owls left until the Chill's arrival in 1991, he traveled to other cities to watch minor-league hockey games.

An African American in a predominantly white sport, Shepard nonetheless lived for hockey season and the friendships he developed over the years.

133

"I've met some wonderful people here," he once said. "I've met Bobby Hull and Gordie Howe. Those are wonderful memories for me. Those things don't happen to everybody."

He spent many years supervising the officials' room, often going above and beyond the normal requirements. ECHL referee Ken Dyar in a 1997 interview recalled when referee Pete Messana's car broke down. "Richie insisted [Pete] take his car to a couple of cities while Pete's was being fixed," Dyar said.

Stories of sacrifice abound among the minor or off-ice officials. Not only they did give up about forty nights a season to work games, but some of the "home games" had to be played in such Ohio cities as Athens, Cleveland, Bowling Green, Troy, and Fairborn.

The Chill was blessed with top notch people from the start, some of whom carried over their responsibilities from earlier Columbus franchises. The help of Bill Fyfe, Bill Woodall, Dick Grossinger, Eric Haines, and Rich Haines in assisting the Chill's training and equipment staffs were invaluable, especially during that first year.

Speaking of veterans, Lester Lyle, like Shepard, was in the Coliseum for the first pro game when the Chicago Blackhawks faced the Checkers. He was a fixture as the west end goal judge and didn't miss a game, once leaving the hospital the day after a mild heart attack to attend. Another time he experienced chest pains before the third period and had to be forced by the Chill staff to leave and be checked by doctors. He, of course, was back behind the goal the next game— all for two tickets and free pregame meal in the press box.

Steve Haller supervised (a loose term) the minor officials from day one of the Chill. Identical twins Ron and Joe Mongolier manned the two penalty boxes, causing many a player to wonder if he had taken one too many punches.

They were part of the group that was there from the first Chill game to the last. Dan Grassbaugh was eagle-eye in doing the unenviable task of plus-minus stats but had a better seat then in the end zones when he used to go to Owls games. Don Gulatta usually handled the shots on goal and in later years his family's business, Mr. Meatball, provided the meal for the hungry and underpaid off-ice officials.

Others who did yeomen work for many years beginning with the inaugural game included Doug Reed and Cliff Alton (clock and scoreboard), Rick Kramer, Jay Coyer, Guy Ventresca, and Craig Ventresca.

Jeff Dillion was the ice-making expert and Zamboni driver, not an easy job considering the aged equipment he had to work with. There were also dozens of others who did behind-the-scenes work that kept the Chill in operation, such as bus drivers Bob "Sharky" Smithberger and Harris Fry, and equipment manager Jason Stypinski, now an equipment assistant with the Columbus Blue Jackets. All who worked for the Chill had a love for hockey and loyalty to the Chill.

Shepard was with the Chill through the good and bad times on the ice to the very end. He drove to Upper Marlboro, Maryland, with his mentally challenged son, Ricky, to see the playoff game loss to the Chesapeake Icebreakers in the Chill's final ever game.

Afterward, with tears in his eyes and a quivering voice, he thanked every player and coach Don Granato as they boarded a bus for the long ride home. Then Shepard buckled his son and also headed back to Columbus knowing he did all he could for the Chill for eight years.

They all did.

Chapter Fourteen

THE BIG SELL

"The Chill is a class organization. They clearly know who their market is and how to appeal to them. This kind of marketing would impress the NHL in receiving an expansion team."

—Kevin Allen, *USA Today,* 1993

Ideas need selling. Selling ideas takes effort and repetition before it will take hold. Whether that notion was promoting the value of the Chill experience or the need for a Downtown arena, we focused on delivering a message that was simple, relevant, and truthful.

We believed that if we could connect with the consumer, we had the chance to inspire action. We enabled the same style with the media, as we know that we needed to connect with them in order to make an overall positive effect.

We always took a proactive, extend-the-hand approach with the media. We knew our place, and understood that Chill hockey was not an automatic publicity magnet like Ohio State football. With the Buckeyes, the media was constantly searching for any story angle. Because one negative story could set off a firestorm, Ohio State was much more inclined to work to control the message. That's not a criticism, just a reality for programs of that magnitude. We, on the other hand, were thankful for *any* coverage we could garner, subscribing to the age-old publicity axiom that "any publicity is good publicity."

Our one-on-one efforts during the summer of 1991 were meant to specifically court the non-traditional media (morning radio, alternative newspapers, the *Lantern*, the *Guardian*, etc.) and were paying huge dividends. It was this group that established the Chill as "cool." The mainstream media had to play catch up that entire first season—not completely comprehending the reason for the overwhelming support but, nonetheless, jumping on the bandwagon in full force.

With the bandwagon rolling, it was now time to shift gears. We were sitting on top of something special and we all knew it. We'd love to believe all the early success was due solely to our marketing savvy, but the truth was that the town was ripe for something big. I could feel it; we all could feel it. The Inmon fiasco had opened the door and it was time for us to step through.

We were fresh voices in the community, providing a sudden burst of change. The national media coverage and sellout streak had handed us the bully pulpit as the central authority on professional sports in Columbus. The question then became: How do we keep that momentum going, and use it to our advantage?

We believed we could begin publicly selling the idea that Columbus was a major league town. Yes it was a long shot, but why not at least try? None of us were career "lifers" in minor league hockey; we all were confident that we'd build successful careers in sports, but this was a one-in-a-lifetime opportunity, so we embraced the moment. What did we have to lose?

We were in a market—being geographically in the middle of the state, with Cleveland to the northeast and Cincinnati to the southwest—that had split loyalties when it came to major league franchises. We had an opportunity to unite central Ohio behind one pro team.[16]

---

[16] The Columbus Clippers Triple-A baseball team of the International League were affiliated with the New York Yankees, causing Indians fans in particular angst; plus, there was a segment who just hated the Yankees for being the Yankees.

Besides, the Ohio teams in other sports had not been doing so great lately. Maybe we could snag a few of their fans. The Reds, who won the World Series in 1990, faltered to 74–88 the following season, while the Cleveland Indians spent the 1991 season in the cellar of the American League East Division with a 57–105 record.

The Cleveland Browns went 6–10 in 1991 under first-year coach Bill Belichick, which was still better than the Cincinnati Bengals' 3–13 record that cost head coach Sam Wyche his job at the end of the season. Even the Cleveland Cavaliers stunk (33–49) despite having a James on their team— that would be Henry James, who averaged 8.1 points for 37 games.

Here was an opening for us to present an edgy and exciting new (to most) product.

Columbus had been a city of inaction or multiple attempts (see 1978, 1981, 1986, and 1987). To us, lack of action was totally unacceptable. Our mission was to be the pesky bug in the ear of anyone who would listen.

There were like-minded business and city leaders who saw the validity of a Downtown arena project and the upside of a major sports franchise. We just had to connect to them and find voices who'd speak out on behalf of the project. The Convention Center, attached to Battelle Hall and the Hyatt Regency, was opened in 1993. Their leadership believed an arena within close proximity to the Convention Center would do wonders to attract additional conventions and visitors. There were plenty of other folks who wanted to rejuvenate the night life that was, at the time, entirely absent downtown. It was clear that the center of the city needed a major shot in the arm, which made our point for attracting a major league sports franchise that much more viable.

One important thing about any great idea or message is that, without the right people pitching these ideas or messages, they can still fall flat. Luckily for us, we had two of the best in Brent Maurer and, in later years, Gary Kohn. In the PR slot, we were looking for promoters—not statisticians or information types—and both of these guys fit the bill.

Brent had the gift of gab, never met a story he didn't like, and had a great feel for how to march the story angle to the media member he knew would be interested. He built a wonderful rapport with the media and bottom line: he knew how to "sell it."

Gary is a southern California native and Arizona State University graduate who oozed openness and a friendly happy-go-lucky style. He is a classic talker who easily picked up the baton from Brent at a critical time when we were working to sell the community on the need for a Downtown arena. As an avid concert attendee and sports fan, he easily related to the audiences who were to benefit from the project. After interviewing dozens of candidates, it took all of ten minutes for us to decide that Gary was our man for the job. Both Brent and Gary had a gift for connecting with people that was priceless to the organization.

While Brent, (later Gary) and I carried the arena message, we strategically pushed our best player personalities to the forefront in marketing the team. The players and coaches were viewed as charming and the guys welcomed the opportunity to help promote themselves and their sport. Hockey players are typically down-to-earth guys, especially in the minor leagues. Even in the NHL, they are less spoiled by the riches of fame and, thus, not considered egotistical.

Morning radio was vital to giving a stage to our newly created celebrities and toward building the Chill brand. What radio could accomplish that television could not was its ability to deviate from the standard interview. In this setting, we wanted the public to see our players as people—not just as professional sports athletes who rattled off the standard clichés. I can't underline enough how important that was for us in forming that bond. As evident in our previous and future advertising campaigns, humor was at the center of the Chill experience, and radio was the perfect outlet in showing this off. The more the public was exposed to their humor and down-to-earth qualities, the more the players were seen as "regular guys." The fans who listened felt like they knew "Smurf," "Pearl," "Sangster, the Gangster," and "The Whopper," all of whom became familiar characters on their morning drive to work. Because of this platform and countless promotional appearances, we continued to form that emotional connection with the fans.

After a few seasons, to keep things fresh for the fans, we created *Saturday Night Live*-style sketches for the players to interact on air with WNCI's Dave Kaelin, Shawn Ireland, and Jimmy Jam. "The Morning Zoo loved what we were doing," said Maurer. "The skits were great stuff."

As we forged relationships with the stations, some were willing to take the partnership to new levels.

At our prompting, alternative rock station WWCD 101 hired Jim Ballantine, a center from the University of Michigan's hockey team, as the morning sports host while he was playing for us. Jim was a perfect fit for their counterculture image. He broke the stereotype many had of minor leaguers—that they were uneducated rubes with no interests outside of hockey. He stood out as someone who was imaginative, intellectual, and in his own way, he easily assimilated within the local college lifestyle.

Jim was one of my personal favorites. He was one-of-a-kind, true to himself, honest, and above all, quotable. He once told a reporter his scoring streak with the Chill was the result of "being on an ethereal plane."

"Strategically we worked the angles to make the right matches with the stations," said Maurer. "Roscoe wowed Wags & Elliott (of Q-FM a classic rock station) with his stories and hockey insight. Smurf and our cast of characters were regulars giggling and hamming it up with the Morning Zoo. Of course, Ballantine's wit was a perfect match for alternative CD 101."

We integrated his ultra-creative writings into our game program. One memorable feature included a photo of Jim standing on the side of the highway with the sign "Will Play Hockey for Food." The guy was priceless.

Jim became the morning show's unofficial sports reporter, sometimes talking about sports, but most of the time talking about life in general. In the spirit of the partnership, Jim wore the number 101 during part of the regular season. He stopped doing so when he deemed the action a "commercialization" that he no longer wanted any part of. That was Jim—pure of spirit. The jersey was later displayed in the Hockey Hall of Fame as the first three-digit uniform in the history of professional hockey.

And, oh yes, he once shot down our remote-controlled blimp that was circling pregame. "Jim is called in for a meeting where he explains [to David] that he 'was practicing my moon shot,' to which [David] reacted, 'Jim, I just don't find your story believable.' It was classic Ballantine," recalled Maurer.

With Jim Talamonti handling the play-by-play and Brent (later Gary) doing the color on our radio broadcasts, we had the perfect platform to drive home every promotional message we could. For an offbeat look at the league and issues effecting the Chill, Craig Merz put aside his notepad for a few minutes and joined Maurer on the radio for a popular and comedic intermission respite.

Though more staid, television provided a few unique creative outlets as well.

Don Granato, in a "trading places segment," became an WCMH NBC 4 weathercaster for a day while their regular weatherman, Jym Ganahl, tried his skills on the ice during a Chill practice. It didn't hurt us that Jym was so crazy about hockey that he built an ice rink in his backyard every winter annually and created a segment in which he teamed with the WNCI Morning Zoo to battle Chill players for pond hockey supremacy.

In time, we developed relationships in television much like we did in radio, allowing us to feed them material frequently. WCMH NBC 4 sports reporter Steve Saunders entered the scene during our third season and was a major part of propelling our momentum and, to some extent, mystique, for being trendy that proved critical once the initial euphoria of a new franchise had worn off. Steve mirrored the young and hip audience we were courting. Over the next few seasons, he created countless MTV-style news reports that continued to build the flavor of the Chill and life as a minor league hockey team.

One of his most memorable pieces included the entire team participating in a music video, "Chillin'," which was reminiscent of the Chicago Bears "Super Bowl Shuffle" of 1985.

In another video that took on a major league look, Saunders spoofed the famous Larry Bird vs. Michael Jordan 1993 McDonald's commercial titled "The Showdown." In the McDonald's commercial, the contest begins as a friendly game of horse between the NBA superstars who are playing for a McDonald's lunch. As shot after shot is hit, the stakes increase to the point that their final shot is "off the Sears Tower, over the express way, through the window—nothing but net." In Saunders's piece, the matchup is between forwards Clayton Young and Mark Woolf, using the same concept in which the funniest scene is the puck bouncing off the desk of a startled Terry Ruskowski—"nothing but net."

"That piece was spectacular. Steve's approach was completely different," Maurer said. "He had that MTV edge and, like us, wasn't afraid to mix popular culture with sports. Channel 4 was a big friend of ours.

"Doug Lessells (WCMH NBC 4 sports anchor) was cut from the same cloth as we were, recreating sports highlights on Sega," said Maurer. "Doug gave Steve a lot of space to be creative. Steve was an unbelievable talent who wanted to be in Hollywood. Steve and the Chill were a match made in heaven." Not surprisingly, Saunders eventually became a personality for MTV, ESPN, CBS, and the Disney Channel.

Our communications team also went at times to extremes in support of our biggest promotions. When we took on the *Animal House* theme for the postseason and sold T-shirts with one word, "Playoffs," it played off the silliness of the plain "College" shirt worn by John Belushi. No controversy there, but we did raise an eyebrow when we distributed "Eat Me" cakes to the morning talk shows to promote the theme.

Hard work also paid off in one of our hokiest promotions ever—a Valentine's Day celebration with Bernie Kopell ("Doc" from the 1970s series *The Love Boat*). Ron Foth Advertising wrote a terrific radio spot for the promotion:

His life was the sea, painting each day and night on a wavy blue canvas.

He sailed the world's oceans looking for love, exciting and new.

He's Doc and he lived on the Love Boat, the biggest and most buoyant aphrodisiac known to man.

Set a course for adventure. Come see the Columbus Chill's Valentine's Day game at the Fairgrounds Coliseum.

This Friday watch the Chill beat on the holy Dayton Bombers then watch love blossom as Bernie Kopell, Doc from *The Love Boat*, helps couples intertwine their lives.

For tickets, visit any Ticketmaster outlet, charge by phone or call the Chill Love Line 614-XXX-XXXX.

Come aboard; we're expecting you.

Chill hockey—blood, sweat and fear and on this night only, love.

ESPN's Charlie Steiner ended an ESPN *Sports Center* report with the Kopell appearance—due in large part to Gary's persistence in sending every item we could to "The Worldwide Leader in Sports."

It just goes to show that principles of marketing and communications remain the same no matter the era, resources, delivery systems, or technologies available.

The Love Boat promo was another instance of expanding our brand beyond Columbus. We spent countless hours building a wide-ranging list of allies that, over the years, would be vital in getting out our message that Columbus was ripe for an NHL expansion team.

For example, when we assisted ex-Chill intern Jason Rothwell and the Ohio State *Lantern's* Chill beat writer Scott Woods to top PR positions in the ECHL and IHL, respectively, we had people in key places, and they played an important part in broadening our reach to hundreds of media across the country. We also maintained positive relationships with all of our coaches. Each was helpful in telling the story to his NHL friends of why Columbus was worthy of the NHL's consideration.

In the meantime, to draw in fans, we kept up the P. T. Barnum sideshow. We were transitioning to becoming a hockey organization and laying down real roots in the community with the building of the Chiller in Dublin in 1993 as our practice facility but, as they say, "the show must go on."

We constantly looked at ways to freshen up the presentation and decided to make a few changes. In season four, Anthony King took over the role of show producer when Larry Lane departed to run one of Horn Chen's new franchises, the Jacksonville Lizard Kings (Jim Morrison lives!), and the marketing team created new promotions and music. We also we hired a new public address announcer.

Anthony, a Columbus-area native and University of Notre Dame finance graduate, had interned for us the previous year and had shown a flair for the role. Years later, he would test off the charts for his Law School Admissions Tests (LSAT) at almost genius levels. He was an aficionado of satire, movie parodies, and popular culture—and had a particular affinity for *Beavis and Butthead* and *Seinfeld*. In stealing a line from *Seinfeld*, seemingly everything he knew about higher culture he learned from Bugs Bunny cartoons. Anthony had a great feel for the comedic timing needed for the role.

Anthony, in his role as the man behind the curtain, was teamed up with the spirited Andy Davis a.k.a. "Andyman," the popular radio deejay and program director at the popular alternative radio station CD 101, who took the reigns as our new "Master of Ceremonies."

We were searching for someone extraordinary, someone who had the spirit to tap into our culture and further define the Chill brand to our fans. The Chill was your unconventional team, and Andyman did nothing but accentuate our avant-garde style.

Andyman

John Andrew Davis, a.k.a. "Andyman," became the Chill's "Master of Ceremonies" beginning in the team's fourth season. He replaced Neil Shapiro, an extremely competent but by-the-book public address announcer.

Andyman was anything but typical, making him a perfect fit for the Chill formula. As an on-air talent and program director for the alternative rock station CD 101, he was uncompromising with the music and dedicated to delivering it with passion and authenticity for his audience. His personality fascinated the Chill, who were committed to consistently freshening up their in-game presentation.

"We took a gargantuan risk in handing over the keys to someone so untested," said Brent, who recalled bringing Andyman's name to the table as a potential candidate for the role. "It was a calculated strategy that proved to be well worth the gamble."

The fact was, he'd never worked as a public address man before and, quite frankly, didn't know much about hockey. That was okay with us; in fact, it was a plus. We liked that he had no preconceived notions or steadfast traditions to follow. Yes, he was handed a script each night, but it read more like a guideline. Andyman's ability to go off-script and improvise is what gave Chill games their edge. With Andyman at the controls, the Coliseum became the place you came to expect the unexpected.

When the Chill introduced Andyman and simultaneously rolled out the "Scream 'til your brain hurts" advertising campaign, (created by Ron Foth Advertising) there was a little sensory overload—even for hardcore hockey fans. Andy's booming voice bellowed the theme every ten minutes or so, encouraging a loud and shrill fan response. There was early backlash to his style, but it didn't take him long to fall into a groove and win over the fans. "Since our crowd was never shy about sharing their opinions, they actually booed him and yelled quite a few other personal insulting comments," explained Anthony King, game entertainment director, and Andyman's partner in crime on the headset. "It did not take long until he got comfortable in his new environment, and once he did, his critics stood absolutely no chance. They had no idea that they'd end up his biggest fans, but I am sure he did. He just had that magical ability—you could not do anything but love him."

"He was the perfect PA guy and great voice for us," said Maurer. "He took the role very seriously and poured his heart and soul into

Chill hockey. Once he had the bug, he bled for the sport and was as much of a fan as any of our diehards."

"Andyman was fearless and not afraid to spoof himself or engage in our across-the-line promotions, despite his public job," added King. "Not many public figures would be caught dead yelling the phrase 'gentlemen, drop your pants' for our penguin races (where our improv comedy team (Midwest Comedy Tool & Die) would, on his command, drop trou and waddle across the ice to the finish line) or get into a scuffle with the San Jose Shark mascot. But that's exactly why he was perfect for us—actually more than perfect. I think we all thought he'd be great for us, but there is not one of us who could have predicted how much he would mean to us and the fans."

Andyman "got it." His charisma, passion, and energy built on the previous momentum to transform the Coliseum into the place to be in Columbus during the 1990s.

Andyman was the face of CD 101 and a fixture on the local entertainment scene. He had endeared himself to the community when, in 1992, he started his annual fundraiser, the Andyman-a-Thon—a 24-hour music marathon, as a way to give back to the community and to allow the rest of the station's staff to spend time at home during the Christmas holiday. He also connected regularly with his listeners at "Andyman's Treehouse," a cozy neighborhood bar and live music venue he owned just southwest of the OSU campus in Grandview.

Landing him for the role gave us another ally who kept a pulse on what was cool in Columbus. "It was big," Maurer said. "Andyman had his own unique legion of followers. We were doing great entertainment without video screens. We needed somebody to tie it together and Andyman became the ring master at the center of the circus."

Each fall brought a battle for mindshare with Ohio State football. In order to grab the media and public's attention, it was imperative for the Chill to start each season with a bang.

Opening Night was always critical to setting the tone. In our second year, with a little help from the WNCI Morning Zoo, we looked to transform the Coliseum into a "white out," borrowing a Canadian tradition started in Winnipeg in 1987, when the Jets (who would move to Arizona in 1996 and become the Coyotes) fans were asked to wear white clothing to home playoff games, creating a very intimidating effect and atmosphere.

We built several items into the "Opening Night, Wear White" theme, including an on-air promotion for which they publicly offered $1,000 cash to anyone who would be willing to part with their used car or truck (as long as it was the color white).

The vehicle would become the grand prize for the intermission contest. To solicit the appropriate vehicle, Alan Karpick and I planted ourselves at 6 a.m. in the parking lot of Westland Mall, checking in with calls to the radio show every thirty minutes or so.

"To be honest, the whole idea probably should have bombed, as we really had no idea what we would attract over the next four hours," Karpick said. "With ten painful minutes remaining, we were beginning to feel a little desperate, as we had viewed a pretty disappointing collection of vehicles. But, as had become our hallmark, we lucked out when at 9:55 a.m. a white Mercedes rolled in.

"We looked at each other in amazement and laughed hysterically," Karpick recalled. "This was it. We'd struck gold! As it got closer and we had a good look we saw why. It had nearly 300,000 miles and was more than a little worn. "

That didn't prevent the us from using the headline "Win a Mercedes on Opening Night." The copy did confess the details. "Yeah, so it has 300,000 miles on it, and it's a plug in, but hey, it's a Mercedes. . . ." We were able to get a local body shop touch up the car a bit and, of course, covered it with Chill logos. It was the exact type of absurdity that Chill fans embraced. The car became a driving billboard for years, although from time to time the front office would receive complaint calls whenever the Mercedes would break down on the outerbelt of Columbus, causing major traffic delays.

Ever wonder what it would have looked like to throw a biscuit into the middle of the Donner party?

Well, that's what it's gonna look like at the Chill ticket window this season. Ugly. Brutal. Savage.

It's a scene you don't want to be a part of. And you don't have to, if you plan ahead.

All full season tickets are sold out. The same with weekend mini-season tickets.

Single game tickets - at $7 for students with a valid college I.D. - are your last chance. And they go

on sale soon. Don't get left out in the cold. The Donner party did. And it wasn't pretty.

CHILL
COLUMBUS

Year two of the Chill in 1992–93 showed the evolving nature of the team and the ECHL as more skilled players made the product better. Sure, there were plenty of fisticuffs, but we actually had 670 fewer penalty minutes (although at 2,081, it still was a robust 32.5 penalty minutes per game) than our first year and improved to 30–30–4 for 64 points.

Unfortunately, that wasn't good enough to again to make the playoffs but it was fascinating to see Roscoe develop as a coach as he handled a more talented group, such as forward Steve Strunk and defenseman Shaun Kane. Both were selected to play in the ECHL All-Star Game.

Jason Christie led the team in scoring for the second straight season with 61 points (20 goals, 41 assists), edging out Strunk (32–28–60). We were a balanced team, as evidenced by the number of players with double digit goals: Kurt Semandel had 27; Rob Schriner came out of Ohio State to score 26 times his rookie season; Frank LaScala netted 19 goals, Jim Ballantine and Kevin Alexander each had 18; Don Granato had 16; Cam Brown had 13 before being traded to Erie; and defenseman Frank Evans chipped in with 11.

Barry Dreger's 301 penalty minutes topped the team while the goaltending duties were handled mainly by veteran Russian import Sergei Khramtsov (16–17–1, 3.44 goals against average) and rookie Jason Fitzsimmons (16–9–3, 4.07 GAA).

Khramtsov was a great story in that he came when players from Russia were just starting to play in North America and at a time when there was still a curiosity about athletes who for so many years had been part of the Soviet bloc.

He knew virtually no English when he joined the Chill on assignment from the Milwaukee Admirals of the American Hockey League and the word was that he was not very good at their preseason camp.

Khramtsov wasn't much of a practice player. However, once the whistle blew for a game, he came alive. That was evident in his first game with the Chill when he was spectacular in beating the Hampton Roads Admirals, 4–3, on their home ice.

There was also an advantage being a foreigner. "I swear in Russian on the ice so the referees don't know what I'm saying," he told the *Dispatch* through an interpreter.

As I said earlier, there was greater emphasis on skill the second season, but there were still incidents that made the ECHL seem like an outlaw league. January 19, 1993, was one of those times. No one in the Coliseum, will forget the night Knoxville's Grant Chorney and the Chill's Sasha Lakovic got into a postgame brawl that began when Chorney punched Lakovic as he crossed the ice from the press box to the locker room. The pair ended up brawling in the corridors underneath the stands as fans scrambled to the exits to avoid the fisticuffs.

Actually, the feud began 13 days earlier in Knoxville as the pair tangled late in the game and then exchanged words in the parking lot.

In the return tilt in Columbus, referee Gordon Buchanan made damn sure they didn't renew hostilities on the ice. He got that part right.

The official gave Chorney and Lakovic minor penalties when they jostled in the first period. In the second, he issued 10-minute misconducts as they eyed each other as a precursor to dropping the gloves.

Then, to the dismay of the packed house, Buchanan threw both of them out of the game for trying to get at each other in the penalty box.

Lakovic watched the third period from the press box on the south side of the Coliseum at the request of our staff. Chorney camped out near the Knoxville bench on the north side.

After the game ended, as Lakovic walked across the rink toward the locker room, he was attacked by Chorney upon leaving the ice. The players scuffled there; Chorney got a cut under his left eye and the security staff escorted Lakovic back to the press box and held them there.

Meanwhile, Chorney tried to get into the Chill locker room but was restrained momentarily. He then raced through the Coliseum in search of Lakovic with State Highway Patrol officers in pursuit.

The building was put on lockdown before Chorney was finally corralled and taken to the Knoxville locker room. The whole incident took about 20 minutes.

Umm, yes, both players were suspended.

Lakovic, by the way, would eventually play 37 games in the NHL for Calgary and New Jersey, totaling four assists and 118 penalty minutes.[16]

He's probably better known for a portraying the star Russian hockey player Boris Mikhailov in the 2004 movie *Miracle*—the story of the US Olympic team's seismic upset of the Soviet Union at the 1980 Winter Olympics in Lake Placid, NY, and subsequent victory in the gold medal game

---

[16] Lakovic passed away at the age of forty-five, on April 25, 2017, from inoperable brain cancer, leaving four children.

against Finland two days later. Obviously, Lakovic quickly earned a reputation in the league, but there were other well-known enforcers as well.

Don Granato was at the back of an unusually quiet bus en route to Nashville in March 1993.

"About halfway through the trip I walk back and ask what's going on," said Granato.

"Barry Dreger said to me, 'Grats, you guys can't start any shit tonight. No, really. This is going to be the most honest game of hockey we've ever played.'"

The reason a seasoned fighter like Dreger was apprehensive? Link Gaetz, the most feared goon in hockey, had recently joined the Knights.

He lived as hard as he fought in a brief but mercurial NHL career with the San Jose Sharks that was cut short after a car accident a few months prior. If there was anybody that came close to the fictional thug Ogey Oglethorpe it was the "Missing Link." Granato continues, "Sure enough, just like in *Slap Shot*, we pull up and one of the stick boys was there. He was talking to one of stick boys in their locker room and came back; we were just getting settled, and said, 'Hey guys, Link just got called back up.'

"There was the biggest sigh of relief possible. It was freakin' priceless, just like *Slap Shot* when they found out Oglethorpe was suspended. The guys almost jumped up and down. They were so fired up Link Gaetz wasn't out there," Granato said.

The 1992–93 season ended the same way it started: a 9–3 loss in Erie, Pennsylvania, against the Panthers. The finale was played under strange circumstances. We made a six-hour bus ride through blizzard-like conditions to arrive 75 minutes before the scheduled 7:30 p.m. start.

What the Chill didn't know was that Erie had decided at 6 p.m. to postpone the game because of a state of emergency. The team was not pleased because Commissioner Pat Kelly had told the Chill in the morning to travel to Erie despite warnings from the Ohio State Highway Patrol that the roads were hazardous and, in fact, during the trip the freeway entry ramps were being closed behind the bus to prevent further traffic.

At 7:15 p.m., Kelly was reached by phone in Toledo and he told the teams that the game had to be played. Erie, at that time, was on the ice practicing because they were already at the arena when management had decided to postpone the game.

Meanwhile, when Kelly's edict came, the Chill was on the bus, ready to head to the hotel. The team stayed at the rink to unload the gear and by 7:55 p.m. was on the ice for the pregame skate, only to be told that Kelly had changed his mind again and the game was postponed until Sunday. The only fans in the stands were those who came by bus and car from Columbus.

The game was played the next day and the Chill, now down to 14 players because of injuries and call-ups, lost in a big way by allowing three goals in the first 13 minutes. That still didn't sit well with Roscoe.

"There are guys you can count on to play, and there are others that you can't," he said. "We had guys filling up the game who wanted to make sure they didn't get hurt."

That comment reminded Brent of another game the previous season in Erie after the Chill had been eliminated from playoff contention. Maurer was sitting at the front of the bus as both teams packed for overnight trips elsewhere. As the players climbed aboard Roscoe pointed toward the Erie bus and said, "winners" before turning to his team with, "losers." And so it went, "Winners-losers. Winners-losers. Winners-losers." It was a long, silent ride.

The challenge for the 1993–94 season was to create a winning culture while also juggling the responsibilities of running a business, operating and programming ice facilities and providing hockey's voice to the downtown arena initiative. We had a remarkable ability to walk that fine line between circus act and legitimate civic leader. It was an unusual combination, to say the least, but it is safe to say years three and four were exhilarating and critical times for the franchise.

Chapter Fifteen

BUILDING FOR THE FUTURE

"There are NHL teams that would love to have a facility like the Chiller."
—Terry Ruskowski (a.k.a. "Roscoe"), October 1993

To make our long-term vision of becoming an NHL city a reality, we understood that we needed to expand our audience by integrating hockey into the community and initiating grassroots participation.

Opening the Chiller Dublin, a $3.5 million, 77,000-square foot dual ice facility in October of 1993 was proof that we were committed to the expansion of hockey in the area. It was a public-private partnership in the affluent northwest Columbus suburb. Dublin, with its 16,000 residents, was exploding with growth and political influence (it had 52,465 residents as of July 2020). With its progressive leadership, we believed this was the "new money" and the future power base of the city. To that point, Dublin was best known in the sports world as the home of golf's Memorial Tournament, founded by Columbus native Jack Nicklaus.

The Chiller Dublin was a historic venture. The Chill became the first minor league team ever to construct, own, and operate an ice facility. At that time, only the NHL's Mighty Ducks of Anaheim could make the same claim. It solidified our credibility with the local community and generated attention in hockey circles.

Yet, opening the Chiller Dublin was fraught with perils from the past. Similar to previous hockey failures, ice rinks, too, had come and gone in Columbus. Past failed ice rink ventures included the Ice Chalet in Westerville, which closed in 1978; Ice Land in Columbus which melted in 1982; and The Centrum, a Downtown outdoor rink at Town and High Streets, which closed in 1986 to make way for the Columbus City Center shopping mall, which also has since come and gone.

The Chiller was vital to the organization on several fronts. First, it provided our team with its own practice facility. We now had exclusive use of locker rooms, offices and a training room. The building also included concessions and a gift shop. There would be no more early morning skates at Ohio State that seemed to always be limited to an hour because it was the lone permanent ice in town and someone else needed to skate.

"It was an efficient, professional operation in Columbus: how they treated us, the facility we practiced in, having the building being full every night," said forward Derek "King" Clancey. "You realized how fortunate you were to play in Columbus."[17]

Second, it started our "cradle to grave" fan development approach by creating hockey-related, or at least-ice related, opportunities for everyone, from toddlers to senior citizens. We cast a wide net for prospective customers. We believed everyone was a potential ice skater at one level or another, even if it was only an annual trip over the holidays for a public skate. Like with the Chill, we knew we'd need to expand upon the existing audience if we were going to run a successful and profitable business and ultimately work to convert those customers into hockey fans.

Third, building in Dublin enabled us to "influence the influencers" by getting their kids on the ice and, hopefully, falling in love with figure skating and/or hockey.

---

[17] Clancey joined the Pittsburgh Penguins' organization in 2007, and was named director of professional scouting in 2010. The club would win three Stanley Cups while Clancey was with the organization (in 2009, 2016, and 2017).

"Soccer moms" later became the buzzword in American politics, but at the time, we were after "hockey parents" who dreamed as big as we did. We thought a good place to start was a place like Dublin.

Fourth, the Chiller proved that our brand could play a role in economic growth. Dublin city manager Tim Hansley attributed the rapid expansion of the southwest quadrant of his suburb directly to the building of the Chiller.

In less than two years, our legal counsel Greg Kirstein, Alan Karpick, and I had worked with the city of Dublin to reach an agreement. During that time we located and leased eight acres of land at a dollar per year for twenty-five years; secured financing for the facility; selected a design and construction team; assembled a formal operations, programming and marketing plan, and constructed and opened the facility.

At Horn Chen's request, Greg had located a handful of local investors to infuse essential start-up cash. As with the hockey team, Chen still owned the majority share of the ice facility. The investment group also included former Ohio State football All-Americans Rex Kern and Tom Skladany. Kern was a godlike figure in Columbus because he guided the Buckeyes to an undefeated season and a consensus national championship as a sophomore quarterback in 1968. Skladany was a three-time All-American punter (1974–76) and enjoyed a six-year NFL career, which included the Pro Bowl in 1981. Their involvement reinforced our message from at least some influential members of the Buckeye Nation that hockey was here to stay.

The dual-rink facility was a godsend to our hockey operation and business. Finally, we had a place to call home.

As part of our due diligence, we traveled the Midwest to research numerous facilities and consulted with ice guru Jack Vivian, considered to be the world's foremost expert in ice arena construction, operation, and management, to assemble our policy and operations manuals. We hired Todd Bell, one of Vivian's protégés from his Sports Facilities Research Laboratory (SFRL) at the University of Michigan, to be our program director; and Gene Lesinski, an ice and refrigeration expert, as our general manager. Gene had been introduced to us by Duke Johnson, of the OSU Ice Rink, during our inaugural season to help keep an eye on the tenuous ice situation at the Coliseum. Julie Fry was instrumental in picking up a majority of the daily administrative and operational duties and making sure that nothing fell through the cracks. During our launch and through the first several months, I even turned to our Chill staff to serve as on-site managers until a comfort level was reached with the newly trained staff.

However, the most important hire was Margy Bennett as our ice skating director. Margy, a native of Knoxville and a graduate of the University of Tennessee, had strong ties with the Ice Skating Institute (ISI), a national non-profit organization for owners, operators, and developers of ice skating facilities. The ISI were the creators of America's original learn-to-skate program and were considered to be more recreationally based than their counterpart, the United States Figure Skating Association (USFSA), whose primary focus centered on higher-end competitive skating. Margy shared our like-minded philosophy, which was to build our programs in-house and control our own destiny.

Our model was simple: Introduce the sport through public skating sessions, convert children and adults to eight-week ice skating group lesson programs, and, ultimately, move them on to youth and adult hockey leagues or more advanced figure skating programs, competitions, and private lessons. To cast the widest net possible, we slotted our most premium ice times to public skate sessions, which would encourage family participation and allow as many people as possible to sample the product.

Based on hourly revenue generation, our financial drivers in order of importance were public skating, group lesson programs, birthday parties, youth and adult hockey leagues, and, finally, private lessons. We received a lot of free advice from "experts" who had different priorities based on their own agendas (effectively reversing our model in order of importance), but our programming philosophy was sound and gave the business the best chance to succeed. We were fortunate to have found Margy, as she may have been the lone skating professional in the Columbus market who "got" what we were trying to do.

During our first year of operation, more than a half a million people flocked to see the new building, and, in short order, we established the ISI's largest learn-to-skate program in the United States. In ensuing years, we created the Columbus Chill Youth Hockey Association (USA Hockey sanctioned) and Chiller Figure Skating Association (USFSA sanctioned).

The Chill players were an integral part of this programming. Monday night public skating sessions were reserved for and free to Chill season ticketholders and included special player appearances. Players such as Jesse Cooper, John Sandell, and Darwin McClelland lent their expertise in skating lessons, refereeing (you can imagine some of their talking points) and conducted coaches' clinics to the absolute delight of eager young fans who were thrilled by the personable approach of the professional athletes.

"The entire project was critical in getting people to think hockey in the community," said Karpick. "It increased our reach far beyond being a little minor league hockey team that also played a role in marketing the facility."

In keeping with the spirit of the Chill, we decided to label our two sheets of ice with keenly appropriate names. The hockey rink was named "Rink-A-Dinka-Do," a take-off of the 1934 classic ditty "Inka-Dinka-Do" by Jimmy Durante. No, the name had no real meaning, but it sounded cool. We named the skating rink "The Columbus Institute for Ice Skating and Higher Consciousness," spoofing the perceived pretentiousness often associated with figure skating.

The timing for making Chiller operational proved fortuitous as well. Luckily, the International Olympic Committee decided to change the way it had conducted its games for the past several decades by alternating the Summer and Winter Olympics every two years rather than stage both in a four-year cycle. That meant the new schedule began with the Winter Olympics in February 1994, as we were still celebrating the opening of our facility.

Months before the start of the Olympic Games, and in our anticipation of their potential impact on our skating programs, we purchased a small portion of WCMH NBC 4's newly created five-second TV ad inventory to run during the final two days of the figure skating championships.

Hard Copy Olympics

Never having followed figure skating until the opening of the Chiller Dublin in the fall of 1993 forced me to learn more about it, and I found myself a few months later fascinated with the Tonya Harding-Nancy Kerrigan story, even though it was not normally my sort of thing.

It pains me to write that I became a regular viewer of the hit tabloid shows *Hard Copy* and *Entertainment Tonight* during that period.

Then it dawned on me to create a promotion out of the whole ugly incident and name it in honor of one of the tabloid shows.

Our edgier stuff was usually reserved for Q-FM's Wags & Elliott because their audience understood us. Such was the case with the Hard Copy Olympics, which debuted in 1994.

The Hard Copy Olympics were an intermission contest narrated by the duo. We created an obstacle course where two fans raced against each other through the maze of tabloid news.

First, the contestants had to strike a female mannequin (representing Kerrigan's plight) on the knee. On contact, Larry Lane, who handled game-day entertainment, provided her infamous "why me?" scream over the PA.

Then the contestants raced to the next location where they shot water pistols at the Menendez brothers (the trials of Lyle and Erik for killing their Beverly Hills socialite parents in 1989 became a national obsession four years later on Court TV).

The third task was to spell "Joey Buttafuoco" on a blackboard (the New Jersey mechanic had an affair with the 17-year-old Amy Fisher. Soon after the dalliances were exposed in 1992, the "Long Island Lolita"—as the press tagged her—shot Joey's wife Mary in the face).

Next on the list was tossing five hockey sticks like a madman (Roscoe became a local legend and even made ESPN earlier in the year for his stick-throwing rampage from the bench after a disputed call).

The final station was the Lorena Bobbitt "chop and lob," where the contestant would chop a sausage and lob it into a basket. (John and Lorena's marital woes gained international attention when in 1993 she severed his penis with a knife and then threw it in a field. In case you were wondering or had forgotten, the appendage was found and reattached).

Wags and Elliott set up of the event perfectly, the crowd loved it, and the Hard Copy Olympics became an instant classic.

It was supposed to be a one-time event but year after year the world just kept feeding us new material and we always tried to include one local celebrity in the mix.

The next year, former Columbus mayor Dana "Buck" Reinhart obliged when he was charged with drunken driving and reckless operation after running his car into a north side dumpster. We recreated the crash by having fans steer remote controlled cars into a pyramid of Budweiser cans—one of our two beer sponsors, and Buck's drink of choice on that ill-fated day.

No one could have predicted at the time how profitable of a buy that would become, because the Olympics were about to become one of the most famous in history due to the Tonya Harding-Nancy Kerrigan feud.

It became arguably the most talked about rivalry on the planet at the time, with the skaters gracing the covers of both *Time* and *Newsweek*, and reporters following their every move.

Their saga enthralled the world and brought unprecedented attention (some would say notoriety) to the event. It's easy to see why.

Harding became public enemy No.1 in early January 1994 when her ex-husband Jeff Gillooly hired a hit man to "take out" Kerrigan with a collapsible baton so that she would be unable to skate in the US Figure Skating Championships in Detroit that served as the Olympic qualifier.

The attack was successful enough to force Kerrigan to withdraw from the championships but she was given an Olympic spot, nonetheless, as a teammate of Harding.

Kerrigan recovered in time to create a "good vs. evil" showdown for gold in Lillehammer, Norway, due to the circumstances. At that infamous moment during the Olympic free skating program when Harding broke her skate lace and pleaded with the judges to replace it, NBC broke for local commercials. With the whole world wondering what would happen in the next few minutes to the distraught skater, the people in Columbus were treated to a Chiller commercial.

Jackpot!

The Olympic skating finals secured a 48.5 rating (the percentage of all TVs in the country) and a 64 share (the percentage of all television sets turned on), making it the third-highest-rated sporting event in history to that point.

Yes, we had planned carefully to take advantage of the figure skating program, but it was just dumb luck in the timing. At $45 per spot, it was the best money we ever spent. As much as a year later we had people telling us they saw our ad over and over. It ran maybe twenty-five times, including the figure skating finals, but the placement made it that much more powerful.

With one successful ice facility (Chiller Dublin) under our belt a few years later, we were dreaming of a location for a second one when I caught wind of a major shopping development project by billionaire Les Wexner. Realizing the magnitude of the project, I reached out to Tim Rollins at Steiner & Associates, the leasing team for information on the development soon to be known as the Easton Town Center, a mammoth retail and entertainment venture on 90 acres in northeast Columbus.

Located more than 20 miles from Dublin, there was enough geographic separation from the initial Chiller. It was a perfect location in what would become the shopping hub of Columbus. Wexner, an arts enthusiast, was not considered a sports fan but could be influential in either making or breaking any project in Columbus. We didn't expect him to support the arena issue when the time came, but if he remained neutral it would be a plus. It certainly didn't hurt us to be doing business with one of his properties.

Chapter Sixteen

THE WALKOUT

"The episode got my close friend traded. That's something new to me. But if you burn too many bridges, you don't have a place to cross."
—Chill Forward Mark Woolf, *Columbus Guardian*, November 3, 1993

In the ebb and flow of life, the christening of the Dublin Chiller (October 3, 1993) was a high point for the organization from a business standpoint, while simultaneously in the fall of 1993 we endured a crisis involving the players that would alter the team's on-ice direction as we entered our third season.

I had missed the end of training camp because I was in Indianapolis attending the funeral of a Pacers' colleague and friend, Roy Hurley. Roy's claim to fame had been as a player who appeared in the first-ever NBA game in the late 1940s. We would later work together with the Pacers and he helped us launch the Indianapolis Ice of the International Hockey League (IHL).

While I was gone, Roscoe completed the contracts with the players and sent them to the league just before the deadline. Roscoe wasn't as comfortable handling the salary cap process as I was and was having trouble living up to earlier promises he made to players while also staying within the salary cap. In short, the numbers weren't adding up.

At some point, several players assumed they would make more than what they ultimately signed for, but in order to stay within the guidelines, Roscoe had to trim the salaries of several key players at the last minute. Not surprisingly, they were pissed.

When I returned from Indianapolis early the next morning, I had five disgruntled players in my office, including the franchise star, Jason Christie. The other veterans were defenseman Darren Perkins and forwards Rob Schriner, Mark Cipriano, and Mark Woolf. They made up three of our most potent offensive stars, a key defenseman and an enforcer.

I spent about thirty minutes with them in my office. They were upset at their perceived lack of compensation, especially in light of the opening of the Chiller and the unquestioned box office success of the team.

The players viewed those two factors as concrete evidence of the franchise's deep pockets and were looking for their share of the windfall. The problem was we had taken the salary cap to the limit and there was nothing legally or ethically that I could do.

I made it clear that we were not going to pay players under the table as I knew, and so did the players, that several other franchises had done so with nod-and-wink agreements. They stated their case in a very straight-forward manner and insisted that they wanted us to bend the rules, but I didn't relent.

It's not that I didn't empathize with their situation. We, indeed, were making money; the players were making peanuts, and without restrictions, the players undoubtedly would have been paid more, but my hands were tied. I knew they could point to other league franchises where they would have made more money, illicitly, than they ever could legitimately in Columbus.

Despite my feelings that it was a closed matter, I told them that I would discuss the issue with Roscoe, who was already fuming because Christie, Perkins, and Woolf refused to practice that morning.

Although the players' meeting had been a bit unsettling, I had turned my attention back to business, when, about twenty minutes later, Brent raced into my office. Apparently, the players decided not to wait for me to discuss the situation with Roscoe. Brent had just received a call from WSYX ABC 6 sports anchor Mark Cooper, who was on his way to the Chiller after learning that five players had walked out of practice in a contract dispute.

It appeared to me that the players obviously had charted their plan all along by using public pressure to force us into a corner to get what they wanted.

I visited briefly with Brent and Alan to assess the situation. A few minutes later, I brought in Roscoe to talk it over. He, too, was pissed and unnerved after trying to work out the contract issues over the previous few days. The feeling was clear amongst us that the patients believed they were in charge of running the asylum and it was time for us take it back.

As a staff, we worked hard over the prior two years to prop up our players' profiles in the city, but our very actions were now working against us. Brent, who dealt most directly with the guys on a day-to-day basis, had grown concerned that the celebrity had gone to Smurf's head, to the point of distraction. Roscoe was upset that Smurf reported to camp in clearly what was less than tip-top shape. If we'd based roster decisions solely on preseason play, he would not have made the team, but because of his play the previous two seasons—as well as the stardom he'd built—he received the benefit of the doubt. Jim Ballantine, who played well throughout camp, scored four goals in our final preseason game and was the last player waived from what was clearly our most talented lineup to date. Even prior to the player walkout there were internal rumblings questioning whether Smurf was the right player to lead the team.

With a wedge now driven between players and management, I was left to make a quick decision that would affect the future of our franchise. From his position as conduit between front office and team operations, Brent had seen the divide brewing for a while and, believing it was insurmountable, lobbied to trade Smurf.

"So much had been handed to him in stardom and becoming the on-ice face of the franchise. He had been entrusted as captain with the responsibility of leadership," Maurer recalled. "In retrospect, it was probably too big of a load for a twenty-four-year-old that early in his career."

I did my best to stay rational, but my blood was boiling. Roscoe had a long history with Smurf, having recruited him out of junior hockey, but he was ready to make a trade. He stated that he also had tired of Smurf's act and felt betrayed by the player's actions.

He also felt that, at this point, he was replaceable. Besides, Roscoe had recruited a new star in Clayton Young, a dynamic, high-scoring forward around whom he planned to build our team's future. Roscoe envisioned him paired with Woolf. Together, they would give us the 1–2 offensive punch we needed to win . . . with or without Smurf.

With the television cameras on the way, we had a matter of minutes to make a decision. We weren't about to give in and, as tough as it would be from a public relations standpoint, in our minds, we had to draw the line.

Tactically, we had to decide whether we would take a proactive or reactive approach with the media. Here we were, making a major decision about the direction of the team, but I wanted to make sure it was a rational one and not based solely out of anger. I was irate for being placed in this situation, both by the players and by my coach, whose actions were culpable in what triggered the issue in the first place, but I still had to determine what was best for the team, all egos aside.

The truth was that Roscoe had absolutely no appetite for the locker-room drama created by the walkout. He had been a leader his entire career, and in his mind the players' response was no way to lead. Plus, there had been rumblings of tensions within the team held over from the previous season. Roscoe hadn't won to this point and realized that by the third season, it was important to field a playoff-caliber team. Nobody was indispensible, not even Christie. From my perspective, the only solution that would satisfy the players was paying them under the table, and I was absolutely clear that wasn't happening. As a marketer, I didn't want to be placed in a position where we would have to trade our highest-profile player, but we didn't force the issue. The players did when they picked up the phone and called the media. That ended it. It was a quick decision, but not a snap decision.

However, if we sat on our hands, I knew we would soon lose control of the story and maybe the team. In the end, right or wrong, Roscoe and I felt the players' actions crystallized that it was time for both parties to move in a new direction. We were confident that we'd be okay on the ice; we'd just have to endure the public fallout.

I decided to suspend all five players indefinitely.

With the players having already tipped off WSYX ABC 6 about the walk out, we decided to use the noon news to release the story to all of the media and do our best to quickly regain control of the situation. Brent called the other media outlets to bring them up to speed, and word quickly spread after several interviews. We took a firm position and knew that there was no turning back. We now had to deal with the expected backlash. Fortunately for us, we were in the pre-Internet and social media era, so we still had the upper hand in steering the direction of the story.

Early that afternoon, after having to deal with the media questions, I decided to stop by Roscoe's office in the back of the Chiller and found the five unhappy players in the locker room. I completely lost it and threw them out of the building, telling them emphatically that they were done in Columbus. I saw from the looks on their faces that they knew I meant it. I had felt belittled by the notion that they thought so little of us that they just assumed they could strong arm the front office into folding to their demands. Walking out and attempting to play the media card was a huge mistake on their parts.

I tried to check my emotions and stick to my guns, but it wasn't easy in the face of the fans' anger. In my mind, the players had crossed a line and the damage was irreparable.

We stayed on the offensive. WSYX ABC 6 invited me to their studio to lead off the six o'clock news. From the news set, I outlined the facts and emphasized that we didn't have a choice in the matter. We couldn't pay the players extra because we were not going to break the rules. There would be no skirting the salary cap, no matter how popular the players were.

"It was classic crisis PR and we all aligned ourselves," said Maurer. "We kept our message simple and truthful. We believed in the rules and we are not going to break them. We also noted that these were still the five highest-paid players on team."

That evening, Dave Kaelin of the Morning Zoo called to give me notice that Smurf and the players had asked to be on his radio show the next morning to state their case. I appreciated him letting me know, but also told him that it was WNCI's call as to whether to have the players on.

All I asked of Kaelin was to be fair with the facts. The players did tell their side on the city's top morning show, but when Kaelin countered with the fact that the guys had signed contracts and we were playing within the rules, they couldn't muster up much of an argument.

The following week was pure hell. We were still in preseason camp so there were no games to be played or discussed. All the attention was on the walkout and the fallout. Fans, by and large, not surprisingly sided with the players. Although we had missed the playoffs our first two seasons, the fans were incredibly attached to the players and were upset that their beloved team was being broken up. We were fielding calls constantly and doing our best to deal with a bad situation. I hated every second of it. The media frenzy nearly equaled the fervor of when Ohio State's star running back Robert Smith walked out right before the start of the 1991 season, claiming the coaches stressed athletics over academics. Cameras were in our faces every day, whether there was anything new to report or not. This was the Chill's mini soap opera, complete with heroes and villains. Unfortunately, I was the villain—a miserable role for me, quite frankly.

In America, we live in a culture where athletes and celebrities are akin to royalty. We crave the satisfaction that comes when our idols confirm our identities. Smurf was "one of us"; emulating the lunch-bucket, hard-nosed, working-class style player our fans personified.

Parting with Smurf was exceedingly hard on our fans. He was immensely popular and had to that point been, along with Roscoe, the face of the franchise. WBNS-TV (CBS) even went as far as to interrupt their afternoon soap operas to broadcast a live Christie tearfully clearing out his locker at the Chiller.

"It was a surreal moment, but Smurf was as high profile of an athlete in this town as any OSU player during that time," said Maurer. "Pop culture declared that we were the hot ticket in town, and he was our most identifiable player. The whole thing was big news."

"At the end of the day, in the midst of all this chaos, we dealt with the player walkout with a calm, sensible business approach," said Karpick.

As unfortunate as the players' revolt was, it showed how ingrained the Chill was in the community that we could push Ohio State football for attention during their season.

In the end, we traded Christie to the Louisville IceHawks for future considerations, but he refused to report and, ultimately, was dealt to the Charlotte Checkers. Darren Perkins was traded to Toledo, where the Storm would somehow not have the same problem that we did keeping him financially happy.

After trading both Christie and Perkins, we decided to keep Mark Woolf, Rob Schriner, and Mark Cipriano.

We felt the latter two, Schriner and Cipriano, were just trying to present a unified front as good teammates and were not instigators of the walkout.

Yes, Woolf was one of the three ringleaders, but he was saved by Young, who went to bat for him. I was against keeping Woolf but relented to the wishes of Young because I could see he was going to be the team's leader, and a good one at that. The players held no ill will toward Woolf and Schriner and voted them as alternate captains to Jason Smart—the third straight Jason (Taylor, Christie) to be captain.[17]

We also gained a terrific player through the Perkins deal in defenseman Joe Cook, a former Miami (Ohio) University standout.

Some ECHL observers speculated that McSorley might have been behind the entire event in an attempt to get Perkins from us. We found it curious when he called Roscoe within minutes of the walkout looking to strike a deal for Perkins. "McSorley tried to be coy, but we held out and got Joe Cook [from Toledo]," said Maurer. It was a complete steal. Funny

---

[17] Per ECHL rules, Young was ineligible because he was the player-assistant coach.

thing was, Cook became among our most anti-Toledo players. He abhorred McSorley and the Storm."

Cook was as good as anyone we ever had at running the power play and racked up 89 points (26 goals, 63 assists) in 63 games for us that season.

If Smurf had truly grown complacent in Columbus, the incident and the subsequent trade to Charlotte may have been the best thing to happen for his career. He would spend part of the 1993–94 season with the Checkers before moving up to the Hamilton Canucks (AHL). In next five seasons, he'd play exclusively at the Triple-A level and did so in fine fashion.

Not surprisingly, the season started with a lot of tension and pressure to win. Fans were on my back in a big way. I had a several invitations for fistfights and the occasional "Paitson sucks" chant would rise up in the Coliseum. It was tough to take, but I took comfort in the fact that at least we knew the fans were passionate about their hockey team.

Fortunately, we went on to have a great season, beginning with a 3–1–1 mark on the road for the new-look Chill. By the home opener, Schriner and Woolf were the only returnees from the 1992–93 club who were on the 16-man active roster.

Unfortunately, the Wheeling Thunderbirds spoiled our first home game in 1993 with a 3–1 win. The good news was the crowd of 6,000 was the 40th straight sellout, another example of their unwavering support. In fact, in a survey of ECHL players the previous season, they voted Columbus as having the loudest and best fans.

The season got better from there, primarily because Roscoe had for the first time secured a very solid group of goaltenders. On November 13, former

---

Limousines and OJ

For Opening Night of 1993, the Chill caught fans completely off guard with a spectacular Opening Night introduction. At my request, Larry Lane secretly had arranged for three white stretch limousines to deliver the team onto the ice from one of the end tunnels instead of their traditional entryway through center ice.

The front office kept the idea very quiet, not telling Roscoe or the team until they completed their morning skate that day.

When the lights and smoke engulfed the limousines as they made their way out of the tunnel, it created an amazing sight. The players inside shook the limos for extra effect, and when the doors opened and the guys hit the ice, the crowd erupted.

"Any description falls flat of how awesome it was, but it was truly one of the most spectacular scenes I'd ever witnessed at a sporting event," Larry said.

Fans pleaded for the return of the limousines the subsequent year, but otherwise, we knew it was impossible to duplicate the excitement and firmly believed true classics are never repeated.

Plus the Chill had other ideas.

We reeled the fans in by executing the smoke and lights in the exact same fashion as the previous year but offered a new twist. It was 1994, and the country was fresh off the infamous O. J. Simpson police car chase witnessed by Americans only six months earlier. Instead of limos appearing through the smoke, the Chill rolled out a white Ford Bronco followed about ten seconds later by a police car with its sirens blaring.

Fans either howled or their jaws dropped in disbelief. *Can they do this?* Sure, why not? What did this have to do with Opening Night? Well, nothing, but in Chill style, we wanted to poke a little fun at America's obsession with the tabloid tale that would enthrall and divide the nation. Once more, we successfully executed the unexpected, creating the type of chatter we loved and craved.

Ohio State goalie Jim Slazyk recorded the first regular-season home shutout in team history (Alain Harvey in 1991 and Sergei Khramtsov in 1992 had road shutouts). He stopped 19 shots to beat the Blizzard, 6–0.

Slazyk (8–5–1, 4.16 GAA) played 16 games in a supporting role, but our two main goalies provided a unique tandem in "Big Sergei" and "Little Sergei." Yes, we had a pair of Russian netminders for much of the season.

"Big Sergei" was the taller, younger, and English-speaking Tkachenko (18–7–4, 4.11). "Little Sergei," of course, was Khrmatsov, back for his second and final season with the club. He was 13–6–2, with a 3.53 GAA.

Another early season highlight came on December 4 at Erie, when we had our greatest comeback to that point, rallying from a 6–2 deficit in the second period to beat the Panthers 9–8 when Woolf scored the winner with 14 seconds left in the third period. It was revenge for blowing a 5–1 lead October 29 in the Pennsylvania city and losing 7–6 in a shootout.

Woolf was overshadowed in the rematch by a team record-tying four goals by Blair Atcheynum, who upped his total to six goals in four games since joining the Chill from a Saskatchewan senior league. He tied the Chill's four-goal mark set by Trent Kaese, Jim Ballantine, and Frank LaScala.

The Young-Atcheynum-Woolf trio led the way and we were dominant as the league's best team for about two-thirds of the season before they were called up to the American Hockey League.

The "Gray boys," so dubbed because they had to wear their gray third jerseys for every game until the black and white ones finally arrived in March (incredibly, as a Double-A team we didn't have the clout with the manufacturer, CCM, to press them for the order placed more than six months prior to the season—very humbling, indeed), were cruising to a North Division title.

We had a nine-point lead over Toledo after 49 of 68 games (32–13–4) and were on auto pilot. But we could not overcome the effects of the promotions of Young (33 goals, 47 assists, 78 points and 98 penalty minutes in 39 games), Woolf (42–29–71, 103 PIMS in 51 games), and Atcheynum (15–12–27 in 16 games).

After going 9–7–3 down the stretch, we lost the division by three points to the Toledo Storm but made the playoffs for the first time in our team's history with a 41–20–7 (89 points) record.

Cook's 89 points led the way, an outstanding number in just 63 games. Smart was second with 79 (29–50). Woolf had a team-best 42 goals and Mike Ross was next with 34 goals, plus 35 assists. Young had 33 goals, as did

Martin Mercier, and Schriner added 29. Mark Kuntz, acquired early in the season from Richmond, had 255 penalty minutes in 57 games.

We were thrilled with our performance during the season and, even better, Coliseum officials had finally agreed before the 1993–94 season that insulated flooring—such as what that had been used in hundreds of arenas for decades—would be sufficient to protect a basketball court over the ice, which opened a few additional home dates for us in the Coliseum.

For the first time, the Chill had March home games (three Sunday matinees) and ice available for the opening two rounds of the postseason.

The moment was made even better for us, as we'd secured WCMH NBC 4 to broadcast our first home playoff game live. Primetime TV for minor league hockey on a network station was unheard of, demonstrating again how far hockey had come in Columbus.

The Johnstown Chiefs came to town after winning the opener of the best-of-three first-round series in Pennsylvania. We wanted the place rocking for the televised game and literally juiced up our home crowd by holding a 90-minute beer party in an adjacent building before the doors to the Coliseum opened.

A good promoter is always willing to beg, borrow, or steal proven ideas . . . and I was no exception. I was a big fan of how the Chicago Blackhawks presented the national anthem at the old Chicago Stadium. It was a bona fide celebration with fans cheering and waving the American Flag, with the noise level rising with each verse until it became near deafening. I wanted to duplicate it for our playoff games.

We brought Roscoe into the party room and, as a former Blackhawks player, he spoke with authority on how the presentation lifted the team. Then we showed an awe-inspiring version of the "Star Spangled Banner" I had recorded a couple of years earlier.

It came from the broadcast of the 1991 NHL All-Star Game at Chicago Stadium during the opening days of the Gulf War. The combination of the pregame party, Roscoe's speech, the video, and the prospect of our first post-season home game in an overflowing building had our fans properly stoked.

"We were getting ready for the game and you could hear how loud the crowd was in the [dressing] room, even before we went on the ice for warm ups," Clancey said. "I remember listening to the excitement when preparing for the game. The emotion gave us such a rush of energy to get out there. It was an incredible environment."

With the TV audience looking on, the Chill fans did not disappoint performing a Chicago-style national anthem salutation. It was spectacular. At the point of the "bombs bursting in air," Larry Lane unleashed one of the ten concussion bombs to rock the Coliseum. The crowd, already at a fever pitch, roared!

The game was over before Johnstown ever hit the ice. Larry unleashed nine more concussion bombs—one for each goal—in a 9–4 victory over the Chiefs.

We took the next game, as well, to win the series before losing three straight—one home game—to the Toledo Storm in the second round.

We would host only one more playoff game in the Coliseum, in March of 1996. In ensuing years, we were forced to take our postseason games to Troy, Dayton, and, in the end, even the Dublin Chiller. While those home-away-from-home games killed us financially, they did provide opportunities once again to shout from the rooftops the need for an arena in Columbus.

It also pounded home the point that this was an embarrassing situation and that it was time for the city to finally step up. After a year of waiting on the Citizens Commission that was assigned to "study whether we needed a study," we were about to get some real action.

Chapter Seventeen

THE BATTLE LINES DRAWN

"The question is not whether the university can support an arena. We can. The question is whether the city can support an arena without the university."
—Ohio State University President E. Gordon Gee, *Columbus Dispatch*,
Spring 1994

I was among a growing contingent who wanted to see Columbus step into the national spotlight. We all felt that it would be a tremendous sense of pride to have a major league sports franchise to call our own. It was with that passion that Downtown arena supporters pushed forward, but we all knew OSU wasn't going to give up their sole possession of the city's sports scene that easily.

While Mayor Greg Lashutka's Citizens Commission was deciding if an arena warranted further inquiry, we were out on the streets spreading the word through any method we could and to any audience that would listen. It became part of our daily dialogue with the media, our partners, and fans. I made regular appearances on morning radio and other in-depth-issues programs to push the point across of how important an arena was to *our* city.

In the May 1993 issue of *Columbus CEO Magazine*, I was a part of a roundtable discussion about the arena issue. The participants included seven-term city councilman M. D. Portman and Ohio State Athletics Directors Jim

Jones and Richard Sheir (known as the so-called "arena slayer," who also was the former spokesman for Citizens for Private Development, a group opposed to using public money for sports facilities). In June, I joined Portman and others on WOSU-TV's (PBS) *Viewpoints* to again debate the matter.

At the suggestion of Columbus titan Ron Pizzuti, I also appeared on WSYX ABC 6 *Newsmakers Sunday* on March 12, 1995. Brent was great at booking us on various talk radio programs, and I became the authoritative voice for the future of hockey in Columbus from that point forward.

In each case, our message was simple: Columbus already possessed the population and demographic base to support major shows and concerts. I had previously worked in Indianapolis, a city supporting two major league teams (NBA Pacers, NFL Colts), the biggest auto race in the world (Indianapolis 500), Triple-A baseball, and that had emerged into the "amateur sports capital of the world." Columbus and Indianapolis were very similar in their makeup. That proved to me that with a serious commitment Columbus could be home to more than Ohio State University athletics.

We made the case for an NHL expansion team by stating several key points:

- We were the largest city in the country without a major league franchise;
- The NHL had no team in Ohio, the seventh most-populated state;
- The NFL and MLB were never going to happen in Columbus due to its proximity to Cleveland and Cincinnati.

Yet, it was our belief that the push for a Downtown arena would have to come from a grassroots effort. I noted that if the public demonstrated a sentiment for the project, the city would be able to "find" the money.

When Polaris Amphitheatre opened in 1994 (Billy Ray Cyrus played the first concert), it started to mark a change in the city's entertainment landscape.

"This was a transformational time in Columbus," said Brent Maurer. "People were getting their appetite whet for major league-style concerts and finally began asking: 'Why do I have to drive to Cincinnati or Cleveland for big-time events?' It was a message we'd been consistently driving home and we were starting to see the payoff."

In each case we argued the point—that a Downtown arena was needed—noting that the city had the ability to grow beyond OSU sports.

It was our strong belief that Ohio State could accomplish its goals and focus on their core initiative (intercollegiate sports) with a significant upgrade of St. John Arena (an aging but tremendous and energetic facility for college basketball) and by building a 6,000 to 8,000-seat facility for their hockey program and other sports. For recruiting purposes, OSU was interested in hosting events like the high school basketball championships at St. John Arena.

On the other hand, a Downtown arena would have a dramatic impact on rejuvenating a struggling area. Downtown had the infrastructure in place (hotels, convention center, parking, etc.) to stage major events and maximize the financial impact to the city. We strongly felt professional hockey, family shows, and concerts belonged in the central city.

This issue was hotter than ever. I felt the public needed someone to drive them to that conclusion. As an organization, we, to the best of our ability, took it upon ourselves to steer the city toward the direction of building an arena.

The spring of 1994 marked a year since Mayor Lashutka appointed the Citizens Commission to look into the arena issue. We were growing a little concerned that his effort might just be for show.

With our Coliseum scheduling fiasco of season two now behind us, and a handful of additional dates opening up with the new permanent ice flooring, our problem may have appeared to have been solved in the public's eye, but it wasn't. In reality, nothing much had changed. Yes, we picked up a few Sunday dates in March, but we still had to shoe horn most of our six-month schedule into the same four-month window. Plus, there continued to be no guarantee for home playoff dates.

Consequently, we had more ambitious objectives. No way were we letting the public forget the need and urgency of a sports/entertainment facility. That's why we kept pounding them with this message.

Behind the scenes, Pizzuti, on behalf of the city, was involved in a series of negotiations with George Skestos—who represented OSU that summer—to determine if there was any possibility of bringing Ohio State into the fold. A few years earlier, Pizzuti had made a serious run at buying the NBA's Orlando Magic but fell short to the DeVoss family who paid cash for the team. Ron was a fixture in the Columbus business community, seen as a leading advocate for sports and the arts, and was deemed fully capable of holding his own in a negotiation with Ohio State officials.

OSU President E. Gordon Gee had signaled his intentions earlier that spring with his statement questioning whether the city could support an arena without OSU. It appeared as though he was clearly suggesting that the university had no motivation or intentions toward participating in a project that was not on his campus.

That sentiment appeared to be confirmed in May 1994, when Ohio State hired Andy Geiger as its new Director of Athletics, succeeding Jim Jones. Geiger had previously served as athletic director at Brown, the University of Pennsylvania, Stanford, and Maryland. While at Stanford, he was credited with building the sports endowment from $4 million in 1979 to $50 million in 1990.

Geiger had a propensity for building sports facilities, and it was evident that his hiring would move Buckeye athletics in a much more proactive direction. Geiger was a force to be reckoned with, and with the new athletic director at the controls, the arms race between Ohio State and those wanting a Downtown arena was unofficially on.

Bill Jennison, who served on the Citizens Commission headed by Bill Hosket, was never sold on the idea that the city and university could build a single arena that satisfied two entities.[18]

"I don't think that was ever a viable plan," said the executive director of the Franklin County Convention Facilities Authority. "I know a lot of people thought that made a lot of sense, but you can't find very many examples where collegiate and professional (major league) sports share a facility."

---

[18] Jennison served as executive director of the FCCFA from 1995 until he left the post in January 2015.

Gee was then—and later in his second stint at Ohio State—a very popular and engaging personality in Columbus and around the state. He's a person who is not afraid to use his considerable influence and works in an environment that historically had few checks and balances by the media. It was evident from the outset of the discussions that tensions existed between the university and the city. "Arrogant" is how one community leader described Gee.

Ohio State's discussions with Pizzuti were a sham. Any talk of a Downtown arena was dealt a major setback in the fall of 1994, when Ohio's powerful House speaker, Vernal G. Riffe Jr., delivered $15 million in state funds for OSU's arena plans. Meanwhile, the city's request for $1 million for a feasibility study on the downtown project was denied.

Gee wanted the university's arena on campus and had no serious interest in having the men's basketball team as a tenant in a Downtown venue.

"Ohio State has the largest athletic program of any university in the country," he later told the *Dispatch*. "The thought of sending any of those programs off-campus would be absurd."

While his representatives were politely talking with city representatives about a shared project, Gee had been quietly lobbying Riffe. In bypassing the Board of Regents, who typically oversees university budget requests, Gee avoided tipping his hand publicly. Riffe, who was exiting office the next year, happily provided his parting gift. Gee had scored a political victory over Lashutka and seemingly a death blow to the Downtown arena project.

Gee's sleight of hand caught downtown arena advocates off guard, so much so that the *Dispatch* ran a cartoon portraying little Gordon Gee stealing a basketball—the 'arena ball'—from a giant Greg Lashutka. The feeling portrayed was that Gee had clearly won the battle, if not the war. The cartoon was significant. At the time there was a belief that there was only an ability to support one building.

Riffe's legacy at Ohio State, which included having a building named for him (Vern Riffe Center for Government and the Arts), grew. Once again it seemed like plans for a Downtown arena or stadium project had stalled. While there had been public discussion of such facilities in the 1980s, the lack of a core tenant made those attempts fraught with pitfalls.

Public skepticism was nothing new for Columbus, after witnessing various arena/stadium issues proposed and rejected by voters in 1978, 1981, 1986, and 1987—the latter two efforts vigorously challenged by Sheir's Citizens for Private Development.

The previous, popular—but feisty and controversial—Mayor Buck Rinehart, a passionate advocate for major league sports (advocating the '81 and '86 countywide sales-tax issues seeking to build major league facilities) was so emphatic to move an arena plan forward that he once tore down a section of the state penitentiary ("the Pen") to get the project started, only to have a court order halt the bulldozers and require him to reimburse the state for the damages.

"I know I probably shouldn't have done it," Rinehart told the *Dispatch* years later. "But we were trying to get the message across that we don't have to be the way we are."

Rinehart was a flamboyant character who had once been seen as the eventual heir to the governor's mansion before a series of highly publicized missteps squashed those dreams.

In one major snafu, he got behind the wheel of a bulldozer (again) and began demolishing a crack house, only to learn that it wasn't. Oops.

Then there was major public backlash when he tried to give away *Brushstrokes in Flight*—the Roy Lichtenstein sculpture at Port Columbus—to Genoa, Italy, as a thank you for its 1955 gift of the Christopher Columbus statue.

Also, the mayor started a city-wide honesty campaign . . . then lied about having an extramarital affair.

As a mayoral candidate, Rinehart suggested turning the abandoned Pen site into a theme park. "This is just a wild brainstorm right now, but it's the kind of thing that makes people think." Yes, think, indeed.

Lacking leadership that people took seriously, many of the city's previous efforts at building a civic arena were seen as silly, unrealistic, or saddled with a "build it and they will come" rhetoric, but with no clear vision or business plan behind it.

"If you look back, I really think the city of Columbus had been shortchanged by the state on athletic facilities," said John Christie, board chairman of the Franklin County Convention Facilities Authority and a former president of the Columbus Area Chamber of Commerce. "Maybe they prioritized COSI (Center of Science and Industry) or some other things that took place," Christie said. "If you look at the [sports] facilities in Cleveland and Cincinnati, they both have state money behind them.

"After the Vern Riffe thing, it wasn't a war but [Ohio State's] thinking was one of, 'We're going to beat the Downtown arena to the punch.'"

He was skeptical from the beginning that OSU was looking to build an on-campus arena with the thought of sharing it with a pro team.

"Ohio State was bound and determined not to cooperate, but if they were going to do something, they were going to be totally in charge," Christie said. "Of course, it's hard to have an NHL team or an NBA team or whatever as the second fiddle in the arena. It would have been a very odd situation."

He wasn't the only one who felt that way.

"We didn't set out to want two arenas, but there were too many conflicts between the town and gown—between the university and the city," noted Pizzuti, who balanced his personal friendship with Gee during the negotiations. "Did I agree with him [Gee]? Absolutely not. I was on the side of the city and never deviated from that, so there were times you just don't mix friendship and business. This was a time there were a lot of tense moments between the mayor and the athletic department of the university and the president of the university. Lots of folks took sides."

The whole Downtown project could have fallen apart right then and there, but the city leaders shook off the setback and kept going. If the wishes of the OSU folks had been realized, I sincerely believe that it would have been generations before any talk of a major league franchise in Columbus could again be taken seriously.

Clearly, we felt otherwise, that under the right plan, a major league franchise and the Buckeyes could happily coexist.

We believed the NHL was the right plan, and Downtown was the right place. However, the reality was that we were headed for a two-arena solution, but the prospect of competing facilities separated by only a few miles would be a hard sell to the public. With Ohio State now in the driver's seat, city officials sought an essential compromise.

As a requirement of the state's capital-improvement budget legislators, OSU officials had to visit with the city about "specific site, use, and operations" for the OSU arena. The university agreed to not compete with the Downtown arena for major concert and entertainment events. According to an OSU planning memo, dated September 20, 1994, "The primary use will be for OSU basketball and other campus events (and) should not compete with a city arena, should the city decide to move ahead."

The memo states it was reiterating principles "previously articulated by President Gee." OSU also agreed not to build sky boxes in their arena, according to the *Dispatch*'s reports at the time.

"Early in the process we were assured by Ohio State that, if they built an arena, it would largely benefit Ohio State sports and the Ohio State students," said Jennison, who worked with Lashutka's Citizens Commission. While more of a gentlemen's agreement than a binding contract, John Christie was one of those who took the university at its word, that Ohio State would not have a venue that would compete with a Downtown arena for bookings.

If OSU was serious about the non-compete memo from September 1994, it would be critical to Columbus' efforts, as that plan would ensure the Downtown arena the opportunity to make money on non-hockey events as well as increase revenue through the sale of suites, club seats, and other amenities associated with professional sports.

Ohio State also agreed to limit the number of concerts, family shows, etc., that were non-school-related events to approximately ten per year at its facility. That was not a concession per se. OSU's proposal was to fund the arena with tax-free bonds and federal law limited the use of profit-making entities to 10 percent of the dates, so their options were limited anyway.

The restriction gave the Downtown contingent an important victory to reclaim a bit of momentum toward funding an arena. Still, most felt the "dueling arena" scenario was unsellable and unsustainable.

Jennison didn't agree with that assessment. He was among those who felt that Ohio State's proposed arena didn't hamper the efforts of the city to fund and build a major league caliber venue of its own because the original plans for the campus facility didn't have many of the amenities that were later added.

"What OSU was doing didn't feed into the belief that said, 'Don't build a professional sports facility for the long term.'[Ohio State's arena] would have fallen short of the needs of the NHL or NBA. It really wasn't a workable solution. It's an awesome intercollegiate sports facility but it falls short of what a major league team would expect—the suites, the clubs."

Meanwhile, the Chill continued to be at the center of the dialogue. In October 1994, I continued the pitch for a Downtown arena, telling the *Dispatch* that we were a major metropolitan area being held back because of a lack of a facility. I noted that the makeup and market of Columbus was as major league as Indianapolis, Tampa, St. Louis, or Portland. The only problem had been the lack of vision and political will to see it come to fruition.

"When you look at the demographics, we're major league by any means," Jennison said. "We had a lot of factors that would make us attractive to professional sports."

Indeed, Columbus had just demonstrated its interest in major league sports by making a commitment to Major League Soccer's Columbus Crew earlier that spring.

While the Crew would begin play two years later in Ohio Stadium, founder Lamar Hunt knew that playing in the Buckeyes' facility was just a temporary fix. Hunt, owner of the NFL's Kansas City Chiefs and the Kansas City Wizards (now Sporting Kansas City) MLS franchise, also had his long-term sights set on a new facility.

Next, we made our first real steps toward a solution. For a Downtown arena to succeed, it had to have an anchor tenant. That tenant would be the Columbus Chill.

In December 1994, six months after the formation of MLS, I joined Pizzuti and Chamber of Commerce President Jonathon York as the featured speakers at a press conference to announce plans for a Downtown arena and adjacent soccer stadium.

The Chamber's feasibility stated that with the Chill as the main arena tenant, the Downtown venue would break even financially. They needed our commitment to play there to justify continuing with a more in-depth analysis, and Horn Chen was able to provide that. With this all in play, it was enough ammunition to provide city leaders with the confidence to move the project forward.

As the president and general manager of the Chill, I was thrilled by the prospects of bringing our team into the center city, but also cited that our ultimate goal was to reach "the highest level possible," speaking to the NHL's forthcoming expansion.

Lashutka, still reeling from the Ohio State debacle, did not make any public comments about the plans that day, I suspect causing some in the media to question the seriousness of the project.

We were faced with the same pessimism from the onset, but at least the arena issue was beginning to attract the attention of key business leaders.

Courtesy: *Columbus Dispatch*

Chill president and general manager David Paitson and the team's promotional strategy were profiled with the story titled "Pulling no Punches" on the front of the features section of the *Columbus Dispatch*, the day of the first-ever home game, November 1, 1991.

Courtesy: Lance Parker, Parker Studios

Opening Night 1993 was replete with the players exiting from three white stretch limousines prior to the introductions. Despite annual pleas from the fans, the spectacle was never repeated.

Terry "Rosco" Ruskowski coached the Chill for their first three seasons and molded the team in his hard-nosed image while having the perfect offbeat personality to match the team's zany marketing.

Jim Ballantine was a darn good player, a true character, and his jersey made the Hockey Hall of Fame when he wore the first-triple digit number (101, not shown) in hockey to promote the Columbus radio station, CD 101.

Defenseman Barry Dreger (left) is on the Chill's All-Time Team. He had 636 penalty minutes in 94 games over the Chill's first two seasons.

Jason "Smurf" Christie was the first player signed by the Chill and led the team in scoring their first two seasons. He returned for the Chill's final season in 1998–99 and is on the All-Time Team.

The Chill celebrates its first playoff series triumph in 1994 versus the Johnstown Chiefs.

Former Ohio State player Rob Schriner is a member of the Chill's All-Time Team and went on to work for the Chiller ice rinks upon his retirement.

Gary Coupal, once dubbed "the baddest man in hockey" by The Hockey News, played part of two seasons for the Chill from 1995–97.

The ultimate hockey photo. Defenseman Corey Bricknell racked up 407 penalty minutes in 79 games from 1995–97.

Courtesy: Greg Bartram, Better Image Photography

Moe Mantha followed Terry Ruskowski as coach and guided the Chill to playoff appearances in his two seasons (1994–95, 1995–96). Moe's intensity matched his ability to develop young players.

Courtesy: Greg Bartram, Better Image Photography

Moe Mantha (left in toga) played along with many of the front office's stunts, including allowing himself to be part of the "Turn Back the Clock" game to the Roman era.

Late Show with David Letterman's favorite shop operators, Mujibur and Sirajul, embraced the Columbus Chill-Toledo Storm rivalry during their 1993 appearance.

Lorne Toews was a rugged forward from Winnipeg, Manitoba, who had had 111 points (57 goals, 54 assists) and 511 penalty minutes for the Chill from 1995–98.

We're going to need a bigger box.

Brian McCutcheon, the Chill's third coach, calmly guided the team to a 44–21–5 record to win the North Division in 1996–97 (the first division title in Columbus pro hockey history), his only season.

The Fairgrounds Coliseum, site of a then-record minor league sellout streak of 83 games in the 5,700-seat building that opened in 1917.

Keith Morris is pictured after what he did best—score goals. He tops the Chill chart with 104 in 189 games and set the single-season mark of 46 in 1995–96.

The Chill became the first minor league hockey franchise to build, own, and operate its own facility when it opened the Chiller Dublin in 1993.

Nixon on the power play.

The "Scream 'til your brain hurts" theme left many wondering what it meant. It's exactly what the Chill wanted.

You knew another Chill victory was going in the books when Judith Kielkopf, aka "The Fat Lady," started bellowing from the top of the stands. Many opposing coaches were not amused.

Derek Clancey is the Chill's career leader in points (313) and assists (218) and is on the All-Time Team. He was named director of pro scouting for the Pittsburgh Penguins in 2010.

As part of the annual New Year's Eve "Turn Back the Clock" game, defenseman Brad Treliving went Latin, and the team wore Roman numerals in homage to the gladiator days. Treliving was named general manager of the Calgary Flames on April 28, 2014.

Chill fans provided important grassroots support for the Downtown arena issue.

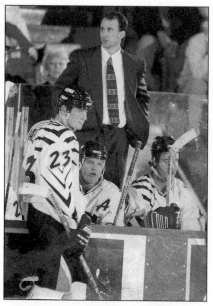

An original Chill player, Don Granato returned as head coach for the 1997–98 season and the following season, the last for the franchise, took the team to a Northwest Division title.

From the "Blood, Sweat, and Fear" marketing campaign.

Jeff Salajko is the goalie on the Chill's All-Time Team. His 74 wins are the most in team history and he set season marks for wins (35 in 1996–97) and goals against average (2.30 in 1997–98).

Courtesy: Greg Bartram, Better Image Photography

David Paitson announces the Mad Cow name switcheroo in October 1997. Players Mark Turner (left) and Matt Oates (right) were not as enthralled with the stunt.

Courtesy: Greg Bartram, Better Image Photography

Two fans during the one-time only Mad Cows game get into the spirit.

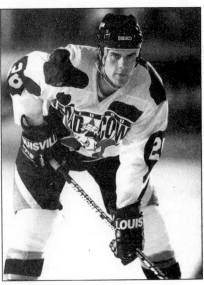

Courtesy: Greg Bartram, Better Image Photography

Mark Pivetz played 119 games for the Chill, this one in the "Meadow of Doom."

Popular radio personality Andy "Andyman" Davis was the ringmaster of the Chill's three ring circus.

The Chill front office staff and off-ice officials.

The players, wearing throwback jerseys from the first season, make one final skate around the Coliseum to salute the fans on April 4, 1999.

Last Call left a lasting memory for players and fans alike.

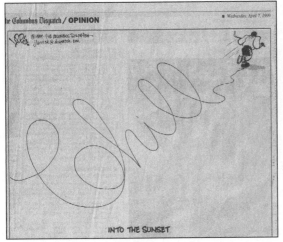

The *Columbus Dispatch* recognized the Chill for its eight-year run in this editorial cartoon on April 7, 1999.

An aerial view looking north in the 1990s of the area now known as the Arena District. The state penitentiary is in the lower middle portion (surrounding a water tower) while the current site of Nationwide Arena is to the upper right.

The Penitentiary site today. Nationwide Arena (arched roof) is middle left.

Blue Jackets fans party in Nationwide Plaza before a game in October of 2014.

Nationwide Arena was packed for the 2007 NHL Draft.

Fireworks celebrate a division title moments after the Chill's last regular season game ever ("Last Call") on Easter Sunday, April 4, 1999.

Courtesy: *Columbus Dispatch*

Chapter Eighteen

MOE KNOWS HOCKEY

"If I go three or four days without having someone on the air from the Chill during the season, people call and ask when we're going to talk about hockey."
—Sports director George Lehner speaking of WTVN's radio call-in show, 1994

Winning sure beats losing, and we had done enough of the latter the first two seasons to eagerly embrace our first playoff appearance in 1994.

Still, winning wasn't the "be all to end all" for our franchise. Our goal was to be competitive every year in order to satiate the appetites of the true hockey fans; yet, we never varied from our firm belief that minor league sports are as much about entertainment as they are about wins and losses.

The 1993 player walkout and its aftermath proved to us that we could be successful on the ice without sacrificing our integrity. It wasn't easy, but we could win within the rules and intended to do so in the future.

After reaching the playoffs in our third season, the job done by Terry Ruskowski in building the franchise did not go unnoticed, and in the summer of 1994 he earned the head coaching position of the expansion Houston Aeros of the International Hockey League.

Just as we reluctantly, but happily, bid adieu to some of our best players when they were promoted, it was bittersweet to say goodbye to the only coach the franchise had known.

Roscoe guided the Chill from the ground up to a three-year record of 96–80–20 (.540), including a 41–20–7 mark during the 1993–94 season.

When Roscoe passed the baton to Moe Mantha, it was another example of how much credibility our franchise had gained in just a few years.

A 12-year NHL veteran, Moe was selected from seventy-five applicants, many of whom had NHL playing and coaching experience. He represented the United States in international hockey as a member of the national team in the 1981, 1985, and 1991 World Championships, as well as being assistant captain at the 1992 Winter Olympics.

We had strongly pursued a couple of former NHL players: Vancouver Canucks goalie coach Glen Hanlon and Washington Capitals color commentator Craig Laughlin.

Despite Moe's credentials, he wasn't our first choice—we initially wanted Hanlon.

We were impressed with Hanlon's hockey pedigree and saw a tremendous coaching upside, but, ultimately, his interest in the position waned. We also were enamored with Laughlin, believing he fit right into our promotional wheelhouse. Laughlin was a natural in front of the camera and we felt he would have been a plausible voice in pitching our big picture vision for the city. He also had a strong background in ice rink programming, which broadened his appeal.

However, it was hard for Laughlin to justify giving up his high-paying television gig as a color analyst with the Washington Capitals, so we continued on our search.

Moe had waited patiently through the entire process and, just as importantly, he had lobbied hard for the job. He wanted to be here.

In the end, it was a great and natural fit. Moe had American and Ohio roots because his Canadian father, Moe Mantha Sr., played for the Cleveland Barons of the AHL when his son was born, thus giving Moe Jr. dual Canadian/US citizenship. It also didn't hurt that Moe Jr. had Columbus ties by skating in his first youth hockey game at the Coliseum during the time his father was a player for the Columbus Checkers.

He had a strong reputation for developing young talent and promoted twenty-one players to the AHL and IHL during his two seasons with the Chill. One reason he was selected as an alternate captain of the 1992 USA Olympic team was to serve as an example to his younger teammates.

However, Moe's passion bubbled up during the '92 Games and caused a bit of an international incident when he instigated a brawl with the host French team as time expired.

"A guy happened to spit on my sweater," Mantha said at the time. "For the last 37 minutes, I kept telling him, 'I'm coming. I'm coming [at you].' He kept saying, 'NHL tough guy.'"

The skirmish nearly got Moe dropped from the team until he explained to his US contingent, "You don't spit on the red, white, and blue and get away with it." The sentiment was hard to argue with and earned Moe the heartfelt support of his teammates, and most Americans.

His wealth of contacts was also impressive and proved important to the bigger picture. The more reach we had into the NHL the better, and Moe had a lot of friends there. We'd tap into those contacts to assist us with our youth hockey efforts as Moe served on the board of directors for USA Hockey.

Moe's first season in Columbus was also the time of the 1994–95 NHL lockout that stretched over 104 days and cost a total of 468 games, along with the All-Star Game. As the city-wide conversation for a Downtown arena began to make headway, we dealt with the ramifications of the 1994–95 NHL strike. "It fueled the fire for those who wanted to make the case that professional sports 'is all about greed,'" Maurer said.

With the NHL players sidelined, Moe invited his friend Dale Hawerchuk to our training camp to hang out with the team for a couple of weeks during the early part of the Chill season.[19]

---

[19] Hawerchuk passed away from stomach cacer at the age of fifty-seven, on August 18, 2020.

It was an honor having the future Hockey Hall of Fame member spend time with us. The former No. 1 pick of the Winnipeg Jets in 1981, Hawerchuk was the Rookie of the Year and the youngest player to reach 100 points. He retired in 1997 as the 17th-best scorer in NHL history. Even cooler, he had a rock band named in his honor, Les Dales Hawerchuk.

The closest a lot of the Chill players ever got to the big leagues was in their dreams. Interacting with Hawerchuk on a daily basis gave the guys first-hand insight on the journey to the big time. It made the goal seem possible for some of our guys.

He even went on a Saturday night trip to Johnstown, followed by a matinee game in Columbus the next day. Hawerchuk seemed to enjoy getting back to his roots and the camaraderie built by riding the team bus.

"I've been in a lot of airports and it's not all that great with the delays and canceled flights," Hawerchuk said. "You spend a lot of time sitting around. At least on a bus you're moving."

Moe fondly recalled the time spent with his buddy, "He was looking for some ice time, wanted to get away and reconnect a friendship, come here and help the young guys. He came in and spoke about what it takes to be an NHL player. Dale was more excited [than the players]. The league was on strike. He was used to being around a team atmosphere and he was always a team guy."

Hawerchuk wasn't the only NHLer with the Chill during the lockout as Florida Panthers forward Jeff Daniels also skated with the team to stay in shape.

Obviously, and unfortunately, he and Hawerchuk couldn't suit up for us.

While the NHL season was in limbo, pro hockey continued elsewhere and we were expecting help in the form of a few talented prospects from the parent Chicago Blackhawks and our IHL affiliate the Indianapolis Ice. Because of that, Moe needed a right-hand man, so we named point-producing forward Derek Clancey as our player/assistant coach.

Moe got off to an inauspicious start. During a preseason game at Huntington, he walked off the ice and the team followed him late in the game after a disputed call. He was suspended the first three games of the regular season—all losses by a combined 22–6 score. He could, at times, let his passion and coaching inexperience get the best of him.

Once, after a god-awful 7–0 loss at Erie, Moe stewed for a while before ordering the bus to stop in the middle of nowhere on I-79 South, where he proceeded to give the players a tongue-lashing. He told the players to replay the mistakes in their minds and he was tired of watching the same errors on videotape after every game.

"Moe pulls out the tape," forward Jamie Spencer said, "swears at us a couple of times and says, 'I don't ever want to see this again.' He opens the door of the bus and launches that tape about 50 yards into the cornfield."

The next afternoon, the Chill lost 7–3 at home to Dayton. Afterward, Moe ripped the team a new one that left him with a cut on his hand after tearing his office door off its hinges.

Another time he delivered a most memorable line to Columbus reporters after a game when he challenged his players to "reach down between their legs to see if anything was there." The comment raised a few eyebrows when sports reporter Jeff Hawthorn recorded the comment and his radio station WTVN played it "every hour, on the hour" for the next two days.

We once placed cameras in the locker room to capture the vibe for later use in a video or commercial. What we got that night was Moe in a full tirade, complete with a barrage of expletives as he shredded the players for a lack of effort.

Moe's rants were too good to be kept inside the hallowed walls of a dressing room, or so we thought, because a few years later someone hatched the idea of making his tirade into a TV spot. I don't know, maybe we were running out of fresh ideas at that point, needed a little controversy, or just wanted some comedic relief.

We turned his verbal assault on the language into a "Chill classic" commercial spot and bleeped the profanity. Yes, it was one of those times we crossed the line and we did receive some public backlash.

Of course, we were a few years ahead of the curve as it turned out. HBO for three years (2010, 2011, and 2013) went inside NHL dressing rooms with their wonderfully insightful and entertaining *24/7* series leading to the Winter Classic, and someone like former Washington Capitals coach Bruce Boudreau became a star because of his profanity-laced tirades. Some twenty-five-plus years after Moe's outbursts all-access sports shows such as HBO's Hard Knocks at NFL training camps are the norm. Times have most certainly changed.

One of Moe's famous traits was his passion, which would sometimes get the best of him—especially especially when he would threaten to make a trade for trade's sake if the team wasn't performing up to his standards.

As general manager, I technically always had the final say in any deals but, frankly, left the player personnel decisions in the coach's hands. They were the experts on evaluating talent, so I relied on their judgment.

What I *did* do was consistently challenge the coach's thinking. If he made a rational case, then it was an easy call. It was his team and he was the ones who would be accountable for the results. That was my philosophy: let the coaches do their jobs but challenge their rationale and serve as a sounding board. In Moe's case, I always asked him to "think about it for 24 hours" to ensure his decision wasn't based solely on emotion.

Yet, I allowed him to deal forward Darwin McClelland, an excellent two-way player. He was hot under the collar after he learned McClelland allegedly told one of his teammates that Moe's trade threats were just talk. After a few days passed, he continued to press the issue, insisting that the comments were not the underlying reason for the deal. I had my doubt, but begrudgingly consented.

One very poor decision on Moe's part happened when we dealt one of our top scorers, Mike Ross. Not only was Ross good on the ice, but he was a first-class guy. Moe seemed to be pissed off that Mike had a girlfriend and was a "little too comfortable" for his liking. He also misjudged how skilled his new signees were at the forward position. As it turned out, not so much.

Mike went on to win the league scoring titles in back-to-back seasons and was voted the 1996–97 ECHL Player of the Year for the South Carolina Stingrays.

I learned trades based on zeal or those intended just to "shake things up" typically come back to haunt you.

On the road, Moe would often have the bus driver stop short of the arena and walk the final few blocks to the rink—usually in a trench coat and *Indiana Jones* hat while puffing on a cigar—to mentally prepare for the game. Even though he was in his mid-thirties, he had an old-school mentality. I learned as our relationship progressed that he required more vigilance than I previously thought.

Moe's greatest attribute, however, was that he was a good man, a character guy completely committed to the effort. No matter how many tirades, he always got the most out of his teams, improved his players' individual skills, and instilled a professional mindset that would serve them well in their future endeavors in hockey, or not.

While going along with our many wacky gimmicks proved he was a great sport, he showed the ability to maintain some order of professionalism with the team. I mean, what other coach would have the humor to be dressed in a toga and a laurel wreath while being pulled by two huge gladiators on a chariot for a New Year's Eve promotion?

"I remember getting booed and hearing 'Fire the coach. Feed him to the lions,'" Moe recalled years later. "We had lost five in a row or something like that. [David] made a nice picture of it. I've still got that picture. It's hanging on what I call my 'hall of shame' wall in my house," he joked.

Moe was known for his sense of humor, but we realized, despite his willingness to work with our off-beat ideas, that we were, at times, testing his limits, so we always appreciated him playing along.

Some of his best contributions were to the local youth hockey scene that at that point was still in its infancy because of the lack of available ice rinks.

Because Columbus had been without pro hockey from 1977–91 and the OSU Ice Rink was the lone sheet of ice in town for much of that time, a generation of kids grew up without being able to experience hockey. It wasn't like the soccer boom of the 1990s when all it took to play the sport was a nice patch of land, a ball, and a net.

We were playing catch up to other cities and Moe opened the doors to important USA Hockey officials when we looked to establish a new youth organization—the Columbus Chill Youth Hockey Association (CCYHA). Our legal counsel, Greg Kirstein, and I visited with regional representatives to make sure were making the correct long-term decision for the community.

At the time there was one youth league, the Capital Amateur Hockey Association (CAHA). It was based out of the OSU Ice Rink and used the Chiller Dublin simply for overflow. We had been driving hundreds of kids through hockey classes but they were falling through the cracks because CAHA felt no sense of urgency to make room for those kids.

To build youth hockey to the level we wanted (and needed), we had to take matters into our own hands. The advice we received from the regional USA Hockey representative convinced us we were on the right track. He indicated that youth organizations were challenged to keep up with managing their leagues if they had more than 300 players. We believed, like we had with so many areas of the team business, that matters were most effectively dealt with when we could control our own destiny.

We moved ahead, despite some strong opposition from CAHA; yet, in the end we felt it was best for the community to involve more parents and create an association for each rink.

With Moe's help we knew we wouldn't have any trouble getting the organization sanctioned by USA Hockey. The CCYHA continues today and is one of Moe's greatest legacies.

By now the city's love for hockey could no longer be written off as a trend.

Between the CCYHA, CAHA, and the program in nearby Newark, youth hockey participation increased from 150 kids in 1991 to 950 players in 1995. Adult-league teams were flourishing as well, and tens of thousands of kids and adults were trying their hand at public skating or taking skating or hockey lessons.

"People were excited about hockey," Mantha said. "We had our players get involved. We brought a lot of the [youth] coaches in and had a little chalk talk with them. We did that a couple of times. We did summer camps. We did hockey schools with [players] Keith Morris and Rob Schriner and some others."

As coach for the Chill, Moe turned in two fairly uneventful seasons. In the 1994–95 season, he hit rock bottom at 7–14–2 on December 1, but finished with a respectable record of 31–32–5. The following season he made further strides as the Chill went 37–28–5. We made the playoffs both years, only to exit in the first round.

Moe displayed his knack for evaluating young talent in the 1994–95 season when he teamed rookie forwards Chris Gotziaman and Keith Morris with veteran Derek Clancey for the "GMC Line" that stayed together for the first half of the season.

Gotziaman, from the University of North Dakota, finished his one season in Columbus with 54 points (35 goals, 19 assists) in 56 games. Morris, a University of Alaska (Anchorage) product was second on the team in points with 73 (32–41) in 62 games, and would net 46 goals the next season and 26 in 1996–97 to become one of the Chill's all-time great scorers.

Clancey, in his second of four seasons with the Chill, had 21 goals and 66 assists in 1994–95 and would top the century mark (32–77–109) the next season for Moe.

One of the most prolific players in Chill history was forward Bobby House, who in two stints with the team in 1994–95, had 11 goals in nine games before being recalled each time to the Indianapolis Ice of the International Hockey League.

He was a "sniper"—using a hockey term for a great shooter—just like Trent Kaese was for the first-year Chill. Kaese (pronounced Casey) scored 28 goals in 28 games (plus 22 assists) and recorded hat tricks in three straight games to tie a pro record after joining the team midway through the season from the Norwich and Peterboro Pirates in Great Britain.

Yet, despite the offensive weaponry Moe's first season the team struggled to a 7–14–1 start. Disgusted with the team's play, he said he put his entire roster on waivers.

"I'm tired of this," he told them. "The guys who want to get on this page and program, fine. The guys who don't—I walked into the room and said, 'You think I'm full of shit. I just posted everyone up for trade right now.' I posted it right on the wall."

The players must have gotten the message because they finished the season strong, ending just one game under .500 to set up a postseason first-round matchup against the Richmond Renegades. The first two games were in the Virginia city, and the hosts took the opener 10–4 in a penalty-filled game (we had 115 of the 197 minutes, which was unusual because we had the second-fewest PIMs in the ECHL in the regular season).

With two Chill players suspended for Game 2 and injuries preventing their replacements from playing, we dressed only 14 players (four under the maximum)—including the two goalies.

"I had to put [forwards] Keith Morris and Derek Clancey on defense a couple of shifts," Mantha said.

In maybe the greatest example of how Moe could rally his team's effort, the Chill lost 9–8 in double overtime in the second-longest game in ECHL history at the time (95 minutes and 5 seconds), ending at 12:16 a.m. The defeat spoiled a league-record 69-save effort by Brett Abel.

We led 8–6 with two minutes left, but the Richmond Renegades scored twice, including the tying score in the final seconds after a Chill icing.

Afterward, our team not only faced elimination in the best-of-five series, but had to play the third game two days later 70 miles west of Columbus in Troy, Ohio, at Hobart Arena.

"It's ridiculous," Clancey said then. "If I'm a Columbus Chill fan I'd be very, very upset."

We lost that game 6–1 before 1,304 fans.

After all the time put in, it was sad to say that our scheduling problems were still *the* story. One headline in the *Dispatch* at the end of the 1994–95 campaign read, "Chill woes underscore need for arena in city."

Moe offered his support to Bob Hunter's accompanying column.

"It's a shame," the coach said. "I think this is a perfect example of why the city of Columbus needs to build a new facility. We have all these events and everybody's fighting over a 75-year-old building. For a city of a million and a half people, it doesn't make any sense."

The Chill got off to another slow start in 1995–96, but won 10 of the final 13 games to finish fourth in the North Division before being swept in three playoff games by Wheeling.

Moe's second-season adventures included trading all-star defenseman Aaron Boh after he missed the bus to start a road trip. Moe made the deal via cell phone—a first for the team—shortly before the ECHL trade deadline while sitting at the front of the bus as the team played cards in the back.

"We could hear Moe on his cell phone," Spencer recalled. "He was trying to be discreet, but you knew he was making a deal."

Boh was one of those characters who bounced around the minors and Europe for years (24 teams in 14 leagues, encompassing four countries, until retirement in 2006) and early in his career he was aptly labeled as having "a million-dollar terminal and a hundred-dollar control tower." In other words, Boh had all the talent in the world but no sense of how to use it.

"His antics grew old," Moe said. "There was something always going on. I think I traded him for a hundred dollars just to get him out of the organization."

Boh was nothing if not colorful and the media gravitated to him because they never knew what he would say. He loved to tell of the time in Johnstown, Pennsylvania, when a puck glanced off a spectator sitting in the stands, then richoted onto the ice to an awaiting Chiefs player for an easy score.

"I said to the ref, 'Didn't you see it go off the fat guy's arm?'"

They didn't, and the goal stood.

Chill forward Jamie Spencer couldn't believe it, "This guy's arms were like 40 inches in diameter. He had an undershirt on. It hits his arm and goes back into play. All of our guys stopped. You could hear it hit his arm. It literally hit his arm and went right down in front of a (Johnstown) defenseman."

And another Boh gem: Shortly after he was traded by Medicine Hat to Tri-City in the junior Western Hockey League during the 1993–94 season, his former club traveled by bus to play his new team.

"I knew what hotel they were staying at," Boh recounted. "The second day I got (to Tri-City), I canceled Medicine Hat's rooms. So they roll in about 4 a.m. and they don't have any rooms. I got lucky because there was a big convention in town and all the rooms were booked. Half the team slept on the bus. Half the team stayed at a Motel 6."

Boh couldn't let the deed go unmentioned at the game that night.

"I skated by their bench with a big smile and said, 'Hey boys, how was the sleep last night?' A lot of the boys smiled. The general manager didn't."

Moe had other problems besides Boh that season. He once had to send the team back onto the ice for a five-minute, puke-till-you-drop skating session after a particularly brutal home loss to Richmond.

"Moe came in and said 'I want you to take your jerseys off, hang them up, and get your asses back in the rink,'" said Spencer. "We did, thinking, 'this is weird.'"

"He basically said, 'If you're not going to burn all your energy during the game, I'm going to make sure I burn it with you.' It was like the Herb Brooks *Miracle* movie. We didn't know when it would end."

Then there was the time forward Spencer knew he and his Chill teammates were in for a long night when the bus pulled up to the Wheeling Civic Center.

"It was Boy Scouts night. We got to the rink early and we were getting taunted by about 4,000 boy scouts. It was so out of character. They weren't swearing or anything but would say things like, 'You guys suck. You're going to get killed.'

"We had a really short lineup that night. I had to play defense and forward. We were double shifting. We kept losing guys to injury. I think we had the flu, too. By the end of the game, we had eight or nine guys skating. I think we lost seven or eight to one (actually, 9–5).

"Moe got pissed. He ran into the stands as we were coming off the ice. As he got up to the section, he was looking for one specific guy. He took off his sport coat and handed it to one of the fans. The guy he handed the sport coat just took off running like it was his Christmas present. Now Moe's without his sport coat and can't get to the guy. The police are coming."

Moe picks up the story: "The fan was badmouthing the guys coming off the ice. I went up there and said, 'You're pretty tough up here. I've got no skates on so I'm coming up. Now tell me how bad these guys are.'

"[Equipment manager] Rusty Pearl went after the guy and got my coat, my black coat, back."

Moe guided the team to its second-best record (37–28–5, 79 points) in the five-year history of the franchise, but, once again, the Chill was swept out of the first round in three games by the Wheeling Nailers, although we had one playoff game in the Coliseum.

After just two Chill seasons with mixed success on the ice, Moe was offered the head coaching position for the junior Ontario Hockey League's London Knights. After briefly accepting the offer, he changed his mind to take the head coaching job with the AHL's Baltimore Bandits. The Bandits, with Moe in tow, later became the Cincinnati Mighty Ducks. Moe had a hard act to follow in Roscoe and there were some fans who never warmed to him; yet he was a winner in my book.

After being eliminated in the 1995 playoffs by the Richmond Renegades in Troy, a disappointed Moe strolled out of Hobart Arena toward a Chill fan bus. He knew there might be some derisive comments but he boarded it anyway and thanked the followers for coming before he exited into the offseason.

That's the kind of guy Moe was.

Chapter Nineteen

A SEAT AT THE BIG BOYS' TABLE

"It's one thing for our citizens to look the other way and pretend that the Fairgrounds Coliseum is a first-rate facility when the in-laws from Cleveland, Cincinnati or Indianapolis visit, but it's quite another to put its hockey team on a bus in the middle of the playoffs and send them over the river and through the woods to Hobart Arena (in Troy, Ohio)."
—Bob Hunter's column in the *Columbus Dispatch,* March 28, 1995

Baby steps were necessary if the goal of getting a Downtown arena was to become a reality.

In March 1995, I was appointed as one of two private businessmen to represent entertainment and sports on the 10-person Multipurpose & Sports Facility Work Group (a.k.a. the Downtown arena commission). It was where the real work of the city and county began after the Chamber's press conference supporting a downtown arena and soccer stadium set the stage four months earlier. By this point the Chill organization had established itself as a serious player and I was the chief voice on the Columbus professional sports landscape. We had gained national media attention, built a significant fan base while establishing a record sellout streak, and laid the foundation for hockey's future participants and followers through the building of the Chiller Dublin.

Another private business member of the commission was Doug Kridler, president of the Columbus Association for the Performing Arts (CAPA). The group also included representatives from the Chamber of Commerce, Franklin County, the city of Columbus, and the county's convention facilities authority.

The idea of an arena close to the convention center to attract more visitors and business was gaining momentum. The Franklin County Convention Facilities Authority was funded by the local bed tax (a tax on hotel room rentals) and it wanted the arena, pro sports, and major entertainment acts to attract more visitors. Ohio State's plan was to build an arena to serve as the home of its men's and women's basketball teams and men's and women's ice hockey programs. Its wish was to also host various Ohio High School Athletic Association championship events. This would draw many of the state's top athletes, in various sports, to campus and showcase their new facilities. In essence, it would indirectly bolster recruiting.

The Ohio State arena plans were being considered for vacant land northwest of the Buckeye's football stadium, at the corner of Lane Avenue and Olentangy River Road. The arena was to anchor a sports complex, with facilities for baseball and track and field. The supporting infrastructure of hotels, restaurants, and shops was more or less non-existent. Located about three miles north of the center of Columbus, a campus arena would have a minimal positive impact on convention business and Downtown growth craved by city and business leaders.

The city's most desirable site was the state penitentiary, known as "the Pen," which closed in 1984 but stood as a vacant eyesore for more than a decade. The site encompassed 90 acres of land in the northwest quadrant of Downtown, just west of the convention center and Nationwide Insurance's national headquarters.

"We looked at other sites in the Downtown area but quickly concluded the site where it is today was the best," Bill Jennison said. "I don't think there was a close No. 2."

By bringing in all the key voices to the arena commission, we had a good cross section of perspectives. I had the sports background; Kridler was in tune with the performing arts community, which had concerns about monies being directed away from their projects. There were business people from the Chamber with a pulse on the economic sectors and local government officials to guide us through the bureaucratic red tape that would attach itself to such major undertaking. Also, if we eventually recommended going to the public for support, it was important to cast as wide a net as possible to include not only the city but the county as well. That way we could better spread the cost and hopefully have a better shot to win the vote.

While skeptics were still plentiful we were winning supporters one by one. The *Dispatch* sports columnist Bob Hunter wrote in May 1995: "You have been a skeptic of Columbus' chances of getting any kind of major league franchise, but now you're not so sure. Nashville? Hamilton? In a game being played by cities like that, doesn't Columbus at least deserve a seat at the table?" The Downtown arena commission wanted to answer that and other questions by visiting several cities.

One tour was of the Arrowhead Pond of Anaheim, California. I had arranged a meeting with then-Anaheim Mighty Ducks President Tony Tavares to provide insight into NHL expansion.

I had publicly pointed to Anaheim as a great example of how skeptics had been proven wrong. The Mighty Ducks were a smash success and the Pond was voted as America's New Venue of the Year by *Pollstar* and *Performance* magazines in 1994.

"The mayor [in Anaheim] lost an election because of it," I told the *Dispatch.* "People in Anaheim said the guys were idiots for doing this thing. Then, two weeks after the election, Disney announced that they had acquired a team and all those idiots were suddenly declared visionaries. It shows you what can happen."

It was interesting to watch the light bulbs go on over the heads of folks in Columbus when they began to see the project and the NHL as a real possibility.

"What [David] did was prove to Columbus that sports were more than just sports," John Christie said in an interview for the book years later while serving as president of JMAC, a John H. McConnell family owned entity. "Sports had to provide an entertainment venue and sports had to entertain the whole family, not just the hardcore fan, and through the development of the family experience behind it, you would develop hardcore fans."

What surprised me was that not all of the group's members felt the way I did. I falsely assumed they were all on board. As it turns out, they had to be convinced and, over the course of the next several months, we worked to make sure they were.

As with everything we'd been working to accomplish, there would be several crises of confidence throughout this process. Our group felt the full weight of Buckeye hype in September 1995, when, after six decades of waiting, Ohio State football fans got their wish when the Buckeyes met Notre Dame in Columbus.

The nationally televised game was hyped in excess and a then-Ohio Stadium-record overflowing crowd of 95,537 attended the contest. Scalpers commanded six times face value for a ticket.

It was no contest. Behind All-American running back Eddie George, Ohio State rolled up 535 yards total offense to lead them to a commanding 45–26 win, and Buckeye Nation was on top of the world with their swagger in full force.

The Fighting Irish weren't the only ones who felt run over.

As I've said, I wasn't a Buckeyes fan but wished them no ill will, except when they played Purdue (my favorite team). Of course, I witnessed my all-time favorite Purdue moment inside Ross-Ade Stadium, when Drew Brees pulled a victory out of the jaws of defeat with his 64-yard touchdown bomb to Seth Morales in the final minutes to beat Ohio State and propel Purdue to the 2000 Rose Bowl. Sorry Buckeye fans, but it was awesome! With the Chill schedule being what it was, I didn't have time to fully invest myself in Ohio State football, even if I wanted to.

On the other hand, many in the Downtown arena commission were all in for the support of their local team and were overwhelmed by the hysteria before, during, and after their team's victory. It caused them to wonder why

Columbus needed a major league franchise and arena when we had Ohio State sports, specifically football.

The week following the game, one of our committee members said only half kiddingly that he "felt like throwing in the towel."

To make the already daunting task more intimidating, our campaign and Ohio sports fans received an additional punch in the gut on November 6, 1995, when their beloved Cleveland Browns announced plans to pick up and move to Baltimore the following year. We were just a year removed from Major League Baseball cancelling the 1994 World Series due to a labor dispute and fans were growing weary of greed run amuck in professional sports. Cleveland fans had every right to be skeptical. Browns owner Art Modell had coerced city officials into agreeing to step up to the tune of $175 million to refurbish the outmoded and declining Cleveland Stadium—needed, according to Modell, to recapture revenues lost when the Cleveland Indians moved to Jacobs Field in 1994. Incredibly, with the ballot initiative only a day away, Modell announced his team's move to Baltimore (presumably to maintain his leverage with the city of Baltimore in case the Cleveland stadium vote failed). The public vote for the funding was overwhelmingly approved by Cleveland voters the next day; yet, this was professional team owners' greed at its worst and a complete betrayal of the city. The fans and city officials were justifiably furious. Modell became the poster child of professional sports greed and the most hated man in the state.

Nationally, this was the time of Newt Gingrich and the Republican Party's "Contract with America." Scrutiny over government spending was at an all-time high. The political showdown peaked with the United States federal government shutdown from November 1995 to April 1996 as result of a conflict between Democratic President Bill Clinton and the GOP-controlled Congress. This was the landscape in which we were working.

During this time period, I worked through a friend of mine, WTVN radio general manager of sales Jeff Rehl, to arrange for a visit with its influential morning show host Bob Conners. He was the major radio voice for the conservative news and information station that was always at or near the top of the ratings in Columbus.

It would be a big get if we could convince Conners to back the project. He and I visited at length over lunch and I learned that he would be supportive of the arena plan if he could be certain it was good for Columbus.

It turned out that he was an easy sell. He felt in his heart of hearts that Columbus needed to progress as a city and viewed this as a perfect opportunity to do so. As a result of our discussion, Conners's on-air endorsement was a big shot in the arm and helped our group with its confidence issues.

Another boost was the findings of a Deloitte and Touche, LLP, economic impact study for the Downtown arena. In the short-term construction period, the arena project would create 2,500 jobs and bring $1.8 million in new tax revenue. The annual potential operating revenue once the doors opened was also impressive. The city stood to generate $100 million, establish more than 1,400 new jobs, and secure more than $1 million in new tax revenue. The impact study was music to our ears.

With that report as our foundation, and after more than fifty meetings over eight months, we recommended on December 13, 1995, that a 0.5 percent three-year sales tax be placed on the November 1996 ballot. The Franklin County Commissioners, who required 20 percent in private financing as a prerequisite for the ballot initiative, later moved the vote to May 1997, which was to be known as Issue 1.

Chapter Twenty

THE EVIL EMPIRE

"Each film is only as good as its villain. Since the heroes and the gimmicks tend to repeat from film to film, only a great villain can transform a good try into a triumph."

—Film critic Roger Ebert

One of the best ways to unite a group is to pit it against a common enemy.

Baby Boomers who grew up in the midst of the Cold War learned to fear and loathe the Soviet Union. Perhaps that is one of the reasons why the 1980 US Olympic hockey team's "Miracle on Ice" victory over the Russians that propelled them to the gold medal game two days later (in which they were victorious against Finland, 4–2) was named the Top Sports Moment of the 20th Century by *Sports Illustrated*.

Our country's improbable team, made up of collegiate players, stunned the Soviet professionals, unquestionably the best hockey team in the world at the time. Winners of twenty-one straight Olympic contests, the Russians were assumed to be indestructible. The USA upset was a David-versus-Goliath triumph and was considered by fellow countrymen as a win over Communist tyranny.

With Al Michaels's now-famous final countdown call culminating with his signature line "Do you believe in miracles? YES!" there was now a sense of fairness and predictability in the world. Americans' pride soared to new heights. We took a certain satisfaction when that vexing rival that we love to hate loses.

Rooting together against a bitter foe creates instant camaraderie. It's also a great way to sell a ticket. We even worked to manufacturer a rivalry with the Wheeling Thunderbirds by poking a little fun at the West Virginia hillbilly stereotype. In the case of the Columbus Chill, our real villain was the Toledo Storm.

Top Ten List

The Chill picked on opponent players via sound bites during the introductions and played on the stereotyping of hockey players as mindless, toothless goons in its print ads and commercials... but that wasn't crazy enough for us.

Speaking of toothless, why not jab an entire team's city and region at the expense of the Wheeling Thunderbirds?

We caught the ire of the Wheeling City Council with our "Top Ten List of Wheeling" promotions that included a real zinger at No.1. I guess they didn't appreciate the joke.

10. <u>Front Yard Washer Night</u> $2 off admission when you present any broken-down major appliance at the door.

9. <u>Black Lung Night</u> Anyone with a bottled oxygen pull cart is admitted free. Full medical insurance coverage to the winner of the Brown Phlegm Distance Spit between periods.

8. <u>Deliverance Night</u> Come one, come all to see the postgame screening of the Appalachian equivalent of *The Rocky Horror Picture Show*. Squeal like a pig for a buck off admission.

7. <u>Shoot for Shoes</u> A between-periods promotion in which contestants fire pucks at the net, with the winner just grateful to hang on to all ten toes through another hard winter.

---

6. <u>Indoor Plumbing Night</u> Bring in ten (unused) corn cobs and get a free estimate from Ted's Terlet City.

5. <u>Trailer Night</u> Bring in Polaroids of storm damage and get a free hot dog.

4. <u>Haircut Night</u> Three working barbers in attendance with a variety of bowls to choose from.

3. <u>Root Canal Night</u> Contestants eat roastin' ears between periods. Entrant with the most kernels left on his cob is the winner of the major orthodontic procedure of his choice.

2. <u>Bowhunter's Night</u> A 12-point buck is released into the arena shortly after the game starts. Three arrow limit. No field dressing in the facility.

1. <u>Uncle Daddy Night</u> 'nuf said.

A few weeks later, two of our players—Steve Strunk and Shaun Kane—appeared in the ECHL All-Star Game in Wheeling and were booed out of the arena. The players were pissed, as they went to be honored and ended up fearing for their lives. Sorry guys, it was all meant to be in good fun.

The truth was, following the Wheeling incident, other teams actually requested we throw a little playful rivalry banter their way, but we reserved our best venom for our one true rival—the Toledo Storm.

Rivalries were nothing new for Columbus and Toledo, or for that matter the states of Ohio and Michigan.

Dating back centuries, there was something about the city of Toledo that stirred passions.

Maybe we've not gotten over the Toledo War (1835–1836), also known as the Michigan-Ohio War. The quarrel was over a narrow strip of land that is now Toledo and the surrounding communities that nearly two centuries ago was prized real estate coveted by the two states.

Imagine that, fighting over Toledo.

Eventually, the disagreement was resolved without a single casualty, and Ohio was awarded the land after the state of Michigan was given a larger portion of the Upper Peninsula in exchange. However, the debate continued and, as recently as 1972, the US Supreme Court heard arguments from attorneys who maintained that *Toledo belongs in Michigan.*

To this day, the loyalties of those Ohioans living in the northwest corner of the state are still questioned.

The conflict is still brought into focus through the Ohio State-Michigan battle over recruits in this key football territory. Buckeye fans believe Ohioans who desert the state for greener pastures up north are traitors. Plenty of Toledo-area players end up as Wolverines, much to the chagrin of the Buckeye faithful.

Anyone who lives in Columbus understands that no matter what else happens during an Ohio State football season, whenever the Buckeyes beat the Michigan Wolverines, it's considered a successful year.[20]

On the ice, the dislike between the cities dates back to the Columbus vs. Toledo battles in the IHL during the 1970s.

If you wanted to be fair, it's hard to blame the folks in Toledo for wanting to follow Michigan-based sports. Ann Arbor (40 miles) and Detroit (55 miles) are about an hour to the north compared to a 125-mile drive down Route 23 to Columbus.

---

[20] While Michigan holds 58–51–6 advantage in the series since the first meeting in 1897, Ohio State has a 51–46–4 edge in the Big Ten era (1918–present). Unlike the coach John Cooper era during the Chill's existence, the Buckeyes have dominated the rivalry this century, winning 16 of 19 games, including a program record eight straight victories through the 2019 season.

While Toledo residents may have split allegiances between other Ohio and Michigan professional sports teams, the absence of an NHL team in Ohio led to an almost universal backing of the Red Wings among Toledo residents.

With that as a backdrop, it's easy to understand why the Storm copied the Red Wings' signature look for its uniforms.

While Columbus also had a long history with Dayton in hockey (the IHL's Gems) and we had our share of brawls with the Bombers, there was never quite the vitriol as when the Chill and Storm collided.

"Dayton was a rival, but we respected their owners Bud Gingher and Arnie Johnson," Maurer said. "Their front office folks and coaches were all nice people. We didn't feel that way about Toledo. It was a legitimate hatred."

We saw red every time we faced the Storm—from a 9–2 defeat in the first meeting of the expansion teams in 1991, to our 6–4 victory in the 70th and final regular season showdown on March 26, 1999. By the way, our final regular season record against the Storm was 32–35–3.

The cultural differences between the cities is striking. Toledo is a conservative city well known for its industry, particularly in glass and auto assembly. It's also home to Tony Packo's (made famous in *M*A*S*H* by Toledo's own Jamie Farr), its signature chili dog, and authentic Hungarian food. Toledo is blue collar and proud of it.

Columbus, on the other hand, is a progressive metropolitan market with a diverse economy built on education, government, insurance, banking, and fashion; is home to the world's largest private research and development foundation (the Battelle Memorial Institute); and has emerged as one of the up-and-coming tech cities in the nation. Its famous residents include Limited Brands founder Les Wexner, Wendy's founder Dave Thomas, golfer Jack Nicklaus, and humorist James Thurber.

There was a lot not to like about the Storm, from our perspective. Their rink was a hell hole, their original coach was haughty, and Toledo won ECHL championships in their second and third seasons; with hockey personnel throughout the league speculating that they had violated the ECHL salary cap rules.

That was the crux of our relationship with them. As has been stated before, we didn't believe in the sleight-of-hand, secret envelope or, in some cases, or overtly stretching the rules when it came to paying players.

"Every time before we made a trade we had to ask the guy 'What are you getting under the table? What are you getting for scoring goals?'" an exasperated Mantha said.

Did Toledo bend the rules? Brent had his opinions.

"They were always rumored to be pushing the envelope on the salary cap," he said. "We played by the straight and narrow so their antics always put us in a bad position with our guys come contract time."

In so many ways, Toledo was our antagonist. To compete for a title, the Storm was the obstacle we had to overcome.

The early years of the Chill vs. Storm rivalry emanated from the head coaches. Both Roscoe and Storm coach Chris McSorley loved hard-nosed, fists-ready players, and the ECHL—heck, nearly all of minor league hockey— still acted as if the Broad Street Bullies of the mid-'70s were the formula for success. The truth was that in most new hockey markets at our level, fighting was still considered a part of the draw to fans. And with the Chill and Storm, it didn't take long for the two in-state rivals to set new standards for hostility.

During an eventful Sunday afternoon matinee in November of our second season, the teams combined for an ECHL-record 301 penalty minutes—158 by the Storm in the three-hour, thirty-minute marathon. The teams smashed the previous penalty mark by 38 minutes, and the 67 infractions were also a new high, or low, depending on how you looked at it.

We couldn't have picked a worse day for the bloodlust to be unleashed in full fury for the first time. It was Family Day, to be precise, when many parents introduced hockey to their children. And, oh yes, Commissioner Pat Kelly was in the house.

McSorley and four of his players were ejected, as were five players from the Chill.

The main donnybrook took place late in the second period and involved every player on the ice. The trouble began after Jason Christie—our lovable Smurf—was cross-checked to the ice by Storm enforcer Derek Booth. No penalty was called.

Without delay, an incensed Roscoe countered with enforcer Mark Cipriano. Mayhem was unleashed when Cipriano took all of seven seconds to even the score by picking up his own cross-checking penalty. Chill forward Cam Brown then plowed over Toledo goalie Scott King and the full battle ensued. Booth went after Brown. King jumped in. Our goalie, Jason Fitzsimmons, skated the length of the ice to join the fracas. Dreger pummeled Booth, who went into a shell and took his beating. "Booth was on an ego trip; Dregs put him back to reality," recalled Christie.

Both players were given double-game misconducts and the entire altercation resulted in 75 minutes to the Chill and 63 for the evil Storm. McSorley was thrown out after berating the officials for not throwing out Brown.

"We're back to playing Chill hockey," declared forward Rob Schriner after scoring two power-play goals in the 5–2 win.

Don Granato, a scorer not a fighter in his days at Wisconsin, went to dinner that evening with his father, who was in town seeing him play for the Chill for the first time. The elder Granato was no fan of the gratuitous violence that had seeped into a sport at which so many of his children excelled.

"Halfway through dinner, he looks at me real serious, 'Did you actually have fun out there today?'" Don said. "He was disgusted."

"Yeah, I did have fun."

He looked at me and shook his head: "There's something wrong with you."

McSorley fielded talented and physical teams that befit the Toledo Sports Arena, a bandbox built in 1947 that housed a variety of hockey franchises in several leagues, producing a rich and colorful history that was on display through the banners that hung from a ceiling that you seemed to be able to touch with an extended hockey stick.

While our home Coliseum had an arched roof and concourses around the ice surface and above the seating, there was literally no room to breathe in the Sport-A-Let, so aptly named by Brent, with no walkways inside the seating area.

The place seated 5,230 for hockey, and hundreds crammed into the little-available standing room on a regular basis to create a cacophony of sound because from the height from the floor to the lowest steel beam was only 33 feet, 8 inches.

How low was the ceiling? Well, whenever Ringling Bros. entertained in the building, they had to eliminate the human cannon ball, restrict the trapeze artists, and perform not-so-high-wire acts.

Not only was the arena compact, but the ice surface was about 15 feet shorter than the regulation 200-foot length and was perfectly suited for the physical style McSorley wanted.

"It was a small rink. They were a big team. You had to stay on your toes at all times," Chill forward Derek Clancey said.

Added Chill forward Jamie Spencer: "Toledo was freakin' tough, so every shift literally if you came out with your teeth you were feeling pretty good. The sticks were up; the elbows were flying."

Contributing to the misery of the Sports Arena for visiting teams was the squalor of the dressing rooms that spilled onto the walkways underneath the stands with curtains being the only things separating the players from the fans.

"In the locker room you had to go in shifts to tie your skates," Chill forward David Hymovitz remembered. "It was so narrow, so old; you're literally hitting the guy next to you or the guy across the bench from you. Then you walk out and it's the [cigarette] smoke, the food smell. It was a great hockey atmosphere."

Teams had to traverse the beer stands and jeering mobs separated only by a thin rope to reach the ice where the opponent's bench was practically part of the paying crowd. Unlike most arenas, there wasn't any glass on the back of the visiting team bench, allowing Storm fans an up-close-and-personal view of the opposing teams.

"People would line up to yell at you. They would spit and throw things at you," Clancey said.

The claustrophobic feeling continued on the ice with fans right on top of the action.

"I remember we beat them one night and the fans were throwing things on the ice," Spencer said. "We had to go through the beer garden to get back to the locker room. I didn't think we were going to make it out of there. Fans were coming over the glass. [Chill goaltender] Jeff Lembke turns around and everybody's hanging over the glass giving us the finger. He takes his stick and is chopping fingers along the glass. He's trying to break finger after finger. It's like we are going into the hornet's nest to get from the locker room to the bus.

"Moe led the way. We put all the bigger guys up front. He said, 'Okay, get us out of here.' And off we went to our bus. People were throwing stuff and swearing. There weren't any incidents, per se. There was a lot of jaw jacking and shoving but we got out of there in one piece."

Moe agreed that the Storm fans were relentless.

"The first time we won at Toledo, walking off the bench, I got doused with beer. I remember finding the owner, Barry Soskin. I said 'I've got a nice suit here drenched in beer. I'm going to send you the damn dry cleaning bill.'"

There was no respite after the game.

"The locker room was the worst I ever experienced as a pro athlete," Clancey said. "I remember after a game trying to shower. You had to get in and get out, because after ten minutes the water was up to your ankles."

Of course the building was home sweet home for the Storm, who lost only 11 of 36 regular-season home games to the Chill. It earned the respect of our players.

"They were a tough, intimidating team," Chill enforcer Barry Dreger said. "Those were always tough games, a lot of physicality. They probably had a more skilled team than we did.'"

Spencer agreed with Dreger's statement. "I feel like every game was a one-goal game. The fans were way into it. Playing in Toledo was a whole different world. They were really good. They had a good mix of scoring and grit, but they had a lot of guys and you had to watch your back everywhere."

Moe said playing in Toledo was always a good measure of how his players would react to adversity: "There was no place to hide. You found out what kind of man you were on that small ice surface. It was 'play the game, get out quickly.'"

Chill forward Kurt Semandel likened the rivalry to that of when he skated in college for Wisconsin against Minnesota. The big difference was that fighting got you tossed in college hockey, while a good bout earned a standing ovation and five minutes in the pros.

While fighting may seem barbaric, it historically has become a necessary ritual. For the most part, fighters are there to protect the skilled players and allow them to operate on the ice without the fear of being blindsided by some goon. Inevitably, when the game intensifies, the enforcers "drop the gloves" to the pleasure of many of the fans. Although not as common as it is in hockey, retaliations do happen occasionally in other sports, most notably baseball's bench-clearing brawls when players charge the mound if they believe a teammate at bat was deliberately struck by the opposing pitcher. In hockey it's common knowledge that if you cheap shot somebody, you better be ready to back it up with your fists.

Dreger described one titanic mismatch between the Chill's Phil Crowe and the Storm's Pat Pylypuik: "Phil grabbed Pylypuik and sliced him open for a gazillion stitches." Pylypuik, who later became the Storm's general manager, to this day bears a scar on his upper lip from the encounter.

Through the years, players and coaches changed, but the hostilities and fierceness continued, culminating with each team winning all five games on their home ice our final season in 1998–99.

Every athlete or team needs a rival to bring out the best or, in some cases, worst in each other to lift their game to another level. For us, the Toledo Storm was our juice.

The remnants of the series are all gone—the Storm ceased operations in 2007, the same year the Toledo Sports Arena was razed to make way for a new arena and another ECHL team (the Walleyes) in 2009—but not forgotten. Speaking of harboring memories, one final story illustrates our eight-year war with that team up north.

The rivalry got personal for me, too, when McSorley called me after Roscoe had moved on to the Houston Aeros and, surprisingly, showed interest in the Chill job. McSorley and I had a relationship from his playing days during our inaugural season with the Indianapolis Ice.

I was surprised and a bit disturbed that McSorley was interested in the job. For the life of me I couldn't quite figure out why. It was strongly rumored that he was indirectly responsible for our player walkout, as he was attempting to entice Darren Perkins to the Storm while we owned the player's rights. McSorley obviously did not fit our formula and during our phone call I blatantly told him so. He continued to lobby by telling me that the accusations were just hearsay started by opposing coaches who were jealous of his success. I responded by telling him, "Chris, I don't believe you." After an awkward pause we closed the call, but McSorley wouldn't forget or let go of that moment of rejection.

A few weeks later, McSorley called our game entertainment guru, Larry Lane, and offered him an opportunity to become the entertainment coordinator for the Buffalo Stampede, of the Roller Hockey International team he coached that summer. To ensure the offer was tempting, McSorley offered Larry $1,500 per game for each of the eight home games and would pay for his travel to and from Columbus. Don't get me wrong, Larry was outstanding in his role, but the offer was outrageously over the top.

Larry was both stunned and obviously fascinated by the opportunity to augment his salary. He gingerly approached me about the subject and outlined the particulars. My response was take his money if he's that foolish to spend that for a vendetta. The Stampede job was during the off-season, on the weekends, and wouldn't interfere with his job with the Chill. If McSorley was also hoping to coax Larry into a full-time role with Toledo as some sort of payback, it was because he didn't know Larry. I understood Larry's loyalties and knew he had no interest in getting knee deep with an operation like that. Larry took the job and picked up an extra $12,000 for an eight-weekend gig.

To top off the story, he was paid personally by McSorley after each game. When Lane was handed the check from the Stampede, McSorley added his favorite line each week, "Tell Paitson to go fuck himself."

Say what you want, but McSorley was nothing but a class act all the way.

Chapter Twenty-One

THE DRIVE TO THE FINISH

"It would be very helpful to us to have an NHL expansion team being awarded, but I don't think it is fatal [to the arena issue] if that doesn't happen. We've already shown that the economics of the arena work as an entertainment facility and with the Chill."
—Columbus Mayor Greg Lashutka, the *Dispatch,* October 25, 1996

When Ohio State broke ground on the Jerome Schottenstein Center on April 2, 1996, and the NHL formally announced the availability of four expansion franchises on June 15 of that year, it put us in full campaign mode.

By the start of the 1996 training camp in October, things were falling into place. The Downtown arena commission had recommended a sales tax to fund an arena/soccer stadium complex and the Chill had committed to the indoor venue so that the venture would be a break-even proposition from the get-go.

Earlier that summer, I joined six other Columbus representatives for a meeting in New York with NHL Commissioner Gary Bettman on the viability of our city for an expansion franchise. The entourage included Mayor Lashutka; City Councilman John Kennedy; Greater Columbus Chamber of Commerce President Lee Johnson; Franklin County Commissioner Dewey

Stokes; John Christie, JMAC; and Cathy Mayne Lyttle, vice president of marketing for the Chamber of Commerce.

After presenting our case, Bettman responded by saying, "We know all about Columbus." That was what we wanted to hear, and we left heartened by our chances. The media sensed that vibe and finally gave serious discussions to the possibility that the NHL would come to Columbus.

While we were in high hopes, this wasn't the first time a delegation from Columbus had gone before a major league commissioner. In the late 1980s, Columbus made a pitch before Major League Baseball.

John Christie was with a group that included Mayor Rinehart and Dan Galbreath, a Columbus businessman who was an international real estate executive, sportsman, and a civic leader. The Galbreath family owned the Pittsburgh Pirates and horses from their Darby Dan Farms near Columbus won the Kentucky Derby twice.

Christie said Columbus was not on a list of possible expansion cities but Galbreath's connections helped obtain a meeting with baseball commissioner Peter Ueberroth.

Fortunately, George Steinbrenner was a critical ally for Columbus. The volatile New York Yankees owner placed his Triple-A baseball players in Columbus with the Clippers franchise and whenever they were in town on the Fourth of July, he would spend some time at Franklin County (later Cooper) Stadium before visiting his mother to celebrate his birthday in the city.

"We made this presentation on why Columbus should be considered for major league baseball," Christie said. "In that meeting the expansion committee started asking a lot of questions of us and Ueberroth said that's not for them to answer; that's for us to answer.

"Mr. Steinbrenner said, 'I can just tell you I've had a Triple-A team in Columbus, Ohio, for a number of years and it can handle major league baseball.'"

Well, with the Cleveland Indians and Cincinnati Reds casting a wary eye toward Columbus, and the possible loss of fan base for each club, there was never a serious reality that Columbus would get a Major League Baseball franchise. Eventually, Miami (Marlins) and Denver (Rockies) were awarded expansion franchises in the early 1990s.

In 1987, Columbus also enjoyed a brief flirtation with Bill Bidwell, owner of the NFL's St. Louis Cardinals, but again, without an NFL stadium plan in place, central Ohio was not a serious contender.

"It was a charade [referring to the NFL]. It was never going to happen," said Lashutka, who at the time was involved in the Columbus sports commission. In 1988, the Cardinals moved to Phoenix, and later about nine miles northwest to Glendale where they currently play at the University of Phoenix Stadium.

Following his unsuccessful run at purchasing the Orlando Magic, Pizzuti approached NBA Commissioner David Stern about the possibility of securing an franchise for Columbus. "He [Stern] laughed at the notion," recalled Pizzuti. "Basically he said there was no way."

Even the city's first run at Major League Soccer was met with skepticism. In 1989, soccer's governing body, Fédération Internationale de Football Association (FIFA), granted the 1994 World Cup to the United States on the condition that the US Soccer Federation develop a first-division domestic league. Four years later, MLS was formed with more than 30 cities bidding to host the first 10 or 12 teams.

Pizzuti approached a friend, Harley Frankel, who worked for the new soccer league as senior vice president and asked his opinion on whether Columbus would be considered. "He said, 'No, you're not even on the B-list,'" recalled Pizzuti. "He said, 'I'll run it by the powers that be, but I don't think you've got a snowball's chance.'"

Columbus would be awarded a franchise in 1994 on the strength of a season ticket drive that produced more than 11,000 deposits and secured the ownership of fabled millionaire owner Lamar Hunt, founder of the AFL and owner of the Kansas City Chiefs. It was a coup for Columbus to have the investment and interest from a Hall of Famer in three sports—football, soccer, and tennis. The Crew and MLS began play in 1996.

Bolstered by Bettman's comments to our group in New York, I felt a sense of relief even though the months prior to the start of the 1996–97 ECHL season had been a whirlwind of activity around our franchise.

Brian McCutcheon, the former Cornell coach and captain of its 1970 hockey team—the only NCAA Division I men's national champion to go undefeated (29–0)—took over for Moe Mantha as our head coach. Brian Farr, from the OSU athletic training program, took over as trainer, and Jason Stypinski joined the staff as equipment manager. Brian was the head coach at his alma mater from 1987 to 1995 and led the Big Red to a 108–105–24 record before taking an assistant's job for the Los Angeles Ice Dogs of the IHL for one season.

In addition to a stellar playing career at Cornell, McCutcheon was a career minor league player in the 1970s, earning only cameo appearances with the Detroit Red Wings over three different seasons. Brian proved to be a steadier and a more focused leader than Moe or Terry Ruskowski.

"Brian was a no-nonsense, no-bullshit type of guy," recalled Chill public relations director Gary Kohn. We of course immediately set out to project that image in a radio spot created by Ron Foth Advertising:

If the measure of a man was intensity, this man would be a giant.

A rugged warrior who never backed down from a challenge, he now accepts a new mission as motivator and intimidator. In the heat of battle his men don't match wits with the enemy, they bang heads.

(Brian): "Let's go ladies. This ain't no Ice Capades."

Come see the toughest coach in hockey, new Chill head coach Brian McCutcheon.

On Opening Night, this Friday at the Fairgrounds Coliseum, see the Chill put the hurt on the Johnstown Chiefs at 7:30.

New coach Brian McCutcheon, now this guy is cold blooded.

(Brian): "Now let's get out there and bring me back some teeth."

Chill hockey—blood, sweat and fear.

As McCutcheon took charge, the proposed arena/stadium and NHL expansion dominated the public conversation. We entered the season on the road once again due to the All-American Quarter Horse Congress. We were hoping for a positive year and a playoff run to successfully drive the business, but also to support our efforts heading into the stretch drive of the ballot initiative (Issue 1) for a Downtown arena/stadium in the spring of 1997. We knew we were shut out of the Coliseum for the playoffs once again, but by now we were pretty good at turning that annual travesty into a hammer to drive the pro-arena message.

November 1, the same day we opened the 1996–97 ECHL season at home to another sellout crowd, Columbus' NHL expansion application was submitted to the league.

The ownership group on the document was identified as Columbus Hockey Limited (CHL), which was comprised of Pizzuti Sports Limited; Columbus businessman John H. McConnell; Wolfe Enterprises, Inc.; and the Hunt Sports Group.

Meanwhile, we were still busy with facility projects of our own, and two weeks later we announced our intention to build the Chiller Easton with, hopefully, an official agreement coming in the near future.

Earlier that year we held private meetings with John H. McConnell, founder in 1955 of Worthington Industries—a manufacturer of processed steel products, pressure cylinders, and metal framing on the northern edge of Columbus—to discuss partnering with Horn Chen on the project.

McConnell was a business titan in the city and an avid sports fan who was a Michigan State graduate. To have him in our corner was a very big deal. He showed interest in the ice facility and we continued to lay the groundwork for a partnership throughout the fall and winter.

Despite all of the excitement off the ice, the season didn't start out well for McCutcheon.

We had to play short-handed due to suspensions in 10 of the first 26 games, going 5–5 while down a player on the roster.

Eight of the short-handed games were the result of the actions by forward Gary Coupal, who sometime later was assigned the moniker "the baddest man in hockey" by *The Hockey News*. Coupal got kicked out of the ECHL for life when he concussed Hampton Roads' Aaron Downey with a clubbing to the head on December 3.

It was eerily similar to the Jason Taylor incident of the first season, including happening in the Admirals' rink. "We're not the most welcome team in Hampton Roads, I can assure you of that," I contritely told the *Dispatch*.

Coupal swung at Downey while they were on their respective benches. Neither the referee nor the two linesmen saw the incident but it was on video for review in the ensuing days. Coupal was given a two-minute unsportsmanlike conduct penalty, the same infraction given to Downey earlier in the game for spearing Chill forward Peter Vandermeer while Vandermeer was sitting on our bench. Coupal later said that's why he went after Downey.

Hampton Roads head coach John Brophy called Coupal's use of the stick, "The most gutless thing you can do in hockey." This coming from a coach who was suspended for three games the previous season for throwing a hacksaw at a fan—after a home game, no less.

Still, that didn't change the gravity of what Coupal had done.

While Coupal was suspended for the remaining 49 games of the ECHL season, he came back the following year and played in the United Hockey League and the Western Pro Hockey League. He even received a tryout invitation to the 1998 Philadelphia Flyers' training camp from general manager Bobby Clarke but was released when the AHL said it would not allow him in the league if he was assigned there.

We assembled a strong team for McCutcheon, led by player/assistant coach Mark Turner; scorers David Hymovitz, Derek Gauthier, Keith Morris and Matt Oates; and a solid defense including Beau Bilek and Corey Brick-nell. In goal for us was rookie Jeff Salajko.

McCutcheon took command of the team and, after a slow start, molded the talented group into the most solid and consistent unit the franchise had ever put on the ice.

One of the early season highlights was Gauthier playing against his older brother by two years, Sean, a goalie for the Pensacola Ice Pilots. Derek scored the Chill's first goal and Columbus won 5–2 to improve its franchise-best start to 11–3–0.

"That's the first time I've beaten him," Derek said afterward. "This is the sixth time we've played."

By mid-season it became apparent that the Chill had a chance for a first-place finish.

With the possibility of once again having to take our home playoff games on the road, I said to the *Dispatch,* "If we don't make it an issue, it won't be an issue."

In other words, we were preparing one more time to shout from the rooftops.

Unlike our early years, we weren't alone in voicing the need for an arena. On February 18, 1997, the Franklin County Commissioners put a 0.5 percent sales tax on the May 6, 1997, ballot to fund a $277 million Downtown sports complex with an arena (18,000 seats) and adjacent 30,000-seat soccer stadium.

In conjunction with the public funding for Issue 1, the private sector needed to raise $57.5 million for the project.

Thankfully, the private funding was raised in plenty of time. Bank One agreed to pledge $35 million in exchange for naming rights for the new arena. Nationwide Mutual Insurance Company committed an additional $17.5 million to be generated through parking revenues, and Worthington Industries committed $5 million to get us to the 20 percent in private funding required to get the issue on the ballot.

In an effort to allay voters' tax concerns, the levy would expire after three years (commonly referred to as a 'sunset clause') and could not be extended or used for other purposes without another vote. This was an important clause; yet, many people did not believe it and opponents tried to use that fear to their advantage.

"The anti-arena groups didn't believe the sunset clause," said Maurer. "It played right into people's mistrust of politicians. The old adage 'there is nothing more permanent as a temporary tax' had political legs."

Doug Kridler of the Columbus Association for the Performing Arts (CAPA) was chosen to lead the Issue 1 campaign. Kridler had done an extraordinary job of building CAPA into a one of the most highly respected theatrical organizations in the country. He had taken control of the association more than a decade earlier, expanding CAPA from overseeing one theatre in Columbus to six and placed the organization on sound financial footing.

His reputation in Columbus was impeccable. With Kridler taking the lead on Issue 1, we opened the door to those who had no real interest in the NHL but could legitimately support the project, knowing it was for the benefit of the entire community.

To win public support, this venture needed to be seen as broad based, and Kridler's culturally diverse background gave us that clout. Yes, we were trying to attract the NHL, but this project had to be about more than just a Downtown arena for hockey.

Now, it was time to make the final sale to the community, which we knew wouldn't be easy. Although the project had gained its share of public support, it was still a tax initiative. Therefore, it faced cynicism from those who had been down this road before with four other failed sports venue ballot issues from 1978 to 1987. Adding to that skepticism was Richard Sheir and other local activists who opposed the tax issue.

Sheir, a former state employee, was a politically shrewd and intelligent man. He wasn't anti-arena as much as he was of the opinion that it was a rich man's responsibility, not the public's to fund a new area, which was a sentiment that many shared. In the end, voters either believe there are times civic arenas are important public investments or take the stand that building sports arenas is nothing more than corporate welfare.

"Quite frankly, for anybody who is trying to raise your taxes on anything, it's an uphill battle, especially when you're trying to raise enough money to build an arena and soccer stadium in three years," said Bill Jennison, of the county convention facilities authority. "That's a lot of tax push, a lot of money in a short period of time."

We were working to build the case that public backing was necessary to secure projects of this magnitude and that the positive effects from the arena and accompanying new businesses would be worth the investment. Of course, the national and international media attention the arena/soccer stadium would bring was also in play.

Sheir's group, Voters Against Stadium Taxes (VAST), stirred hostility by drilling home the anti-tax sentiment. This small faction attended various citizens' gatherings to present their case but was not particularly well organized and, at times, was loose with their facts. Still, they found themselves front and center as the voice of the opposition.

Whenever a story would appear on the issue, the media turned to Sheir to show that they were providing a balanced view point, whether what he said was true or not. I certainly had no issue with the opposition voicing their opinion. Sheir had some legitimate arguments. The arena project would shift millions of dollars of capital expenditures Downtown and potentially delay other neighborhood projects for years. It was a matter of how and by whom the priority is defined. I empathized with his point but believed that this was the city's top priority at the present moment.

The problem was that Sheir and others were never held accountable for their statements, and the media did virtually nothing to follow up on any misinformation. One memorable claim made was that it would cost $50 million to clean up the penitentiary site in preparation to rebuild. Our estimates had it at around $15 million.

There were times like this when Sheir's group was pulling numbers out of their asses, all the while shouting them loud enough to be perceived as facts. Unfortunately, the media chose not to challenge them, which, in turn, made our job that much more difficult.

"Sheir found the sound bites that resonated with the people," said Maurer. "It's not always about the facts in a campaign but what resonates [with the voters]."

It was painful to admit, but the opposition was succeeding in promoting the negatives to undecided voters. Why let facts stand in the way of a good protest?

The pro-arena forces had significantly more resources, appearing to be the Goliath to their political David, but in reality we were the ones fighting the uphill battle. (For the record, even our estimates overstated the cost—The Pen was cleaned up for less than $10 million.)

"Sheir played the politics adeptly," said Maurer. "He was a sympathetic figure and he didn't come across as a politician. It was a true grassroots effort. He understood that any tax initiative was polarizing and played it to the hilt. It just shows that it is not always about the big campaign war chest."

Even OSU Athletic Director Andy Geiger pitched in on the misinformation. When asked on a morning radio show how much each Columbus Crew game meant financially to the university, he replied less than $10,000 per game. I immediately called Jamey Rootes, the president of the Crew, and asked him for his estimates. The reality was that each game produced at least five or six times that amount. Geiger publicly stated that this number took parking, concessions revenue, merchandise percentages, etc., into consideration, when, in actuality, he was only referring to the rental income from the Crew and conveniently left out the rest of the benefits. This was obviously a misleading appraisal.

Additionally, when Ohio State ran radio advertising promoting their arena seat licenses and promoted access to major concerts and shows, it came off as undermining the Downtown arena effort and created further friction.

Mayor Lashutka said that the OSU arena use "flies in the face of the commitment made back in 1994. There was a clear indication that OSU was pursuing its arena for gender equity in its sports programs and as a convocation center and that it would not be pursuing activities in conflict with what would be offered at the arena being pursued Downtown."

Ohio State eventually pulled the radio ad, but Geiger continued to stir the pot when he said that the campus community needed a wide variety of entertainment, "and those interests should be reflected in the university arena's schedule."

How far did the Ohio State University Athletic Director work behind the scenes to deliberately undermine the city's campaign to secure major league sports? He pressed influential media—including those at the *Dispatch*—to disparage the arena/NHL movement. In Geiger's pitch, Columbus was not ready for the major leagues and would always be a small market, unable to survive with the likes of New York, Chicago, and Los Angeles.

To make matters worse, there was a contingent of preservationists who felt the site of the Pen, built in 1834, should be saved.

Famous inmates of the Pen included William Sidney Porter, better known as the short story writer O. Henry (he wrote *The Gift of the Magi* while there), and Cleveland doctor Sam Shephard. He was incarcerated for ten years for murdering his wife before the conviction was overturned. His story was the basis for the TV show and film *The Fugitive*. The prison population peaked in the mid-1950s at 5,200 prisoners, but the facility became obsolete by 1972 and closed twelve years later.

This "preserve the Pen" story was drilled home time and again, much to our disbelief. I mean, nobody could take this seriously, right? As someone who appreciates history and preservation, I support saving historic monuments, but in this case I never agreed with what they saw as the value of keeping the Pen.

After all, the Pen site was a decaying blight on the edge of Downtown—sidewalks were closed around it because of the falling concrete and rocks from the walls—and this was our chance to get rid of it and open up the heart of the city. The 50-plus acres would be put to great use in transforming the entire Downtown area. Conversely, if the arena wasn't built, I'm convinced the penitentiary would still be sitting there, rotting away with no sign of improvement.

In addition to the anti-arena crowd and preservationists, there were plenty of naysayers who just didn't view Columbus as a major league city. This was a shame, since most of these folks lived here all their lives and couldn't see the forest through the trees.

Then there were those who claimed they'd vote for the arena but didn't want the soccer stadium.

"A lot of people were concerned about an open-air facility Downtown with concerts and other things," Jennison said. "They were concerned about the noise and traffic. And a soccer stadium is twice the size of an arena so that's twice the traffic, twice the parking demand."

Foremost in the opposition was the "not in my backyard" crowd in Victorian Village, a progressive yuppie-style area to the immediate north of the proposed arena. They thought the project would destroy their property values—yet there was data supporting the notion that this project would dramatically increase them.

And, of course, there was the chest thumping and blindly loyal Buckeye contingent who considered it blasphemy to have anything that would compete with their beloved school.

Chapter Twenty-Two

PUCKS, POLITICS, AND THE ART
OF THE POWER PLAY

The Chill's Top Gun: David Paitson never takes the ice, but he's the driving
force behind the phenomenal success of pro hockey in Columbus. Now he's
pushing for an arena and NHL franchise.

> —Headline from *Columbus Monthly*, December 1996

The Chill had the megaphone as the sole voice for hockey and as a forerunner
proponent for Issue 1, and we used it accordingly.

Brent Maurer, Gary Kohn, and I had gained the trust of the media, the
business community, and area sports fans on Issue 1, as we talked the talk and
added no fluff. Through our six-year history as a franchise, we actually did
everything we said we would do, including having box office success unlike
any previous professional sports franchise in Columbus. The Chill built
strong relationships with nearly every radio and TV in town, the newspapers,
as well as our corporate partners and city leaders.

"We were at the core of the arena story, so we had the credibility to sit
down with radio icon Bob Conners or a George Lehner and make a case,"
Kohn said. "Doug Kridler, Lamar Hunt, the Mayor, and many other power
players were well-liked and respected, but the radio, TV, and print media interacted with David, Brent, and me on a regular basis. We weren't titans to them.

We were real people talking about changing our community and that's why we could be very influential, because we had a track record of making things happen. We didn't represent ourselves as 'corporate' but rather as professionals with some form of hockey 'street cred.'"

Because of our reputations, we were able to get general managers of many of the TV and radio outlets to assemble their staffs so that I could present updates on the arena campaign and NHL expansion. These were the on-air personalities, producers, and sales people who had a deep reach into the community. By all rights, they also had a major stake in the arena issue, themselves. If we were successful, it would be good for their business, as a slew of new events—concerts, family shows, etc.—in addition to the NHL, would all need to be promoted and advertised.

Brent and Gary played a major role in this campaign. They were proactive press agents and brought their typical enthusiasm and energy to our message. They were out front every day stating our case and doing so convincingly. With Brent having moved to director of corporate sales and promotions, Gary took over the PR duties and was recruited to assist the campaign with the day-to-day communications efforts.

While Brent and Gary were at the front lines, we knew there were other ways for us to get the word out. Speaking at a Chill pregame party, I told the crowd, "We're going to be looking for fan involvement. This needs to be a real grassroots deal. [You] fans need to lead it, not us." While most of the Chill faithful were on board, some didn't want to see hockey leave the Coliseum.

"Some of the fans enjoyed the mom-and-pop access to the players and the community spirit of the team," said Maurer. "That doesn't necessarily translate at the NHL level."

"There were Chill fans who were unhappy about the move to the NHL," said Kohn. "They loved the team, the environment, the players, and the fun. For them, moving to the NHL was similar to a hippie taking a corporate job. No NHL team could handle the kind of edginess the Chill was known for, and the die-hard fans knew that once the Chill left town, they would never have anything like it again."

The fans understood NHL tickets were expensive and their seat proximity would likely not be as close as it was in the minor leagues. But, for the most part, the fans saw the bigger picture and their support was unwavering.

Following the all-out media assault led by Gary, Brent, and me, the entire front office staff, led by Amy Reese and Ted Van Zelst, enthusiastically got behind the grassroots campaign. We were all in, even though the passage of Issue 1 and the possibility of an NHL team meant we could all be out of jobs.

"The grassroots support from our fans was unbelievable," said Reese, our marketing executive. "They tirelessly typed letters to the media and politicians, campaigned via phone banks, going door to door, and placing signs in yards. Issue 1 laid the groundwork for the support of the building project and expansion team."

We registered voters at Chill games and promoted the topic in our programs and on our radio and TV broadcasts. Like the team, the community campaign was coming together through a tireless effort. In our minds, it was all setting up perfectly.

On the ice, McCutcheon calmly guided the Chill through the early-season suspensions, call-ups, and injuries to a North Division title, keeping us in first place for 22 of 25 weeks—including the last 17—although we never led by more than three points at any stage of the season.

It wasn't easy for him, with the constant juggling of the lineup. On the day of our New Year's Eve 1996 home game against the Toledo Storm, *Dispatch* hockey writer Craig Merz chronicled the Chill's travails, which included the most recent injury to David Hymovitz, our top goal scorer who had a fingernail torn off and sustained a small fracture and lacerations on a finger after a shot by teammate Corey Bricknell ripped through Hymovitz's glove.

In the month of December alone, leading scorer Mark Turner missed seven games with a groin injury and top defenseman Marc Dupuis was promoted to the Indianapolis Ice, leaving us with only five defensemen. We endured the banning of Gary Coupal and had Derek Gauthier suspended twice for a total of six games. Also, forward Eric Manlow (broken nose) and Mike Rusk (concussion) each missed a game.

Even though we were 20–10–1 and in first place, I was anxious to put that month behind us and hoped January would bring some relief.

But wouldn't you know it, before the ball dropped on 1997 we were punched in the gut again when forward Peter Vandermeer got the worse of a collision with a Toledo player and broke his left leg, possibly putting him out for the season. Fortunately, we still won the game, 5–2, before another festive standing-room only crowd of 6,000.

There were some positive vibes that December, though, because one of our all-time greats rejoined the team midway through the month. Derek Clancey was playing for the Waco (Texas) Wizards in the Western Pro Hockey League when the opportunity to return to Columbus opened.

He even got his old No. 27 back and after a few weeks of adjustment he was the same Clancey who terrorized ECHL goalies for years. He finished the season with 59 points (26 goals, 33 assists) in just 46 games and was a big reason we experienced a special moment on the last day of the 1996–97 regular season.

Columbus had been through four pro hockey teams in two leagues, encompassing 16 seasons over a 31-year period beginning with the Checkers in 1966, but had never won a league or division title — until March 30, 1997.

Playing before a hostile crowd of 5,350 in the decrepit Toledo Sports Arena, the Chill got two second-period goals apiece by Gauthier and Keith Morris to break a scoreless tie en route to a 4–1 victory and finished a point ahead of the second-place Peoria Rivermen.

It was particularly gratifying to clinch the division by beating our long-time nemesis. The Storm had won ECHL championships in 1993 and again in 1994, the latter title coming two series after sweeping us in the second round of the playoffs.

But this was our year. We won the last five meetings to win the season series 6–2. "They've just played better than us, no doubt," Toledo coach Greg Puhalski said after the finale. "They deserve to win the North."

The Chill compiled a 44–21–5 record, and McCutcheon was named ECHL Coach of the Year, a first for our franchise, as was my Executive of the Year award. And what was the team's reward for this dream season?

Just one month before the arena vote, the Chill was forced into "home" playoff games in the Nutter Center in Fairborn, Ohio—a Dayton suburb 55 miles to the west of Columbus—on the campus of Wright State University. It was also home to the Dayton Bombers, but fortunately our first-round opponent was that other in-state rival, Toledo.

The timing for a playoff run couldn't have been better. I turned our staff loose and we browbeat the message that Columbus desperately needed a Downtown arena so "home" playoff games could *actually* be played at home. It had been a great season and our fans were losing out on the best part of the year because we had no place to play in our own town.

"We used this success as a platform for our venue problems; i.e., first place team with a chance to win a title has to play on the road? We posed that question to every media member that would listen," said Kohn. "We hosted an information session for the media just before the playoffs to inform them of the different venue scenarios. We created radio stunts. We sent direct-mail pieces to our fan bases letting them know the arenas issues and suggesting they get on the phone to call TV, radio, and print media to voice their displeasure at the situation. By the time the playoffs were about to begin, the Chill having to play in Dayton became a main talking point for everyone involved in Issue 1."

While Toledo had the edge in the rivalry over the years, we were able to exorcise a few demons when we ousted them in a nail-biting best-of-five, first-round series replete with three straight overtime games and a few "interesting" calls.

Our guys won the opener, 5–2, in Fairborn to end a nine-game playoff losing streak which dated back to 1994. Team captain Matt Oates scored twice for us in the game, including once shorthanded, as we jumped to a 2–0 lead in the first four minutes before a quaint gathering of 690 in a building seating 9,950 for hockey.

"To tell you the truth, it felt like Dad dropped me off at a Saturday afternoon game—pee wee hockey—it was so empty," Oates said afterward.

Game 2 in Toledo began at 7:30 p.m. on April 3 and ended at 12:25 in the morning of April 4, with the Storm prevailing 3–2 in double overtime to tie the series at 1. The goal came 8:32 into the fifth period, making it the second-longest Chill game (88 minutes, 32 seconds) in history, behind the 95:05 marathon against the Richmond Renegades on March 25, 1995.

We trailed the Storm 2–1 entering the third period but Derek Wood fed Joe Coombs for the tying goal after five minutes and both teams buckled down from there. We survived a Toledo 5-on-3 power play in the first overtime but couldn't pull out a win.

Afterward, our goalie, Jeff Salajko, had to spend several hours in a Bluffton, Ohio, hospital on our way overnight to Fairborn to be treated for dehydration. It's no wonder. The Toledo Sports Arena had a cloud of cigarette smoke hanging from the low ceiling and the early warm spring temperatures created a sweltering situation in the non-air conditioned building.

Yet, just twelve and a half hours after the completion of Game 2 in Toledo, he was on the ice as the teams battled, with the Storm winning 3–2 in overtime (again!) in front of 1,411 transplanted Chill faithful in Fairborn.

Just like Game 2 in Toledo the previous night, Toledo got a two-man advantage on the power play in overtime, and this time Rick Judson converted at 2:57 to give the Storm a 2–1 series lead, leaving the Chill incensed at the referee for calling the two penalties in overtime, as well as at Salajko's claim that he had the puck tied up for a faceoff before Judson poked it free and scored.

Of course, complaining about the officiating is standard operating procedure.

Former Chill intern/emergency goalie Jason Rothwell was working in the ECHL office when retired Hockey Hall of Fame referee Andy Van

Hellemond, the league's senior vice president of hockey operations, called the staff into his office.

"He said that we've got to hear these two voicemails. The first message is obviously right after a game. I mean maybe a minute or two. The head coach on the phone is livid about the officiating. I think we counted fifty cuss words in a two-minute message," Rothwell said. "The second voicemail is from the same coach, but about twenty minutes later. The first thirty seconds is a heart-felt apology to Andy about the previous voicemail. But as he's apologizing, his anger is coming back and then the final thirty seconds of the voicemail includes another twenty cuss words. That sums up life as an ECHL official."

Several players and McCutcheon were given misconduct penalties at the conclusion of the Game 3 loss to Toledo, although none would be suspended for Game 4 the following day back in Toledo.

As it turned out, that game was our biggest road win ever, in my estimation, and maybe the top victory of all-time considering the opponent and the circumstances.

The atmosphere was so intense throughout the series that we took our own security guards to Toledo for Game 4, as the crazed Storm fans braced for what they expected to be the end of the playoffs for us.

Trailing in the game 2–1 with just ten minutes left in the third period (and from us being eliminated), the hockey gods finally rewarded us with a lucky bounce off the glass that squirted past Toledo goalie David Goverde for the easy put in by Hymovitz.

Chill defenseman Beau Bilek cleared the defensive zone with a pass to Bricknell, who chipped the puck off the glass in the Toledo end so the Chill forwards could chase it. Goverde came out of his crease to handle the puck but it squirted by him, leaving Hymovitz with the puck and an open net. He buried his shot before a stunned Goverde could get back to the goalmouth.

The sound of silence in the Toledo Sports Arena was deafening.

Hymovitz then ended the drama at 16:13 of overtime by taking a pass in stride from Mark Turner and, spotting an opening against the challenging Goverde, quickly ripped a shot into the back of the net to even the series at 2–2.

"It was great to go up there and beat them," said Hymovitz. "There's nothing better."

As the players rushed the ice to mob him, McCutcheon, in a display of relief and exhilaration, found the closest thing to him on the bench, a water bottle, and flung it in the air, watching the plastic pieces shatter on the ice like Toledo's hopes of ending the series at home. The Toledo fans threw bottles and wooden folding chairs on the ice as the Chill celebrated.

How crazy was this series, with three straight overtime games? Of the other seven best-of-three, first-round series in the ECHL, only three of the 23 games went to OT.

We finished off the Storm 5–2 on April 9 in Fairborn in front of 1,760 "home" fans.

Two goals from Turner and another by Gauthier gave us a 3–0 lead through 40 minutes, but the story was Vandermeer. He scored twice in third period against the Storm, the opponent when he sustained a broken leg in two places on December 31. At the time, he was told he would miss eight months, but he returned for the season finale on March 30.

Exhausted from the Toledo series, we lost three straight to Peoria in the second-round, best-of-five series (5–2, 3–2, and 5–2). Games 2 and 3 in Fairborn drew 1,170 and 654 fans, respectively. In all, the Chill played 27 of its final 34 games outside of Columbus. The guys did a great job but eventually ran out of gas. It had been a memorable season.

The playoffs had been in full force when we finalized our deal with McConnell to build a second Chiller in Easton, 21 miles from the Dublin Chiller.

This burgeoning relationship with McConnell reinforced the Chill brand as an important player in the community and further enhanced our chances of partnering with him in some form if Columbus got an NHL franchise.

We had signaled our intentions back in the fall to build the rinks but completing the agreement one month before the arena vote sent one more significant message about our organization's commitment to Columbus. The Chiller served as the anchor of a section of Easton devoted specifically to youth sports, just as the Dublin Chiller was surrounded by sports facilities.

Because of that we had some leverage with the fledgling development. Our legal counsel Greg Kirstein had the idea of naming the street leading into the facility "Chiller Lane," and successfully negotiated it into our contract. It had to be another first for a minor league hockey team.

Easton's Chiller opened a new section of the city for ice skating and hockey enthusiasts, while also expanding the Chill's fan base.

The dual ice rink facility included an Olympic-size ice sheet (200 feet by 100 feet), the first of its kind in Ohio. The Olympic rink became a draw, especially for figure skaters. We would also develop our second youth hockey organization—Easton Youth Hockey Association (EYHA)—with an eye on the December 1997 opening of the rinks.

Of course, we were counting on a meteoric rise in participation based on Columbus receiving an NHL team with the passage of Issue 1.

Building the Chiller at Easton and partnering with McConnell had another subtle (to the public, anyway) effect. Easton owner Les Wexner was a deep-pocketed supporter of everything Ohio State, but he did not voice opposition to the arena/stadium because it was backed by fellow titans, namely John F. Wolfe, Ron Pizzuti, John McConnell, and NFL owner Lamar Hunt.

And there we were, the Chill organization hobnobbing with the big boys and heading toward a grand finale on May 6 at the polls. We were really gaining traction with the voters, until . . .

WNCI'S April Fools' Joke

The first day of April 1997 dawned and the WNCI Morning Zoo played host to several Chill players in the studio. The players appeared during the prime, seven o'clock slot to promote the team's upcoming playoff series and to plug Issue 1.

Unbeknownst to Chill PR Director Gary Kohn, who planned to meet the players at the station but was running late, the Morning Zoo did their damnedest to give Gary and Issue 1 supporters a heart attack.

Midway through the segment, the radio personalities urgently described how one of the "players" got into a fistfight with Zoo co-host Jimmy Jam. This "player" was then pulled off Jimmy Jam and tossed out of the studio.

This was great theater for the station and the remaining players spent the rest of the interview apologizing for their buddy but, of course, WNCI played up the incident over the next two hours.

Listeners were hammering the station and the Chill offices with calls upset over the vicious attack. They "couldn't believe the players would conduct themselves that way," and they were "not supporting hockey if this is the kind of athlete the NHL was bringing to town."

Gary was mortified and raced to the scene but arrived after the players had left. That's when the gag was revealed—it was a fictitious player in a made-up fight. He promised not to say anything about the stunt until after 9 a.m., when the truth was revealed as an April Fools' joke.

Ironically, the next day, the Morning Zoo hosted a pep rally in front of the Nationwide Insurance building and left their high jinks behind. The event was part of NHL commissioner Gary Bettman's final visit before the vote and was engineered to gauge Columbus' support for an NHL team, as well as hype the passage of Issue 1.

While WNCI's gag momentarily had Chill officials and everyone associated with Issue 1 on pins and needles, in the end it was harmless. In turn, Bettman's appearance gave the Downtown arena and soccer stadium campaign an added lift and, according to one poll, Issue 1 had a five-point lead with just over a month until Election Day.

Chapter Twenty-Three

THE ENEMIES WITHIN

"It is difficult to say who does you the most mischief: enemies with the worst intentions or friends with the best."

—E. R. Bulwer-Lytton

During the final stages leading to the May 6 vote on Issue 1, the group leading the campaign made the dumbest damn decision I've ever seen. Worse than letting the enemy through the back door, we practically invited them in!

Ohio State's Gee was named co-chairman and became a major face of Issue 1. The idea was to provide a unified front, but who were we kidding?

I thought, *Come on folks, the public is smart enough to see through this.*

In my opinion, Gee was a phony. Value City Arena on the Ohio State campus was scheduled to open the next year, and here we were putting the fox in charge of the hen house. It may have been well intended, but it was a boneheaded decision by the campaign's leadership.

There seemingly was a resistance from OSU to the change that was happening in the community. Our friends in the media told our staff on several occasions that OSU officials were working the back channels, sending a message of why pro sports would be bad for Columbus. It seems that they feared the unknown of what the NHL could do to their monopoly on the market. I couldn't help but ponder this simple question: *Why would Gee campaign for another arena to compete with the new one on campus?*

Instinctively, I felt we were headed down the wrong path with Gee as co-chair and felt the political types making these calls were clueless when it came to understanding the vibe of the average citizen.

Still, I was optimistic leaving the pro-arena rally Bettman attended on April 2. However, our momentum was short lived, as we were about to be derailed through a series of misadventures that could have been easily avoided.

Peter Karmanos, the owner of the NHL's Hartford Whalers, rolled into town one month before the vote to pitch the idea of moving his team to Columbus. Karmanos had made an earlier visit the previous October flirting with the idea and was back now for a public push. His lease in Hartford was to expire in 1998, and he was shopping around for a city. On April 8, he met with representatives from the Franklin County Convention Facilities Authority in an attempt to strike a deal.

I was agonizing over Karmanos' plans to bring the transplanted Whalers, believing we had the right ownership in place with Lamar Hunt and the local contingent. I felt Karmanos was at best a distraction and at worst a symbol of professional sports owners' greed. It was perhaps well intended to cover all options in case of an Issue 1 failure but, as far as I was concerned, we needed this like we needed a hole in our heads.

John Christie, who by then was president of McConnell's JMAC, Inc., a private investment company, gets the credit—or blame—for inviting Karmanos.

Christie said the perception that Karmanos was just playing the city for a better deal elsewhere for his hockey franchise at the expense of Issue 1 was wrong. "All along he was doing everything he could to help us," Christie said in an interview for the book.

Christie, no relation to our player Jason Christie by the way, said that skeptics wanted Karmanos to put his money where his mouth was and support the Issue 1 campaign.

"They said if he's so supportive of Columbus, why doesn't he give any money?" Christie said. "He doesn't live here, okay? So I actually sat down with Peter Karmanos on a visit and said, 'Peter, you're getting really bad rounds here. People think you're trying to hurt us and we need to prove you're not. I need a check.'

"He asked what amount. I said $50,000. He wrote the check that day and said don't cash it for two days because I'm not a guy who keeps $50,000 in my checking account."

Christie was warned by those in the campaign not to get involved further with Karmanos.

"I got a lot of crap for bringing him. Trust me," Christie said. "I did it not as a representative of JMAC; I did it as the chairman of the convention facilities authority.

"I was told not to bring Karmanos in for that April visit. I was going into a meeting at seven o'clock in the evening, and Mr. Bettman called me and said, 'You know, John, if you don't get an [expansion] franchise, this [the Whalers] is you're only hope. This is your shot.' I wouldn't tell Peter not to come in and I got a ration of shit."

"Peter was genuine in his interest but also his statements clouded the issue," said Columbus Mayor Greg Lashutka, in an interview for the book.

Even if Karmanos' interest in Columbus had been legitimate, it didn't play well with the public. Honestly, I was among those who were leery about the situation. It was clear to me that we needed someone who was right for Columbus, and Hunt was our man. In my opinion, this distraction did more harm than good.

Yes, Lamar Hunt was a player in the American sports scene even in his later years.

Hunt, who died in 2006, was not only a pioneer and a founder of many professional franchises, but the NFL's AFC Championship trophy is named in his honor. Today, the oldest annual team tournament in the US in any sport, soccer's US Open Cup (founded 1914), now bears his name in honor of his pioneering role in that sport stateside. His credentials were big league, all the way.

Plus, it was clear he had the deep pockets needed to sustain a start-up NHL operation.

There's the tale that I enjoyed that probably was first told about some other millionaire in a different setting but has long been attributed to Hunt:

It seems some friends of Hunt's father had gone to the old man worried that Lamar had lost a lot of money in one year of ownership of the Dallas Tornado, in the North American Soccer League, in the late 1960s. "At a million dollars a year, aren't you concerned he is headed to financial ruin?" a friend said.

Haroldson Lafayette Hunt, founder of Hunt Oil, leaned back in his chair and in a slow Texas drawl said, "Well, I guess he'll be broke in 400 years."

As much as I believed in Hunt, I also firmly felt we needed adequate time to prepare the market for the arrival of an expansion franchise and that the two or three years between the Issue 1 vote and the first NHL game would be a great opportunity to let the product simmer before consuming. If we rushed it out too quickly, we could spoil it altogether.

Hunt signed a letter of intent on April 10, committing to a twenty-five-year lease for both the stadium and the arena, with a guaranteed annual profit of $200,000 to the Franklin County Convention and Facilities Authority.

However, it was later reported that Hunt apparently had confided in Commissioner Bettman that if the ballot initiative failed, he would pull out of the effort.

Richard Sheir weighed in from the anti-arena campaign. "How are we to know that Hunt Sports is the best bidder for the project when this wasn't put out to public bid?" I guess he wasn't sufficiently impressed with Hunt's credentials.

Undeterred by Hunt's letter of intent, Karmanos on April 20 announced the harebrained idea of retrofitting an abandoned airplane hangar to seat 20,000 for the short-term until an arena could be built. City officials did their due diligence. "We looked hard at the airport as a temporary facility and it just wouldn't work," recalled Lashutka. To many, Karmanos came across to the public as another owner looking to fleece the city or play one market against another for his financial benefit.

Karmanos' presence clearly disrupted our effort, and it was evident the public distrusted the guy. I could feel our poll numbers sinking like a stone.[21] Christie disagreed with my assessment.

"Karmanos saying he would move the team here, everyone said was a negative. I didn't take it as that. The city was going to get a team. We were either going to get [expansion] or a get a franchise, but we had to have an arena," he said.

"Some people involved in the campaign believed that [Karmanos] hurt the campaign. I don't believe it."

Kohn said Karmanos presented a problem. His presence in the city confirmed that the NHL was serious about Columbus as a site for a team, but "he came across to many as another greedy owner who just wanted to line his pockets."

When the television media approached me to comment on the airplane hangar concept, I did my best to redirect public attention back to the idea of Columbus securing an expansion franchise led by Hunt.

I was hopeful the campaign could begin to put this silliness behind us and regain our momentum in time for the vote. Kridler and the Issue 1 campaign team also were pushing a message that the tax issue was good for all of Columbus, but we still didn't know if all of our efforts would be enough.

Eventually, the Karmanos proposal was scuttled—and as some predicted, he used Columbus to leverage a better deal in Raleigh, North Carolina (coincidentally, he would announce the move on Election Day), after temporarily playing in Greensboro, North Carolina, while an arena was being built.

If Karmanos' entry was seen as harmful to the effort—in boxing terms, it might have been described as a combination of a right jab followed by a left hook—then what came next was the sucker punch.

---

[21] A survey of voters after the election showed that 54 percent had a "favorable" view of Hunt, compared to 18 percent for Karmanos.

In an editorial piece published in the *Dispatch* just three days before the vote, Constance B. Gee, the wife of "our friend" Gordon Gee, came out against Issue 1.

Like many associated with the campaign, I saw this as a well-calculated statement. Gordon Gee attempted to write it off as having a relationship in which his wife was an independent thinker. B. S., I never bought it and never will.

"The conflict with Ohio State was definitely a negative," John Christie said. "Always has been. There was a lot of background backstabbing in the arena vote effort. Ohio State never, ever committed 100 percent to help. In fact, they undermined us. I think they undermined the whole thing."

Christie cited OSU's decision a few years prior to build their own arena instead of partnering with the city as still resonating with the voters. "It hurt the ballot initiative because people said, 'You're already going to have an arena; why build two?'"

Gee's involvement in the campaign, in my opinion, was an obvious conflict of interest, as Ohio State would be the big winner with Issue 1's defeat. It ultimately damaged Gee to those in the business community who saw through the charade, but was also another negative that would overturn the momentum we had built heading into voting day.

Greg Haas, the campaign manager for Issue 1, had told our group that in order to win we needed to drive turnout—getting to 30 percent was our goal. He argued that the more folks that came out, the better.

The May ballot was historically a time for low voter participation, typically drawing less than 20 percent to the polls. We'd been beating the drum publicly for almost two years and were confident that all our work would help us beat that number with ease.

"I referred to Issue 1 as Columbus' O. J. case," said Kohn, referencing the hype of the infamous trial two years earlier. "It was everywhere. It dominated all conversation."

He recalled that days before the Issue 1 vote, a polling service gave an update at the pro-arena headquarters. "According to their numbers, turnout was expected to be big, and we were actually trending 1–2 points ahead of the no-vote."

Election Day finally arrived on May 6, 1997, and we were all over the airwaves trying to help win the vote.

We kept a close eye on turnout throughout the day. The news was optimistic. It was looking like a historic numbers were casting ballots.

"Our biggest concern was weather, which day of turned out to be perfect," said Kohn. "We had a HUGE, get out the vote, crew organized and the media exposure was massive. You could not move in Columbus without knowing it was the day of the Issue 1 vote."

Around 3 p.m., I pulled the Chill and Chiller staffs together and gave them an update on the expected turnout and what it meant. Many of us planned to gather later at the Downtown campaign headquarters for what we hoped would be a celebratory event.

It was not to be.

"About 11 a.m., I got a call from Munch on Sports (WTVN radio)," Kohn said, referring to talk show host Mark Bishop. "He asked me if I was worried about the exit polls. I said I had not gotten any information yet about how we were doing. He said we were getting killed. I was worried, but I kept the call to myself."

A record 43 percent of the registered voters went to the polls. The problem was that Haas and his poll numbers were way wrong.

We lost by almost 13 points—56.3 to 43.7 percent.

"The mood was grim," said Kohn. "I was stunned."

"It was evident early on that evening that things were not going to go our way," added Maurer. "The campaign threw in the towel at 9:30 p.m. I remember seeing Sheir on television celebrating. It was a punch in the gut.

"We'd been pounding the message for five years, long before there was an official campaign," Maurer continued. "In one defining moment, the Chill stopped being that transcendent vehicle to change the city. The clock had struck midnight and we were back to being just a Double-A team playing in a cow barn."

We were all devastated. It appeared as though our dream of a Downtown arena and landing an expansion franchise had vanished before our eyes.

I told the *Dispatch*, "As far as growth, we'll maintain being a nice little hockey city, but we're never going to get a building. We flushed that opportunity down the toilet."

We were not the only ones who believed it was over. According to reports later run in the *Dispatch*, publisher John F. Wolfe told editor Mike Curtain that evening, "I will never in my lifetime see a Downtown arena."

The NHL was scheduled to announce its four expansion cities three days later, on May 9.

Chapter Twenty-Four

STRIKING BACK

"I'm sure they're having a big laugh down on Lane Avenue right now."
—David Paitson, *Columbus Business First*, May 9, 1997

The day after the vote, the feeling of defeat was devastating.

I truly believed Columbus was ripe for an expansion franchise, but with no arena to play in, the bid was pretty much dead in the water.

It was a sinking feeling and I found myself in a state of limbo. While I loved the Chill, I certainly had no plans to be a minor league hockey general manager forever. This would be the end of this road for me . . . and much of our organization.

For years the Chill front office had put their heart and soul into the effort, but it looked like Columbus voters decided they were okay with the status quo. The decisive vote against the issue played right into the hands of critics who believed the city lacked vision. It was no wonder that many of its own residents frustratingly referred to Columbus as a cow town. The city was seen by outsiders as a back woods, uncultured throwback to the days when farm animals roamed the streets and sophistication was too big of a word for such a small town. If you check the definition under Wikipedia, Columbus is one of five US cities listed. *Seriously!* [22]

From the moment that Issue 1 was announced, we did everything we possibly could to get it passed. We triggered the entire arena discussion five years earlier by bringing attention to our Coliseum scheduling fiasco; we were an active voice and participant throughout the process; and we put the franchise's future on the line with our public support of the issue; and we cultivated support within the business community, the media, and fans.

The vote was a bitter setback and the next day the media was in follow-up mode and I received a number of calls locally and nationally, including one from Kevin Allen of *USA Today,* who would publish an account of our plight in the following day's paper.

"In a way the Chill was fighting for its life," said Maurer. "We pinned it all on the arena issue. [Years earlier] we had decided to define a new course, knowing otherwise we'd either burn out or die a long, slow, painful death."

Another story was by Dan Crawford, of Columbus *Business First.* He had been following the story for quite some time and we had developed a good rapport. He was looking for a comment and I gave him a doozy.

As Janis Joplin once sang, "Freedom's just another word for nothing left to lose."

It was one of those moments in which I was still smarting from the loss and just let the unvarnished truth fly, repercussions be damned. Without mentioning their names, I let the Gees have it with a one-line quote:

"I'm sure they're having a big laugh down on Lane Avenue right now."

Lane Avenue is the corridor to the OSU sports complexes—Ohio Stadium, St. John Arena, the OSU Ice Rink, and Value City Arena among them, and, at the time, the offices for the athletics department. While my remarks were aimed at the Gees for what I believed to be their hypocrisy, it also blanketed Athletics Director Andy Geiger.

---

[22] Also mentioned: Fort Worth, Texas; Wichita, Kansas; Vacaville, California, and the Kansas City metropolitan area covering Kansas and Missouri.

Clearly, Ohio State athletics was the winner with their blockage of the Downtown project and elimination of pro sports as a direct competitor. My quote in Crawford's story, "Vote opens rift between OSU, arena backers," was published just three days after the defeat of Issue 1 and was highlighted in bold type on the front page of *Business First*.

I also said that Constance Gee's letter to the *Dispatch* criticizing Issue 1 supporters and suggesting the city council was trying to "bribe" possible pro-voters showed OSU was clearly against the issue, despite a counter public stance by her and others within the university community.

My quote caused an immediate uproar throughout Columbus. The Gees' response within the story only made them look guilty in my mind.

"Mr. Paitson's comment was a knee-jerk comment and certainly an unfortunate one," she told *Business First*. "I spoke only for myself as a private individual. My husband had nothing to do with the letter."

She again went on to criticize pro-arena backers by saying the plan was another example of the "patchwork" design of the Downtown and the leaders should have included more community support.

Are you kidding me? We had all corners of the community covered in the Downtown arena task force and the issue had been fully vetted through years of public discussion.

Gordon Gee also reacted in *Business First* to my comments: "I find that quite extraordinary that he would say something like that."

The OSU president painted Karmanos as the "villain" and "a well-known vagabond" that caused the defeat. "People who invited him are equally at fault," Gee said.

Gee noted how he co-chaired the campaign for the arena/stadium issue and that he voted for it. He said he did not know how his wife voted and she declined to say as much to *Business First*.

The idea that Gordon Gee's wife coming out against Issue 1 just three days before the vote didn't have a contributing effect in derailing the campaign was simply preposterous. Of course it did! This was the de-facto first lady of

Columbus accusing the City Council of trying to "bribe" the voters. Her characterization of the pro-arena effort was outrageous. The Gees were enormously popular and their influence was vast, but their "hidden agenda" to defeat Issue 1 as reported in the *Dispatch* would catch up to them the following year. As the *Dispatch* would write, "His lukewarm support—and the public opposition of his wife, Constance—for last spring's civic arena ballot initiative strained political relationships in Columbus."

We had to be realistic; as it turned out, our margin of error to get a tax issue approved by the voters was zero, or maybe infinitesimal.

John Christie felt that many voters just could not vote for taxes that they perceived provided no direct benefit to them because they would never go to the arena or stadium. Also, "We just have a lack of vision as a city," he said.

The Karmanos-Gee combination provided the knockout in my opinion. The final result is all the more maddening because it may have been preventable.

Were we doomed from the outset? Maybe so; it's certainly possible the campaign's polling numbers suggesting a possible win with a big turnout were just flat- out wrong. Maybe the soccer stadium was a drag on the issue. Maybe Columbus wasn't enamored with the idea of the NHL. Maybe our chances of winning were the equivalent of climbing Mount Everest. Or quite possibly, there was a change in the trajectory caused by two distracting messages during those final weeks and days. In the aftermath of Art Modell's move of the Cleveland Browns to Baltimore, who wants to vote for another "greedy sports owner" or who could support a group accused of trying to "bribe" the voters? Perhaps without the distraction of Karmanos and the misrepresentations of Gee, it could have been a closer outcome. Truth is we will never know for sure.

Bill Jennison saw things differently. He felt the soccer stadium portion made it too complicated, and he was also concerned that, while the taxpayers would be on the hook to fund the construction of the arena/stadium for only three years, the goal to be debt-free in three was a bit "ambitious."

"A lot of people were worried about a sales tax that promised to pay off the facility in three years. Nobody buys a house and pays for it in three years. You're building assets that are going to last thirty, forty, fifty years," he said.

"You want to streamline it. If I were doing it in a vacuum, I would have picked a funding source with a much smaller tax, a much narrower tax, and paid for it over thirty years," said Jennison. "It was pretty aggressive to think you could build it and pay for it in cash over a few years.

"Karmanos' perceived meddling was not why Issue 1 failed," Jennison said. "I think it showed that Columbus was a major league city. That a guy who actually owned an NHL team was seriously looking at Columbus was exciting. It gave us credibility that we really were a legitimate NHL city."

Ron Pizzuti believed taxpayers felt two arenas were overkill: "Nobody could understand why we needed to add 38- or 40-thousand seats to a city that basically had (no arena) other than the facility at the fairgrounds. That was not real desirable."

Political warfare also played a role in sealing the fate of Issue 1, Lashutka said: "These are tough sells, even in the best of environments, and we had a lot of sub-currents going on with certain folks at Ohio State. There was also concerns about Karmanos and 'He's not one of ours; do we really trust somebody who's not from Columbus?'"

My "Lane Avenue" statement shook the city, as challenging the OSU machine was a political death wish in Columbus. It was unprecedented and risky.

But at this point I couldn't care less. My feeling was that it needed to be said. It turns out my assertion lent a voice for what much of the business community and arena backers had felt for a long time, that although Ohio State and its athletics are an integral part of the Columbus culture, they shouldn't be the city's singular entertainment and economic focus.

"It represented how significant the Chill and, more specifically, (David) was to the NHL effort," said Kohn. "Gordon Gee, president of OSU, shouldn't have cared at all about what the Columbus Chill says. I had to say we were an ant on the OSU elephant. Instead, the Chill was a lightning rod that struck on the OSU campus to the point where Gee felt he had to comment on (David's) statement. Foolishly, Gee didn't understand that by commenting, he gave the story more legs and perhaps opened a few eyes at the same time."

"A lot of things went on behind the scenes that never came out in public," Christie said. "It set the city back quite a bit and the relationship between Ohio State and the Blue Jackets, or pro sporting entities in town, has been pretty tense. It may have eased up now, but it was tense for the first nine years or so of the Blue Jackets, without question."

I made my statement in a calm and rationale tone as a declaration of fact. It would resonate around town and apparently earned the private praise of one of the most important people in Columbus—John H. McConnell.

Known to everyone as "Mr. Mac," McConnell was an honest, plain-speaking man who lived by the credo that you treat others as you would like to be treated. The son of a steelworker and a World War II veteran, he envisioned early in his life a niche in custom steel processing.

He secured a $600 loan, using his 1952 Oldsmobile as collateral, to found Worthington Industries.

His golden philosophy that "people are our most important asset" led to the company being named one of the "Top 100 Companies to Work for in America" by *Fortune* magazine four separate times. Worthington Industries has also been listed among *Fortune's* "Most Admired Companies" and "Best Managed Companies."

At the time of this writing, the company has annual sales of approximately $3.8 billion, operates 57 facilities in 15 states and six countries, sells into more than 90 countries and employs approximately 9,000 people, according to its website.

Mr. Mac loved Columbus and, after the Issue 1 failure, became the key figure in a last-ditch attempt to resurrect the Downtown arena and to help the city secure an NHL franchise.

Commissioner Bettman had always believed Columbus was a good fit, so following the ballot defeat, he called Mayor Lashutka to express his disappointment and ask if there was another way to fund an arena.

"There was no fallback plan," said Lashutka. "That has been rumored, but there was none."

Several of the community leaders recognized that a golden opportunity was about to pass the city by. It was now or never for Columbus—and was time to get creative.

John Christie, who had for years been a tireless behind the scenes advocate for the downtown arena project and NHL expansion, was integral throughout the process in holding all the key players together, and as such, Columbus' chances for an expansion team.

Lashutka and Dimon R. McFerson, Chairman and CEO of Nationwide Financial Services, each met with Hunt the day after the vote to discuss opportunities and the possibility of still building an arena.

"The next morning [after the vote], Dimon McFerson called John McConnell and said 'We can still do this,'" Christie said. "He [Dimon] said, 'You buy the team; I'll build the building.'

"By that afternoon, one of the two called Gary Bettman and said, 'Don't knock us off yet.' He gave us so much time to get back with a plan and we met every deadline," said Christie. "It's amazing what happened in such a short period of time."

Pizzuti agreed with Christie's assessment. "If it had not been for Dimon making the quick decision in committing Nationwide to the arena, we'd still be knocking on doors, maybe looking for a lacrosse team."

Even though the NHL expansion committee was supposed to make its final recommendations only three days after the vote, Bettman provided us an extension until June 4, after hearing positive feedback from the Columbus contingent. "I think I asked for 45 days but Bettman said no, you've got 30 days," Lashutka said.

"I didn't have much time to mourn the loss," Jennison recounted. "The next morning, Bob Woodward (Executive Vice President and Chief Investment

Officer of Nationwide) called. When it [the defeat] happened, people saw that we were an NHL city. The NHL had told us build an arena and you'll get a team."

Other potential cities such as Houston and Oklahoma City, Oklahoma, also needed more time, but none needed the reprieve more than we did to be among the four selected.

"The mayor, John Wolfe, John McConnell, Dimon McFerson—they absolutely would not let this thing drop because they knew if Columbus, Ohio, was to be the Columbus, Ohio—to compete globally—you have to have an arena. You have to," Christie said. "With community leaders like that, it had to move rapidly. The pressure was on."

Nationwide representatives met with Hunts Sports Group in late May, but HSG did not accept Nationwide's lease proposal for the proposed arena. Nationwide then informed them that it needed an answer by May 30.

Feeling the lease was unacceptable, a response never came, and Hunt Sports Group was out of the picture.

Hunt recognized several potential drawbacks to the deal, including a $3 million annual payment to Nationwide to operate the new arena. He viewed the cost of becoming a tenant of the new facility without the benefits of several of the key revenue streams as problematic and was not willing to make a commitment.[23]

After not hearing from Hunt, McFerson then met with McConnell to discuss his privately funded arena plan as the June 4 deadline for expansion applications loomed. McConnell stated that if Hunt would not step up and lease the arena for a team, he would.

On June 2, 1997, Nationwide Mutual Insurance Company unveiled its plans to privately finance a $125 million Downtown arena.

The landmark move put Columbus in position to secure its first big-four, major league franchise through the following partnership:

---

[23] Two years later, Hunt christened the $28 million Crew Stadium he built for his soccer team following a failed stadium vote in Dublin on February 10, 1998. It was the first facility constructed for an MLS team. Coincidentally, the 22,000-seat venue was on the north side of the Fairgrounds, not far from where the Chill played.

McFerson committed Nationwide Insurance to take a 90 percent owner-ship stake in the new arena. The key ingredient making the investment viable was Nationwide receiving the opportunity to acquire and develop property for a mixed-use development of shops, offices, restaurants, and residences on the 50-acre Ohio Pen site. McFerson also counted on revenue from seat licenses and luxury suites to cover about 35 percent of the construction costs.

Nationwide also placed its name on the building—Nationwide Arena—without providing the normal cash outlay that would fund the annual arena or team operation. In essence, the company got naming rights without having to pay for them. The deal also allowed many of the on-site parking and related revenues to go directly to Nationwide Realty, Inc.

While their commitment was essential, Nationwide made certain they protected their own financial interests. John F. Wolfe, whose newspaper, the *Columbus Dispatch* supported the idea of a downtown arena for three decades, committed the Dispatch Printing Company to the remaining 10 percent of Nationwide Arena and also as part of the prospective deal would become an investor in the expansion franchise. The long-time Columbus titan believed that an arena was vital to Downtown development, spurring convention center business and strengthening the city's central core.

Ron Pizzuti, who played a key role in securing potential NHL investors, stepped forward as a secondary shareholder in the franchise. As one of the more respected real estate developers in the country, Pizzuti had already deeply invested in Downtown by creating the swanky Miranova high-rise along the Scioto riverfront.

Years earlier, his attempt to purchase the NBA's Orlando Magic fell short. He then became an original investor in the Columbus Crew in 1994 and was happy to be part of the next sports venture in Columbus.

The Franklin County Convention Facilities Authority committed $11.7 million to buy land for the arena. It would then be leased to developers for 99 years, with a plan to be paid back over the next 50 years. The City Council declared the arena site a blighted area, allowing the county to acquire the land. The Council also earmarked $20 million for infrastructure improvements and cleanup around the old Pen site.

The arena area was exempted from real estate taxes, although a ticket surcharge would be used to provide revenues to Columbus public schools equal to the amount the district would have received in real estate taxes.

City Auditor Hugh Dorrian, a member of our Downtown arena commission (Multi Purpose Sports and Facilities Work Group), gave a lengthy speech on the floor of the City Council to express his support. He pointed to his faith in Nationwide's track record of quality developments, the fact there would be no new taxes used for the project, and the benefits to Columbus schools by the tax surcharge. Still, there were the same old detractors—those who worried about the potential for increased traffic to the neighborhoods adjacent to the new Arena District, the Pen preservationists, and other developers who wanted in on the action. This time, thanks to the hard work of many people, an arena vote passed City Council.

The Columbus expansion application was considered by five NHL owners, including Karmanos. During his visits to Columbus, he and McConnell became friends and that relationship sealed the support of the other owners.

"He knew Columbus. He liked Columbus and was a member of Double Eagle Country Club (as was Boston Bruins owner Jeremy Jacobs)," Christie said of Karmanos. "When we considered applying for a franchise, forget his franchise, we had a meeting at Double Eagle, probably in the fall of '96, where he came in and walked us through all the economics of hockey."

And yes, I'm still amazed that I was there in the room at the meeting among an impressive group that included McFerson, Wolfe, and McConnell.

On June 25, 1997, the NHL announced expansion franchises for Columbus, Nashville, Atlanta, and Minnesota.

"I was in New York City that day with John McConnell and others," Christie recalled. "We made our presentation and I got on Mr. McConnell's plane and we flew to the ranch in Colorado and I picked up the phone sometime later out there and they [an NHL representative] said, 'John, tell Mr. McConnell he's got the franchise.'"

Christie relayed the news that McConnell had been waiting for.

"He couldn't speak a word," Christie said. "Even after all the stuff we had been through with the vote and despite the conflict of ownership (with Hunt) at the end, he was proud. I can tell you that."

Exactly one month shy of six years after we announced the Chill to Columbus under great public skepticism, the National Hockey League was a reality. It was an incredible feat and a huge victory for our city.

"Mr. McConnell pulled off one of the most heroic feats I've seen in the more than twenty years I've been involved in major league sports," Bettman told the *Dispatch*.

"He did it for Columbus," said Christie of McConnell, who died on April 25, 2008, at age eighty-four. "He didn't do it to make a lot of money. He publicly said he did it for Columbus and having dealt with him all the time and having been the point man for him, he actually believed those words in his heart.

"I don't think he expected to lose this kind of money [over the years], but he didn't plan on making a lot. He planned on making Columbus the city it deserves. That's why he did it.

"I will give as much credit to three other guys: John F. Wolfe, Ron Pizzuti, and Dimon McFerson," said Christie. Right back at you, John!

The Chill's role in the drive to secure an NHL franchise for Columbus cannot be overlooked or overstated. We had ignited the city's passion for the sport and spread "the gospel of hockey" to a football-mad region.

"It was minor league, but what they were able to accomplish within the limits of the Fairgrounds was remarkable," Jennison said. "Going to games was fun, but it was a tired facility. But the Chill showed what could happen with a better facility."

While Issue 1 was soundly defeated, the Chill's message reverberated with all of the key decision makers and allowed them to quickly regroup. Within a month, McConnell, Nationwide Insurance, and the Wolfe family were spurred to invest millions of dollars in an expansion franchise and a privately funded arena.

"The real legacy of Issue 1 was convincing the money people (McConnell, Nationwide, Pizzuti, and Wolfe) that building an arena and getting the NHL was a must-do idea," Kohn said. "I don't think these same people would have made the financial commitment they did without Issue 1. The year-long build up, plus all of the information presented through the campaign, convinced the 'Titans' that the NHL idea had to happen with or without the public vote."

Christie said the Chill's role was just as important as those investors in the expansion team.

"The Chill got the hockey world to notice Columbus. We were recognized as having a very successful franchise in the East Coast Hockey League and that the next step would definitely be possible," Christie said.

"The success the Chill had and the attendance records they were setting proved in the eyes of the people in the National Hockey League that hockey was viable in a town like Columbus and in a market this size," said Christie.

We were proud to do our part in making the NHL dream a reality, but as always seems to be the case, there was little time to savor the moment.

During the emotional roller coaster ride from the Issue 1 defeat to securing an NHL team, the Chill had to deal with another important issue that was more personal.

After just one season, McCutcheon took the head coaching job of the Rochester Americans, the Buffalo Sabres' AHL affiliate. He eventually became an assistant and later the associate head coach for Buffalo.

A year earlier, we had failed in our attempt to hire Don Granato as head coach. He passed in order to pursue his quest of becoming the first coach in United States Hockey League (an amateur junior hockey league) history to win back-to-back championship titles (he would win consecutive regular season titles). It made him a hot commodity in coaching circles.

Now the timing was right, and we hired Granato as the Chill's fourth and final head coach. The Downers Grove, Illinois, native came from a family with deep hockey roots. Brother Tony was a 14-year NHL veteran who spent most of his playing career with the Los Angeles Kings and San Jose Sharks, later became head coach of the Colorado Avalanche (2002–2004, 2008–2009).[24]

Sister Cammi was approaching the peak of her national acclaim as the captain of the US women's hockey team that won the gold medal in the 1998 Winter Olympics.[25]

Granato was a big addition for our franchise. I couldn't have been more thrilled to hand the coaching baton to one of our original players, but we still had plenty of business to conduct.

---

[24] Tony Granato was named head coach of the Wisconsin Badgers in 2016.
[25] Cammi and Canadian player Angela James were the first women to be inducted into the Hockey Hall of Fame in 2010. In 2019, Cammi became the first female pro scout in NHL history when she was hired by the Seattle Kraken expansion team scheduled to begin play for the 2021–22 season.

Chapter Twenty-Five

UDDER MADNESS

"Welcome to the Meadow of Doom."
> —Andy Davis, a.k.a. Andyman, the public address announcer on
> Opening Night, 1997

The Mad Cows promotion was the most inventive of them all.

Now that the National Hockey League was a reality in Columbus, it was time to shed our cow town image. *The Other Paper* decided to have a little fun with a tongue-in-cheek feature suggesting the NHL team be named the Mad Cows.[26]

With the city embracing its expansion team, we anticipated the public's inevitable shift of attention away from us.

That's why I recommended to Horn that we begin looking for a buyer and cease operations after the 1998–99 season. This allowed an 18-month window for the expansion franchise to exclusively own the market in preparation for the Blue Jackets' 2000–01 inaugural season.

---

[26] The mad cow epidemic had crippled the British beef industry in the early '90s, with a reported thousand cases a week of the infectious disease. Nearly 200,000 cows were afflicted, but several million more were destroyed to prevent the disease from spreading.

We began planning our graceful exit from the stage but ran into an immediate problem. When the 1997–98 ECHL schedule was released, we learned that our first home game was scheduled on Halloween. That was bad news, as Halloween is traditionally a tough night to draw fans due to competition with trick-or-treating (colloquially called "Beggar's Night" in the Columbus area) and parties.

An Opening Night sellout was always vital in giving us enough early-season momentum to break through Ohio State football's stranglehold on the media. Now we faced a challenging date and feared we would be ignored from day one. It was clear that a capacity crowd was no longer guaranteed. Not only would the game need a big push, but we had to reach into our bag of tricks one more time to find that big hook.

At around the same time, the Columbus majority expansion owners were working closely with the NHL to establish a franchise identity and set up the process to begin season ticket sales. At the urging of league officials, a third party—Sports Facilities Marketing Group—was hired in the fall of 1997 for the rollout of personal seat licenses (PSLs). Essentially, fans were required to spend twice for season tickets; a one-time fee for the PSL to help fund the private portion of the arena construction, and again for the season ticket.

PSLs guarantee the owner the right to buy season tickets for the same seat for games as long he or she retains ownership. The average PSL at Nationwide Arena sold for about $2,000. The kicker is the PSL owner had to buy season tickets for hockey or forfeit the seat. If the owner, though, chooses to stop paying for season tickets, they are able to sell their PSLs for the same amount for which they were purchased.

A saving grace was that the NHL gave the team plenty of time to build a following. Unlike Nashville, who began play in 1998, and Atlanta, who began in 1999, Minnesota and Columbus had three years to make the sales. Each expansion franchise was required to sell 12,000 season tickets.

Our first order of business was to take ticket deposits. We agreed to promote the campaign and encouraged Chill fans to make early commitments by making the $100 refundable down payments at our home games. Similar to our in-arena messaging efforts for Issue 1, we used our games as a platform to help the new team in town sell tickets.

In an effort to be mindful of those Chill fans who couldn't afford high-priced tickets, I worked directly with John Christie of the McConnell ownership group to create a special section with season tickets sold exclusively to our fans for only $15 per game.

The plan had another positive objective—to build a sector of our most loyal Chill fans and continue to harness their energy that was so prevalent at the Coliseum.

To promote the cause, Nationwide and the NHL ownership released an advertising campaign for thirty days (October 15 to November 15, 1997)—costing approximately a million dollars—to build season ticket support in the new NHL expansion franchise. Hockey fever was quickly growing to new heights in Columbus.

To cap it off, our NHL franchise planned to unveil its nickname during the final week of that 30-day window. The city was ripe with anticipation, and our Opening Night fell in the middle of the drive.

Then it hit me.

Halloween, costumes. Halloween, costumes . . .

We'd leverage the excitement of all the hype around the name change to our advantage.

NHL team naming + million-dollar PSL marketing campaign + Mad Cows + Halloween = Opportunity.

I loved the Mad Cows spoof run on the front-page of *The Other Paper*. When Columbus was awarded an NHL expansion team, *The Other Paper* developed a logo that included an image of a snorting cow carrying a hockey stick and wearing a helmet bearing the suggested team name. I had an idea on how to turn it into a Chill promotion. I decided to quietly approach publisher Max Brown and see if we could coax them into a gag.

My idea was to pull our own "bait and switch," playing on the much-anticipated nickname unveiling. I knew if we threw a little mystery around our Opening Night, we could suck the media (and fans) into our trap.

Brown and his staff were a little suspicious of my motives at first. The NHL team and Nationwide Arena each were partially owned by Wolfe's Dispatch Media Group, or in the eyes of *The Other Paper*, the big, bad corporate enemy.

I was able to assure Max that I was not coming at the request of the Wolfes, the McConnells, or anyone else associated with the NHL franchise. I hadn't run the idea by anyone else, and wouldn't. The Chill had a gag and we wanted *The Other Paper* to be a part of it because they had created something fun that had to be shared as only the Chill could, and yes, we had our ulterior motive—to sell out Opening Night. Our request was to bring the Mad Cows to life "for real" for one game.

In true Halloween spirit, we'd simply make a costume change—discard our regular uniforms for one night and transform ourselves into the Mad Cows. Much to our surprise (and delight), they loved the idea. What had been a little one-story lark that got a great response from *The Other Paper* readers would now become part of Columbus hockey history.

It was still a risky move and we had to be careful not to get burned. By building relationship capital with the media over the years, we felt that once they were let in on the gag, they'd give us a pass after duping them. Mishandle it, and we'd have a lot of pissed-off people.

We kept the internal circle very tight on the plan. I entrusted Gary Kohn, Amy Reese, Anthony King, and Jakki Moyer from our staff to begin working on ideas for the in-game execution of the Mad Cows promotion, but sternly told them that they were not to breathe a word to anyone. I decided to keep the "bait-and-switch" plan to myself.

On Monday, October 27—just four days before Opening Night—it was time to unleash our trap. I wrote a one-line release stating "the Columbus Chill will announce a team name change on Thursday at 2 p.m."

I handed the statement to Gary and instructed him to wait until 4 p.m. before sending it to the media. I purposely timed the release for just an hour before the local TV news shows aired. I didn't want them to have any real time to investigate before alerting their viewers.

Gary's face went white after reading it. He immediately understood what the reaction would be. The media could mistakenly assume that our announcement had something to do with the NHL team nickname. The release included no explanation of Halloween, Mad Cows, or what we were doing promotionally.

I intentionally left the announcement maddeningly vague in hopes that the media's imaginations would run wild. If the media overreacted (as I assumed they would) it couldn't be construed as our fault. As we hadn't mentioned anything about the NHL, any connections made would not come back to us.

And, as I had hoped, the media did not disappoint. They bit big time, and the release sent them into a tizzy.

I told Gary that he was not to reveal any information other than the one line in the release. We were about to score big if we stuck to our plan. There would be no interviews or additional information provided until Thursday, and the media would just have to wait. Gary faced having to hold the line for three full days, not a prospect he was all too thrilled about. He pleaded a bit, but in the end he held firm.

"Just a few minutes after our fax went out, I had calls from a half a dozen media," said Kohn. "I hadn't anticipated how difficult it was going to be to toe the company line without deliberately lying. Right off the top [WCMH NBC 4's David] Thompson asked, 'Can you confirm or deny the Columbus Chill is giving the name to the NHL.' I never thought a reporter would actually use those words with me. It struck me as funny. George Lehner's [WTVN 610 AM] questions were much tougher and to the point, but after that I was solid in my responses. Twenty minutes later I had spoken with Craig Merz [*Dispatch*], Mike Gleason [WBNS CBS 10], Carol Luper [WSYX ABC 6], Eric Kaelin [WBNS-AM 1460], and Clay Hall [WSYX ABC 6], and the calls just kept coming. After a while, I was having fun with it."

I ducked the first round of calls until after the Monday early evening newscasts, as to avoid being tempted in any way to tip our hand. Gary also stuck to the script, "Sorry folks, we can't say anything more than what is in the release. You'll have to wait until Thursday." Because we'd always been so transparent and open with the media, it only added to the mystery surrounding the story.

Speculation was rampant. With little time to react and not wanting to get beat by their competition, the television media speculated that the NHL team would be named the Chill. All three stations said so. Our plan was working to perfection.

"I was very nervous," Kohn recalled. "Credibility is everything in media relations, and I was not sure the people with whom I had daily contact were going to be happy to find they were the star participants in an episode of *Punk'd*."

We followed the Monday newscasts with a series of silly deliveries to the TV and radio stations—one per day—to tease the Thursday press conference. The reporters had no idea what we were up to or that the big buildup was that the Chill would be renamed the Mad Cows for just one game. Several reporters began to realize it might be some kind of joke when they were delivered cartons of milk, cow bells, and cow tongues. The speculation continued in high gear all week, with morning radio shows and fans dying to learn what we were up to.

After the Monday report, Mike Gleason and WBNS CBS 10 didn't refer to the story again. They realized they'd been had—they just didn't know how. Dave Maetzold of WCMH NBC 4 also knew it was some kind of gimmick. However, the WSYX ABC 6 crew didn't have a clue. They kept up their reporting of the Chill becoming the NHL team's nickname through Wednesday, when we mercifully called off the dogs and let them in on the fact that it was a joke.

The Thursday press conference was a zoo, as most of the media still didn't know exactly what was coming. When we unveiled the Mad Cows jerseys, the fans ate it up. The uniforms were worn by players Matt Oates and Mark Turner with the song "Raw Hide" playing in the background. Fortunately for us, the public and media really embraced the whole story and had fun with it.

What made this so special was that the media chose not to crucify us. In their minds, this was just the Chill being the Chill. Very few teams anywhere could have gotten away with this, and it was a moment I'll never forget.

"After the first day's coverage, I was floating on air," said Kohn. "Duping the media for those few days was perhaps the most fun I've ever had on the job."

With the whole city now in on the joke, we wrapped ourselves up in the promotion.

The Coliseum would become the "Meadow of Doom," with everything for the game tied to the Mad Cows. The front office staff costumed according to the theme, including sales executive Dale Ball and I, who each dressed up as milk men in full whites. Some of the front office staffers chose traditional Halloween get ups. Evonne Segall dressed up as player Mark Turner and Amy Reese was, of course, a Reese's Cup. The response was terrific, with tons of fans showing up—in cow garb—as well.

Our pregame party in the nearby Round Room was filled not only with enthusiastic fans but with a 40-foot inflatable cow. Mad Cows T-shirts sold out instantly.

The crazies at WNCI took the hook in the form of an intermission contest to bring that special touch to the event.

Playing off the Halloween theme, instead of bobbing for apples, three lucky fans competed in a dunking contest for cow tongues to win one of the exclusive Mad Cows spotted jerseys. The whole thing was a howl. The participants enthusiastically played along, and the winner continued bobbing long after the contest was over.

Before the game, Andyman's booming voice pricelessly welcomed everyone to "the Meadow of Doom," and prior to the player introductions, we gave the microphone to Oates, our captain, so he could say a few words.

Whoops.

While we were all having fun with the Mad Cows concept, some of the players, including Oates, were none too pleased. They didn't like being part of a charade, no matter how hard we tried to sell them on the idea.

"Oates and Mark Turner were not happy about the Mad Cows," recalled Kohn. "Several other players also expressed disappointment and frustration. They felt we were embarrassing them. Minor league or not, they all were professional athletes and what we were asking them to do was mock themselves. Of course, Oates had the last laugh on live TV."

At the end of his short pre-game speech Oates acknowledged the crowd and said Chill fans "are the best fucking fans in the league."

Touché, Matt.

The gag, the hype, the contest, and the fan interaction were all unbelievable. The Mad Cows jerseys were auctioned off throughout the game, with the final bids taking place shortly after the game. Such was the fervor over the jerseys that a fist fight even broke out. It was udder madness.

To top it off, the Chill rocked the 5,700 fans with a 2–0 victory over the Johnstown Chiefs, despite allowing 12 power plays. Goalie David Brumby credited coach Don Granato with keeping the team focused in face of the mayhem created by the front office in the days leading to the game. "He said to forget all that stuff," Brumby said. "I thought it was a great show. Donnie made sure it didn't bother us."

The amount of attention brought to the Mad Cows promotion ensured the sellout and kicked off the season in style. It was a great tribute to the Chill franchise, *The Other Paper*, and the city's ability to demonstrate a sense of humor.

After launching the 1997–98 ECHL season on a high note with the spectacle of the Mad Cows promotion, the team hit a rocky road on the ice, with the entire season being a bit tumultuous. While Don had inherited a division championship team from Brian McCutcheon, the results on the ice were mixed. He had his own unique coaching style and approach, and some of the returnees were not suited for his system. He had a few run-ins with players and eventually made deals to assemble a team of his liking.

"We struggled," Granato admitted. "They had a great year with Brian, and [then] I came in. There were a lot of players who just didn't like that change. They were used to things one way and they didn't [want] to change from that. That was a real challenge the first year."

At age 30, Don was barely older than some of his players who were questioning his authority and knowledge. Others thought his last name got him the Chill job more than merit.

I knew better. Don was smart, insightful, and a class act. I had no doubt he would succeed. I saw him mature as a player and a person during his playing days with Chill and followed his coaching career closely. I was confident in our previous three picks as head coach and this time was no different. That's why when he came to me with possible roster moves, I trusted his judgment.

Through the middle of January we had already used 32 players, seven more than the entire 1996–97 season (by the end of the 1997–98, 36 players had been on the roster). The team started to jell in the second half and went on an 8–0–2 run that was capped with a 5–0 victory against the visiting Louisville Riverfrogs on March 1.

Goalie Clint Owen,—acquired from the Dayton Bombers for $100 the day before when both Jeff Salajko and Marc Magliarditi were unexpectedly called up to the IHL—stopped 36 shots to give the Chill a league-record sixth shutout spread among four netminders. (A seventh was not allowed the next week vs. the Louisville Riverfrogs because ECHL rules at the time did not grant a team a shutout when the score was 0–0 after regulation—there was no overtime in the regular season—if a team loses the shootout.)

As well as we were playing, we faced the daunting task of playing 12 of the final 14 games on the road. Long trips, crammed schedules and a steady diet of fast food while riding a bus can take a toll on any team, which explains the extremes a former Toledo Storm player said his teammates once took to get a day off.

In the spirit of *Bull Durham* when the players hosed the field in hopes of a "rainout," this unnamed player said they once tried to get a game in Roanoke, Virginia, postponed because of their grueling schedule. After the morning skate they purchased bags of salt used to melt a snowfall and dumped the load on the ice. The plan almost succeeded. The game would end up being delayed while the crew repaired the patches of ice damaged from the salt.

We played all our road games as scheduled, although there was a moment during the season when that claim might have been in jeopardy when the following announcement was made during a game in Wheeling, West Virginia, by the Civic Center management: "Because of the high river conditions, you are asked to not use the restrooms. Or, use them as little as possible." Apparently, the sewer system along the Ohio River had reached the flood level and flushing was limited to emergencies—whatever that meant. Many people left at the start of the second period after hearing the warning and didn't stick around for the Nailers' 4–3 win.

Although we were 5–5–2 in the late-season road games we stayed in the race until the very last day, when the Hampton Roads Admirals beat the Chesapeake Icebreakers 4–3 to jump ahead of us by a point and claim the last playoff spot. We could have clinched a berth the night before but lost 7–4 at the Peoria Rivermen, and Hampton Roads took advantage of that slip.

Still, it was a strong finish once Don got the players he wanted. We were 19–24–3 on February 5, but went 14–6–4 in the last 24 games to finish 33–30–7, and Don was successful in promoting eighteen players to the AHL and IHL, a club record.

Turner, in his second and final season with the Chill, had a team-best 60 points, including 25 goals. Tim Fingerhut was second with 59 points and his 29 goals tied Lorne Toews (pronounced Taves) for the most on our team.

While we did not have the success we wanted on the ice by missing the playoffs for the first time in five seasons, our Mad Cows promotion ended up being a great lead into the NHL expansion team's announcement of a nickname by drawing even more attention to it. From that moment on, the Chill started to pass the hockey baton to the team soon to be named the Columbus Blue Jackets.

Chapter Twenty-Six

LAST CALL

"We want no violins; we want no hankies, no tears. It'll be one big party. This team changed the sports scene in this city. It set the table for the major leagues. And you know what? Here we are."
—David Paitson, *Columbus Business First*, September 25, 1998

With the Blue Jackets on the horizon, we shifted gears to make way for our city's new NHL franchise.

We began by completing a deal between Horn Chen and John H. McConnell, paving the way for our official exit. By now the Chill franchise, based on annual profits, had escalated in value from its original $100,000 expansion franchise fee to an estimated $3.5 million—a figure well above the $1.5 million ECHL expansion franchise fee at that time.

Horn supported our efforts to promote the chase for an NHL franchise and by doing so had jeopardized a very valuable property. My proposal to the McConnell family was simple. Make up the $2 million difference between the current value and the current expansion fee in equity in the NHL expansion franchise. To be honest, the McConnell family had no legal obligation to agree to this deal, but Mr. Mac believed it was fair and by the end of the day Horn Chen became a two-percent owner of the Columbus Blue Jackets.

With the deal completed, Horn was free to search for a potential buyer for the Chill. As part of our deal, we agreed that the 1998–99 ECHL season would be our last. In the meantime, we forged onward.

Under the McConnell-Chen co-ownership, we opened the Easton Chiller in December 1997, paving the way to ice skating and hockey in northeast Columbus.

For years we had been committed to promoting hockey at its highest level. Although we were successful in our part of that effort, we were just as committed to ensuring that the city's new franchise also flourished in its launch and to make sure we took care of our fans in the process.

In the spring of 1998, I was asked to join the Blue Jackets front office to help in setting up their new operation. It was exciting to become part of the franchise, but a little bittersweet in knowing that the Chill would be coming to an end. It was a passing of the torch in one respect, but in reality this was just an extension of the project that, in my mind, had started seven years earlier. As for the Chill, I didn't drift far away, as I remained involved with the planning of its final season and exit strategy. I also continued to assist Horn in his efforts to secure a buyer for the Chill.

After consulting with Horn, we placed the responsibility of that final season into the hands of two very capable people. Don Granato was named general manager, assigning him all hockey operations duties and personnel decisions. Jakki Moyer, who joined the staff four years earlier as ticket operations director, was named vice president of business operations. She was entrusted with the marketing and promotion of the final season and the thankless task of closing up shop. Don had a unique perspective in seeing the franchise grow as a player and then returning years later to the front office.

"We clearly had matured as an organization from a level of watching the budget the first year to reaping the benefits of a larger-budget team that had financial means," Granato said. "Also, the locker room and the coach's room at the Dublin Chiller were state of the art."

Something else had also changed from the early years of practices at the OSU Ice Rink.

"We needed to win," Granato added. "We needed to show the credibility in winning for us now, where as credibility in the early stages was based on fan entertainment. I don't want to say sideshow, but it was clear when I came back that everybody valued winning more than in the first couple of years."

On September 24, 1998, the Chill announced the franchise had been sold to Spectacor Management Group (SMG) and that the 1998–99 ECHL season would be the team's last in Columbus. The franchise would eventually relocate to Reading, Pennsylvania, to begin play in 2001 as the Royals. After seven profitable seasons, the Chill's seven-figure sale was just more evidence of the team's booming business success.

When our player/assistant coach Mark Turner signed with the New Orleans Brass prior to the start of the 1998–99 season, we had a void on the roster and Don came up with a great idea. Although I was no longer officially overseeing the franchise, he called to run the plan by me.

He wanted to offer the player/assistant role to Jason "Smurf" Christie. After the initial surprise, my reaction was positive. It was an opportunity to bring the franchise full circle and a tremendous opportunity to reward our die-hard fans with a team icon who was with us at the start.

However, I knew that Smurf and I first had to bury the hatchet. Smurf had exited five years earlier under a cloud of controversy. I was the one who had made the decision to trade him and knew how upset he was at the time. I took the brunt of the negative feedback from the fans and had no intention of reliving that issue. But I was now responsible for promoting the Blue Jackets, and the last thing I needed was a loose cannon bad mouthing me around town. Therefore, we set a meeting with Don, Smurf, and me to discuss the situation.

We put everything on the table and, to my delight, the visit was very encouraging. We agreed to turn the page and commit ourselves to writing a compelling final chapter to close out the franchise.

"It's all water under the bridge," Christie told the *Dispatch* (of the walkout and trade). "It's done and over with. I was captain of the team. We all stuck together. I really have a warm spot in my heart for Columbus."

Smurf's return, as the player/assistant coach, was favorably welcomed by the Chill faithful. We instantly sold a number of season tickets for our final season in Columbus, and his fan mail began flowing immediately.

With two original Chill alumni placed in coaching positions, Don and Smurf got down to the job of placing a team on the ice that could compete for a championship in our Columbus finale.

It was great to have them for one last go-around. They were able to provide some historical perspective on what the Chill meant to Columbus and the path the franchise took to get here, although the message was sometimes lost on the younger players, some of whom were just starting high school when Don and Smurf joined the Chill for the first time in 1991.

After a pregame meal one afternoon in Peoria, Illinois, Don had an announcement: "I told them the bus was leaving the hotel at 5:30, and Bob would be at the bus at 5:15 to load the gear.

"They all looked at me and said, 'Bob? Who's Bob?'

"It was so funny. They didn't even know his real name," Granato said.

That would be Bob "Sharkey" Smithberger, the man behind the wheel for many of the Chill road trips, including the first season when no one knew the way to the arenas in the pre-GPS days.

That's how the legend of Sharkey began. After a particularly circuitous route to a rink, someone during the inaugural season—mostly likely team jester Brad Treliving—said Smithberger was like a shark: "He circles twice before going in for the kill."

The nickname stuck and none of the current players had ever heard Bob addressed differently.

But Don and Smurf weren't there to remember the good old days. From a marketing perspective, we wanted to end on a high note. We were determined to live up to our lofty expectations until the end.

Ron Foth Advertising came up with a great final season theme that our group could hang its hat on: "Last Call." With its implied edge, it summed up the Chill spirit as well as the reality of the situation in just two words. It said it all.

We always believed that the small touches in our presentation made a big difference and in that spirit we carefully selected two songs that would fittingly end Chill games that final season—Green Day's "Good Riddance (Time of Your Life)" and Semisonic's "Closing Time."

With the tone now set, Last Call became a season-long tribute to the fans and to the brief but amazing history of the Chill, as well as Columbus' previous minor league hockey teams. Roscoe returned for Opening Night, as did Moe Bartoli—a hockey pioneer and the legendary player/head coach of the Columbus Checkers—the city's initial hockey franchise.

Naturally, the Chill couldn't let Roscoe's infamous stick tossing incident go quietly into the history books. So in classic Chill form, a contest recreating the moment that got him fined and suspended by the league was held during the first intermission.

Hell, even former Ohio State and Chill standout Rob Schriner, who retired in 1996, laced the skates for five games on an emergency basis.

The Chill honored (Columbus') hockey past by wearing uniforms of the previous franchises—Checkers, Golden Seals, and Owls—on three tribute nights. The replica jerseys were auctioned to the fans following each commemorative game.

The fans also played a major role in Last Call when they selected the all-time Chill team, presented in an intermission ceremony hosted by Chill radio play-by-play announcer Jim Talamonti:

Jason Christie, Forward
Derek Clancey, Forward
Rob Schriner, Forward
Lance Brady, Defenseman
Barry Dreger, Defenseman
Jeff Salajko, Goaltender
Phil Crowe, Enforcer

Don's team was shaping up to be special as well. He and the boys made a run at the division title and it would go all the way down to final game of the season before the Northwest Division championship was decided. We were proud of our team and the strides our hockey operations had made over the years. Everyone knew that a second division title would mean a lot to us.

It took the first 14 games of the season to get above .500 (7–6–1), but once we did, we never looked back. On February 6, we stood ninth in the Northern Conference, one spot out of the playoffs, but over the final 28 games, we compiled a league-best 18–6–4 record to complete a 39–24–7 season. I'm most proud of how we turned around a 1–9–0 start on the road to go 10–9–6 over the final 25 away games. It wasn't a spectacular mark but it was enough to give us a chance at the end to win the Northwest Division title and possibly be the top team in the conference and earn home ice for the first three rounds of the playoffs.

The final weekend began with a heartbreaking 5–4 shootout loss to the Dayton Bombers in the Nutter Center on April 2, 1999. We trailed 3–0 early and 4–2 after two periods but goals by Bret Meyers and team captain Matt Oates tied the score at 4 each midway through the third period.

Although we lost the shootout, 2–1, we still picked up a valuable point in the divisional standings and now stood tied for the lead with the Peoria Rivermen at 82 points. The Toledo Storm was one point back. We still hadn't led the division all season but that was the first time we had been tied for the top spot.

Peoria would complete its season the next night at home against us and if the Rivermen won in regulation (two points) it would clinch the division. If we won in regulation or a shootout (two point for the winner and one for the loser) then we'd be champs. The good news was a shootout loss would still keep us alive. Meanwhile, Toledo, the same night, finished the season at the Wheeling Nailers. We had two games left. First, the showdown with Peoria, on Saturday, April 3, and then finishing with our rival Dayton Bombers on Easter Sunday.

In our Saturday night tilt at Peoria, the Rivermen scored twice in the first eight minutes, but then we rallied to go up 3–2 after the first period. Defenseman Beau Bilek started the comeback with a goal and Richard Keyes tied the score with 1:21 left in the period before Meyers put us ahead with 11 seconds left before intermission. Keyes then added another goal late in the middle period for a 4–2 advantage.

Knowing how we'd come back from a two-goal deficit the previous game, I knew a desperate Peoria team would battle like crazy, and my fears were realized 29 seconds into the third period when the Rivermen cut their deficit in half. However, we were inching closer and closer to the division championship as the game approached the final minute. But the Rivermen, with an extra attacker on the ice for the goalie, tied the game with 59 seconds remaining.

That set up a frenetic end to the game, with Peoria trying to win in regulation to claim the title. That didn't happen and when the clock struck zero we knew no matter the outcome of the shootout, we were going home with a chance to win the Northwest Division.

Peoria won the shootout 3–1. Now it got interesting. The Rivermen were first in the division with 84 points and no games left. The Chill and Toledo, who beat Wheeling 7–6, had 83 points but the Storm was also finished.

Because Peoria held the tiebreaker over us, we had to beat Dayton in regulation or a shootout (two points) to win the Northwest. Pretty simple, huh?

Our team arrived back in Columbus at 7 a.m. Sunday, knowing they would faceoff nine hours later against a Dayton team that did not play Saturday.

We saved our best for the season finale, as Last Call came to an end Easter Sunday, April 4, 1999.

It would be the 191st and final sellout at the Coliseum. In our eight seasons, more than 80 percent of our games were at capacity or above.

A better script could not have been written. The Chill took to the ice in replicas of the road jerseys worn in the inaugural 1991–92 season by Granato and Smurf. The Bombers had no chance in front of 5,856 frenetic fans.

In a perfect blend of showmanship and gamesmanship, we won our second division title in three years by defeating the Dayton Bombers, 5–0. We edged out Peoria by a point and, just as sweet, Toledo by two to earn the second seed in the Northern Conference (one point behind the Roanoke Express) to cap a dizzying weekend.

"At that level you know a lot about a team in the first ten minutes," Granato said. "You can tell whether you're going to win out or it's going to be a battle.

"That day it was clear Dayton just wanted to get home. They're like, 'Shit, we're not going to win this game,' and that was because of the tone we set from the start."

Chill captain Matt Oates told the *Dispatch*, "I had goose bumps, a lump in my throat. Also, being in the starting lineup for the Last Call was special. This was a night you don't ever forget."

Smurf, who had missed more than 30 games that season because of a herniated disc, was not expected to play because of a sore ankle. He could barely skate during warm-ups.

But he took an injection in the ankle and then went and played his heart out. Appropriately, he scored the first goal—the game winner—in the first period and his teammates added three more in the first four minutes of the second.

Don had seen enough from Smurf over the years to not be surprised by his heroics that day: "Hands down for me, I played with him and coached him, that guy was one hell of a hockey player and, beyond a hockey player, a leader. Sure, he liked the accolades that came with it but he never took a shortcut on the ice.

"There are a lot of players on a lot of teams, including the Chill, who like the accolades and that recognition, and they took shortcuts all the time," said Granato. "They never gave it their all. He did."

After the middle-period barrage, it was all over except for the screams, cheers, and tears. For the record, the victory gave the Chill bragging rights forever over Dayton with a 36–34 advantage in the all-time series. The five-goal outburst also enabled the Chill to outscore the Bombers, 273–272. In addition to the Smurf goal, Keyes scored twice, and Oates and Tim Fingerhut scored one apiece while Salajko made 29 saves for the shutout.

Oates topped all of our scorers the final season with 24 goals and 57 assists, for 81 points. Keyes was tops in goals with 38, followed by 33 from Meyers. Salajko had an excellent season (30–16–6, 3.16 goals against average) despite shuffling between Columbus and the Indianapolis Ice.

While the Chill went on to lose a first-round, best-of-five series in four games to Chesapeake (including two games at the Dublin Chiller because, once again, there was no ice in the Coliseum), that was not the lasting recollection of the fans.

The Chill had a tradition for its home finales and this one was no different in that regard: the players skated to center ice and raised their sticks in tribute to the fans.

With a division title in hand and emotions running high, the sellout crowd remained long after the game had concluded, soaking up every last second. The stick salute was always a stirring moment, but knowing this would be the final time the silver and black would ever take the ice in the Coliseum was especially emotional.

With Andyman emceeing the ceremonies at center ice, the postgame ceremony continued with the players presenting the "jerseys off their backs" to selected fans. It was an effort by the Chill organization to recognize and thank those who demonstrated spirit and loyalty over the franchise's eight seasons.

Afterward, front office members, minor officials, and game-day staff were introduced to the fans and thanked for their contributions. It was another touch that wrapped up the occasion with a perfect bow.

Don, Jakki, our show producer Andy Herron, and the staff had made Last Call as good as any event we ever executed. Chill fans would shuffle reluctantly out of the Coliseum for the last time filled with enough great memories to last a lifetime.

As for me, I would soak it all up and was among the last to leave. I exited the Coliseum along with a one of our diehard fans—John Kennedy—with a mixture of sadness, satisfaction, and excitement for the future.

Three days later the *Dispatch* published a fitting cartoon tribute with the image of a Chill player skating into the sunset.

It was the end of an era and the start of another.

"Closing time . . . every new beginning comes from some other beginning's end."

—Semisonic, "Closing Time," *Feeling Strangely Fine*

Chapter Twenty-Seven

THE CHILL FACTOR

"The Columbus Chill deserves its own wing in the public relations hall of fame that could serve as a model for minor league hockey franchises everywhere."

—Bob Hunter, *Columbus Dispatch*, October 30, 1998

It is said that "luck is when preparation meets opportunity."

The amazingly short timeframe between the announcement of the Chill franchise on July 25, 1991, and the NHL expansion team, on June 25, 1997, would imply a fairly easy path for Columbus in becoming a major league sports city . . . but that was far from the case. It was a combination of planning, good fortune, timing, vision, skill, hard work, execution, and perseverance that led to our ultimate triumph.

There are a lot of tremendous minor league sports organizations across the country, but no other team can claim such a direct impact on bringing a major league franchise to a city as the Columbus Chill. None built an infrastructure that continues to attract new participants to their sport as the Chill did in the form of its ice facilities, the Chillers. The Canadian Broadcasting Company declared that the "Chill is the most successful minor league franchise in history."

The second-year scheduling snafu at the Coliseum could have been the death of the franchise, but, instead, it was our big break.

State fair manager Billy Inmon's missteps inadvertently helped get discussions started for a Downtown arena and allowed us to take hold of that vital moment. We purposely stoked the fans into an immediate fury. Their intense support stunned the media and caught the attention of the city leadership. This incident opened the door of opportunity and, once our group had a toehold, we didn't let go until the job was done.

The national media attention from the *Wall Street Journal*, ABC World News Sunday, *Sports Illustrated*, *The Hockey News*, and others highlighting our aggressive advertising campaign and marketing efforts were not things we planned or dreamed of, but this prominent publicity gave us the credibility and the ability to stand on a much bigger soap box needed to lend our voice to ideas of bigger things to come. We were able to influence the influencers.

In retrospect, the key moment occurred when I took an enormous risk and went out on a ledge by writing our own letter signed by the league commissioner threatening our franchise. Our marketing and communication team's unequaled ability to use the bully pulpit and secure passionate grassroots and media support produced outrage among Chill fans and that outpouring forced Mayor Greg Lashutka to take action. We not only secured our dates, but six days later the mayor announced the formation of an arena commission to kick start the process that ultimately led to what you see today in downtown Columbus. Without an incident of that scale, it would have been difficult for the mayor to initiate any discussion that would have been taken seriously involving a Downtown arena or an NHL team. Furthermore, had the process started any later, it is likely Columbus would have missed its window of opportunity to secure an expansion team.

The incident also secured the involvement of two members of the eventual Blue Jackets ownership group—John F. Wolfe and Ron Pizzuti—to solve the short-term (scheduling crisis) and long-term (Downtown arena) issues, respectively. What was a near disaster became the launching point for NHL expansion efforts.

But through it all, we never let the arena conversation fall to the background.

In December 1994, we endorsed a Downtown arena/soccer stadium plan presented by Mayor Lashutka's Citizens Commission. It included a Chamber of Commerce feasibility study that stated that with the Chill as a main tenant, the arena would break even financially. By publicly committing to play in the proposed venue Lashutka, Chamber president Jonathon York, and other community leaders had the ammunition needed to legitimize the idea and continue the discussion.

Because the Chill was included in the ten-person Downtown arena commission as one of only two private entities (and only sports voice), it gave us a seat at the table with the major players and a hand in setting the future course.

When we joined the seven-person contingent of Columbus dignitaries on a private trip to New York in the spring of 1996 to make our expansion case to NHL Commissioner Gary Bettman, it reinforced our influence in the process.

The Chill was front and center in the facilities debate all the way through the vote on the sales tax initiative (Issue 1) on May 6, 1997.

Even in the defeat of Issue 1, the Chill's longtime influence was felt because all of the essential private and public figures were still united to bring an NHL team to Columbus.

We worked for years to bring them together and, less than a month after Issue 1 failed to pass, they produced a privately funded arena plan that soon thereafter would secure the expansion team we had dreamed of.

Chill fans would be rewarded with their own special section and pricing within Nationwide Arena. Horn Chen would earn a two percent ownership stake in the Blue Jackets, and the Chiller partnership would continue to flourish.

When it all started six years earlier, virtually everyone believed we were just another in a long line of franchises that would add its tombstone to the minor league sports graveyard in Columbus. Instead, we set out to create a successful minor league hockey franchise and did it. When we had a goal to build an unequaled fan base and break the minor league hockey sellout in hopes of bringing the attention of the hockey world to Columbus, we did it. When, after hearing OSU Ice Rink operators George Burke and Duke Johnson facetiously say that we were the 25th group in twenty-five years promising to build an ice rink in the community, we proved we weren't pretenders. Skeptics laughed when we envisioned rinks around the community to support the growth of hockey, but we built them.

We believed Columbus was a major league city, even when many of its lifelong citizens didn't feel the same way. We believed that the city was starved for a pro team to call its own. It just happened that hockey was the fit. During the many times that this project could have floundered, we kept our noses to the grindstone and never stopped pushing.

All we needed was about a hundred dominos to fall in perfect order with no mishaps for the NHL to become a reality. You had to have real faith and perseverance. We'd been tested from day one in Columbus, so grinding our way through Issue 1 was never a deterrent. We were in this till the bitter end.

No other minor league sports franchise in history can claim to have had their aspirations impact a community as much as ours. Without the Columbus Chill, there is no Columbus Blue Jackets and no Arena District. That's a fact, plain and simple.

In the movie *Apollo 13*, the undertaking to bring the crew home from the disabled spacecraft after a moon landing mission was scrubbed was called a "successful failure" once the astronauts returned safely to Earth. That's how we felt about our efforts on Issue 1.

The Chill's lasting impact is still far reaching. Today, hockey is woven into the fabric of and makes up what defines Columbus, Ohio. It's evidenced in Nationwide Arena, the Arena District—a billion dollar development—and the Blue Jackets.

Very few arena projects have redefined a Downtown area the way that Nationwide Arena and the Blue Jackets have done for Columbus, but none of that happens without the Chill paving the way.

Pittsburgh city officials and members of the Penguins, including owner Mario Lemieux, visited the Arena District in advance of building the Consol Energy Center (now PPG Paints Arena), which opened in the Steel City in the fall of 2010. Representatives of other NHL teams such as the Phoenix (now Arizona) Coyotes and Edmonton Oilers also studied the Columbus plan in pursuit of Downtown arena developments in their cities.

Major league sports revived Downtown Columbus into a vibrant and relevant area, which the city had been sorely missing. The economic impact is far beyond anything imagined when presented to the voters in 1997, and certainly beyond any dreams of a fledgling minor league team announced six years earlier.

Nationwide Realty, Inc., has overseen a billion-dollar, 75-acre mixed-use of development in this once-blighted area. The Arena District—home to 2 million square feet of office space, 17,000 full and part-time employees, more than 1000 residential units, and 300,000 square feet of retail and restaurants—at last count has generated $30 million in additional tax revenue each year since the outset, with expectations of $60 million before the calendar turned to the second decade of the twenty-first century.

With the launch of the Blue Jackets, annual sales by Arena District businesses rose from $78 million in 2000 to $1.6 billion in 2006. Columbus Public Schools has directly benefited by receiving a check of more than a million dollars annually from ticket surcharges on Nationwide Arena events and visiting players' taxes. The total resulting financial impact on the city is in the billions of dollars and its social impact was in a word: priceless.

The Chill's decision to invest its time and resources into the building, programming, and managing of the Chiller ice rinks led to an explosion of skating and hockey activity in Central Ohio.

Our management team led the effort to build the largest Ice Skating Institute (ISI) program in the United States, and initiated the expansion hockey participation now tenfold. In the ensuing years, the Chillers produced numerous NCAA Division I and III intercollegiate hockey players, including Dublin native Sean Kuraly, Miami (Ohio) University.[27] The Chillers also produced NHL players Dublin's Connor Murphy (Phoenix Coyotes),[28] Bexley's Jack Roslovic (Winnipeg Jets), the first central Ohio player to be selected in the first round of the NHL Draft,[29] and Kole Sherwood (Columbus Blue Jackets) who became the first Columbus player to play for the Blue Jackets,[30] as well as USA National and Olympic figure skater Marcy Hinzmann.

We succeeded because our players created a remarkable bond with our fans. We succeeded because we had four terrific coaches, top notch trainers and equipment managers, as well as a dedicated game-day staff. We succeeded because of an extraordinary front office. Original Chill staffers Alan Karpick, Larry Lane, Brent Maurer, Ken Cohn, David Peck, and Sheryl Kolb helped set expectations at a major league level. As these folks were sought after for bigger and better opportunities, we reloaded with equally tremendous talent. Gary Kohn, Jakki Moyer, Jim Talamonti, Amy Reese, Ted Van Zelst, Mike Slates, Brian Sells, Evonne Segall, Nora Ludwig, Andy Herron, Anthony King, Susie Churchill, Aylish Costello, Paul Schaffer, Kristina Jameson, and others picked up the torch and saw the vision through. The funny thing was that we weren't even supposed to be here!

If Horn Chen was successful in placing the franchise at the Cleveland State University Convocation Center, the story's over before it even began! Simply stated: no Chill, no Blue Jackets.

There's a credo that big thinking precedes great achievement.

---

[27] Kuraly was the 133rd overall pick by the San Jose Sharks in the 2011 NHL Draft.

[28] Murphy debuted for the for the Phoenix (now Arizona) Coyotes on November 16, 2013.

[29] Roslovic was selected in the first round (25th overall) by the Winnipeg Jets in 2015.

[30] Sherwood debuted for the Blue Jackets on February 16, 2019. Brother Keifer also played in the NHL for the Anaheim Ducks.

The ECHL franchise was a cultural phenomenon that brought joy through its sometimes politically incorrect presentation to more than a million hockey fans during its eight-year history. While the Chill's legacy is considered to be more closely related to its in-your-face advertising campaigns or perfecting how to sling shot frozen chickens across the ice at supersonic speed or enticing fans to bob for cow tongues, it indeed became the team that changed a city forever. For those who attended games at the Coliseum, the Chill will always be remembered for its record 83-game sellout streak; hard-hitting hockey; engaging personalities; enthusiastic fans (imagine Duke's Cameron Crazies meets *Slap Shot*); unique fun-filled promotions; and a commitment to an irreverent marketing strategy from start to finish. It was how professional sports, in my opinion, should be presented.

Many franchises talk of a total entertainment package, but the Chill—without the benefit of the bells and whistles of a modern day facility—delivered just that.

To paraphrase the immortal words of Charlestown Chiefs beat writer Dickie Dunn in *Slap Shot*, "We just tried to capture the spirit of the thing."

ACKNOWLEDGMENTS

In 1999, as the Columbus Chill closed its eighth and final season in the East Coast Hockey League (ECHL), I asked public relations director Gary Kohn to assemble and bound all of the news articles that we had collected from the inception of the franchise, which he then distributed to the staff and media. Ten years later, in the summer of 2009, I picked up the booklet and began reviewing the articles. The more I read, the more I realized that we had a very unique story to tell. Two days later, I met with Craig Merz, the *Columbus Dispatch* sports reporter that covered the Chill, and asked if he would consider co-authoring a book about the Chill. Fortunately for me, Craig agreed.

Chill Factor was five years in the making. There are several key contributors that helped make the book a reality. Three key members of the Chill staff—our two public relations directors Brent Maurer and the aforementioned Gary Kohn each lent their two cents to the editorial. Additionally, my key sounding board, Alan Karpick, contributed his ideas and editorial skills to shaping the content of our early versions of the book. Alan, Brent, and Gary's help, morale, support, and commitment in getting the Chill story told paid tremendous dividends.

We were very fortunate to have been connected early on with Kim Weiss of Kim Weiss Publishing Services, who put us on the path to being published. Kim saw enough raw potential in the content to introduce us to her former editorial director at HCI Books, Michele Matrisciani, who had moved on to Moveable Type Management. Michele and MTM worked diligently to sell the book, but after a year were unable to secure a publisher. The typical feedback was that "nobody cares about hockey," or "it's a regional story." At that pointed we parted ways with MTM.

Craig and I were prepared to self-publish, but wanted to ensure the story be polished up by a professional editor. To that end, I asked Michele for a recommendation of an experienced editor who specialized in sports books. Without hesitation, Michele endorsed Mark Weinstein, Executive Editor at Rodale Books, who has worked on more than 200 sports title. A few months after beginning the editing process, Mark introduced us to his former boss Tony Lyons, Publisher at Skyhorse Publishing. A few months later we had a deal. We had a deal because Kim, Michele, and Mark believed enough in *Chill Factor* to assist us with the next steps. Craig and I thank you all.

Ultimately we worked with Skyhorse editor Jason Katzman who assisted us in reshaping the content, identifying any missing gaps, fleshing out the story, and polishing up the book. There were other key contributors—Greg Bartram, the Chill photographer, who documented many of the great Chill images, and Jennifer Gauntt, a colleague and communications professional at Sam Houston State University, who assisted Craig and me with one last review before submitting our final edits to Skyhorse.

Thank you to Mark LeClerc and David Henthorne for securing all of the fun promotion ads, and Anthony King for cleaning up all legal details.

I'd like to recognize everyone associated with the Columbus Chill (players, coaches, trainers, front office, and game day staff) whose contributions not only helped present a terrific product, but also set the stage for the arrival of the NHL Blue Jackets.

Finally, I'd like to especially thank the fans whose enthusiasm, energy, and passion for hockey made Chill games a cultural phenomenon and the Coliseum the place to be during the 1990s in Columbus.

David Paitson, Ed.D.

OVERTIME

"We have a thriving Downtown area where there used to be the [state] penitentiary. I would have never believed it."
—Stephen Buser, Professor Emeritus of Finance at Ohio State and author of
the 2009 impact study commissioned by the Columbus Chamber

When David Paitson asked me during lunch in the spring of 2009 of my interest in co-authoring the story of the Columbus Chill and its impact on the city, I immediately said what a great idea.

I can't say I had the same thought eighteen years earlier, when I first met David and he outlined his plan of how he was going to make a hockey franchise succeed in a market where many pro sports teams—particularly hockey—had crashed and burned.

As a lifelong resident of Columbus, I grew up with the behemoth known as Ohio State hovering over every venture and figured the odds of David sticking around more than a few years were slim. I hoped I was wrong, not because I was rooting specifically for the yet-to-be-named team, but because I was pulling for Columbus, the city. I felt, and saw firsthand in others, the joy of having a hockey team and the disappointment, anger, and pain when it was taken away.

Columbus was ripe for another chance. The city in the early 1990s was just beginning to sprout its wings as the community became more diverse and transient. Growing up, everybody was an Ohio State fan and the media reflected that in their coverage. At our first meeting, David said he knew his franchise had to have a marketing plan that was bold and different in order to stand out. I was skeptical, based on the city's hockey history, but also intrigued by how a fresh approach to a new generation might work.

Maybe some youngsters would get the same excitement I had when attending my first hockey game at age twelve on November 24, 1971. That night, my father corralled me and my three brothers so my mother could be left alone while preparing for the next day's Thanksgiving feast. There we sat in the orange general admission seats behind the goal at the east end of the Fairgrounds Coliseum as the Golden Seals played the Fort Wayne Komets. Although the arena had a dingy yellow glow from the lights and the ice was more grayish than white, it was heaven, as far as I was concerned.

Over the next six years I was a regular at the Coliseum to see the Seals, who were followed by the Owls. When a bad lease and lack of available playoff dates forced the Owls to move to Dayton, Ohio, after the 1977 season, my fears were confirmed—being a hockey fan in Columbus was going to be hard. Prior to the Owls moving, every new season was fraught with skepticism, whether that team would be the last the city saw for pro hockey.

The Owls left behind a decent following, but, listening to David, I wondered how he was going to get them back after fourteen years and, more importantly, increase the number of hockey fans to make a franchise sustainable.

As it turned out my trepidation was unfounded; the Chill came out blazing with its edgy marketing campaign and crazy promotions unlike anything seen before in Columbus. The Chill was a trailblazer in breaking down the barriers between a team and its fans. Ads were provocative because they said what people were thinking. Hockey back then was still considered mayhem on ice played by toothless Canadians with funny accents and even funnier hair (re: mullets). Of course, the Chill made light of these stereotypes.

It was interesting for me to sit back and watch the two divergent opinions of the fans. One side was the old school "I'm here for the hockey" type of crowd, while the rest were the younger and hipper following who wanted—first and foremost—to be entertained.

David and his staff were able to accommodate both, although it was clear from the first frozen Cornish hen slingshot across the ice to the Laker Girls appearance and other promotions that the top priority was creating buzz within the community.

The Chill was a fresh breeze. Ohio State was conservative in marketing and cloistered when it came to media access to their athletes and coaches because they could get away with it. The most successful of all minor league teams in town were the Clippers, but the baseball team, an affiliate of the New York Yankees, was staid and didn't want to ruffle the feathers of Yankees owner George Steinbrenner.

Players on the Chill were accessible and encouraged by management to be out in the public and on the airwaves as much as possible. Big personalities such as Jason "Smurf" Christie, Brad Treliving, Don Granato, and Jim Ballantine quickly became stars in the community.

Was winning important that first season? You bet it was to coach Terry Ruskowski and the players who bled for him. But the reality was that the goal for year one was to fill the building as many times as possible, widen the fan base, raise awareness in the media, and lay the groundwork for long-term grassroots success by exploring sites for the Chill's own multi-rink facility.

The Chill accomplished all that, including opening the Dublin Chiller ice skating facility in October 1993, and the Easton Chiller four years later.

Sometimes outsiders have a clearer vision of what your city can be than you do. That was the case for David Paitson, Alan Karpick, Larry Lane, and Brent Maurer—the gang from Indianapolis who saw how sports had transformed their city. They moved to Columbus and envisioned a potential NHL city while those of us who spent our lives here were disillusioned after all the broken promises and having several failed ballot issues for stadiums or arenas.

I also had an insider's view of the incredible effect the Chill was having on the sports marketing world after only a few home games in 1991. Think back to that period for a second: There was no social media to spread the word of what the Chill was doing to promote itself. My colleagues at the *Dispatch* and I had done stories on the early success at the gate, but there wasn't Facebook, Twitter, Instagram, YouTube, Zoom, or streaming services to instantly show hundreds of thousands of people the craziness of a Chill game, or have the team's Christmas video go viral. Think about this: the ECHL did not have website until the 1995–96 season.

Yet, just two months after the first home game, the *Wall Street Journal* ran a story (thanks *WSJ* for reading my articles) on the Chill phenomenon that was soon followed by an ABC News feature. All that attention for a minor league hockey team in Columbus, Ohio? Remarkable.

Still, at that time I couldn't see a path from the Chill in the Coliseum to a Downtown arena and the NHL. But my opinion began to change with the scheduling fiasco engineered by state fair manager Billy Inmon. That, of course, led to Mayor Greg Lashutka, under pressure from the public at the Chill's urging, to form a committee to look at alternatives to the aged Coliseum.

Suddenly, everybody was talking not about what Columbus *should* do but what the city *would* do to obtain an NHL franchise.

The Mayor's subsequent sports arena task force, with David representing the Chill, brought the town's titans together, and when Dallas millionaire Lamar Hunt considered Columbus for a franchise in the new Major League Soccer in 1994—and because of the prodding of the Chill—the community/business/civic apparatus was in place and ready to execute an ambitious season ticket drive that won over him and the league.

In interviewing Hunt over the years, he said the Chill's success was a major factor in his looking at Columbus in the first place. In my opinion, if there's no Chill, there's no MLS team and the dominoes don't fall in place for the NHL, Nationwide Arena, Arena District, Huntington Park (the home for the Clippers since 2009), thousands of Downtown housing units, and dozens of nearby restaurants and bars.

Having so many business and community leaders united was great, but there needed to be a singular voice—David and his staff led the charge for an arena and the NHL despite opposition from Ohio State as it sought funding for its own venue (Value City Arena).

"People knew it was time to grow beyond Ohio State," Lashutka, a former OSU football player, told me in June 2014. "Ohio State wasn't ready for it. They didn't particularly get excited about competition, but the city had grown. You had people who couldn't get tickets to Ohio State football but there was an interest in legitimate major league soccer and legitimate NHL."

There were setbacks for the city along the way, and the resounding defeat of Issue 1 in 1997 was a kick in the gut. That was a tough pill to swallow and, the moral of the story was able to show itself: When good people have good ideas, great things can happen.

What was a downtrodden Downtown, anchored by a dilapidated state penitentiary, is now the bustling Arena District with a gleaming Nationwide Arena as the centerpiece. Nationwide Realty, Inc.'s concept is so successful that officials from the Pittsburgh Penguins, Arizona Coyotes, and Edmonton Oilers came to Columbus to elicit ideas for developing areas around their new arenas.

Columbus has become a destination city, thanks to Nationwide Arena, home to the NHL All-Star Game in January 2015. In 2018, Columbus was the site for the NCAA Women's Final Four at Nationwide Arena, which has also hosted the 2007 NHL Draft, early round NCAA men's basketball tournament games, Arena Football League teams, political rallies and hundreds of concerts and exhibitions.

Meanwhile, just across Neil Avenue in the Arena District, sits the Clippers' fabulous stadium. In 2009, it was named Ballpark of the Year by BaseballParks.com, beating such competitors in the newly constructed or significantly renovated categories as Yankee Stadium and Citi Field (New York Mets).

For so many years I had heard that there was nothing to do in Columbus. Today it's possible to attend a hockey and baseball game, with a concert at Express Live! (the first indoor and outdoor concert venue in America) happening simultaneously within a quarter mile of each other and the Arena District stays busy all year round.

Also, the Greater Columbus Convention Center continues to expand and renovate with the times to attract more visitors to the Arena District and surrounding areas leading to the development of nearby hotels and impacting the growth of housing and businesses in the nearby Short North District.

Bringing everything full circle from nearly a quarter century after the vision of Downtown venues for hockey and soccer was vanquished with the defeat of Issue 1 is the construction of a new downtown stadium for the Crew which is scheduled to open in July 2021. The $373 million project includes the conversion of the Crew's Mapfre Stadium at the Ohio State Fairgrounds into a training facility and community sports park. The project will be funded with $233 million in private funds and $140 million in public money. The downtown stadium sits on the western edge of the Arena District past Huntington Park and Nationwide Arena and will include more than 400 apartments and 120,000 square feet of office and retail space on a 23-acre site called Confluence Village. Crew owner Anthony Precourt had threatened to move the franchise to Austin, Texas prior. However, Cleveland Browns owners Jimmy and Dee Haslam and the Edwards family of Columbus, after being inspired by the remarkable story of the fan driven 'Save the Crew' movement, purchased the franchise to keep it in Central Ohio.

The success of Nationwide Realty, Inc.'s investment in the Arena District has served as a catalyst in the city's downtown revitalization that now includes a rebirth along the Scioto River that runs through Downtown and west into Franklinton, which is home to COSI (Center of Science and Industry) and the majestic National Veterans Memorial and Museum, which opened in October 2018 at the site of the old Veterans Auditorium.

There are spots for families to play in water splashes on a hot day and enjoy festivals along the evolving riverfront. What used to be a mall near the Statehouse is now Columbus Commons with outdoor concerts and other activities, all while condominiums and business are being built around the green space.

It's been a gratifying transformation and, ultimately, was worth the wait. I used to run in the pre-Arena District area on Sunday mornings when traffic was light and remember having to avoid chunks of fallen concrete on the cracked sidewalks around the abandoned prison. Businesses were few and far between among boarded buildings. Housing options were nonexistent, and it wasn't a place to spend a night out with friends. "If somebody who was in the Ohio Pen got paroled and came back to see the city, it would blow their mind," real estate developer Ron Pizzuti told me.

Today, shuttle buses run back and forth on High Street between the entertainment establishments in the Arena District and the OSU campus. It's practical and symbolic—the city and Ohio State are now partners with the university managing both arenas. Ironic, isn't it?

Hockey is now fully integrated into the Columbus sports scene including collegiately as Ohio State men's and women's hockey programs have seen a resurgence.

In 2018, the Buckeyes men's team, under the direction of Steve Rohlik, reached the NCAA Frozen Four for the second time (1998 being the other) and in 2019 earned their first regular-season title since their Central College Hockey Association championship in 1972.

Women's coach Nadine Muzerall guided OSU to its first Frozen Four in 2018 and a second NCAA berth in 2020, the same season the Buckeyes won their first Western Collegiate Hockey Association tournament since the program's inception in 1999–2000. Columbus is no longer a city under the shadow of the university. It was the norm growing up to always, always say, "Columbus, Ohio," when asked where I was from. No offense to the dozen or so other like-named cities, but I leave the state off now thanks, in large measure, to the recognition the Crew and Blue Jackets have brought to my city.

Amazingly, that progress can be traced back to an East Coast Hockey League franchise that set out with the modest goal of finding a foothold in an Ohio State-centric city. It's incredible that with a vision, a well-conceived plan, and perseverance, the Chill put in motion a series of events that changed the city of Columbus forever.

—Craig Merz

SHOOTOUT

THE COLUMBUS CHILL TIMELINE

1991

July 25: Franchise is announced. David Paitson, thirty-one-year-old sports marketing veteran, is named as team president and general manager. The Chill nickname, logo, and team colors of black and silver are introduced.

July 31: Terry Ruskowski, a veteran of 15 WHA and NHL seasons, is named the team's first head coach.

October 10: Jason "Smurf" Christie becomes the first player to sign a contract to play for the Chill.

November 1: The Chill plays its first home game in front of 6,298 fans at the Ohio Expo Center Coliseum, although (unofficially) there may have been as many as 7,000 in the 5,700-seat facility. Final score: Columbus Chill 7, Erie Panthers 5.

December/January: Within two months of the opener, the Chill's aggressive marketing campaign receives unprecedented coverage for a minor league hockey team through the *Wall Street Journal* (which described the Chill as "hockey for the hip") on New Year's Eve. Later, attention is drawn to the team in *Sports Illustrated, The Hockey News,* and *ABC World News Sunday.* More recognition would follow in the ensuing months and years:

- Named the city's "Best Sporting Event" in 1992 and 1993 by *Columbus Monthly.*
- "Best New Addition to Columbus" and "Athlete you'd most want to drink a beer with," *Columbus Alive* (1992).
- Named "Best Promotion," *Columbus Monthly* (1993).

- Recognized by *American Marketing Association* as "best marketing project" for the Chill (1994).
- The Canadian Broadcasting Company proclaims "(the) Chill is the most successful minor league franchise in history."
- A board game, "A Night at the Chill," is created by team's first season ticket holder, Steve Miller.

1992

January: The first of 83 straight sellouts, more than tripling the previous minor league hockey record.

March: The Chill set an ECHL season record for most penalty minutes (2,751; 43 minutes per game).

September: A near-disastrous scheduling snafu by Fairgrounds officials results in a public fury. The united show of force helps trigger formation of a Downtown arena study and later the talk of possible NHL expansion.

1993

October: The Chill become the first minor league hockey team to own and operate its own ice facility in suburban Dublin. In the first four years of operation, more than 20,000 area residents participate in "learn to play hockey" and "learn to skate" classes, making the Chiller the largest ISI (International Skating Institute) program in the country. From the arrival of the Chill to its end in 1999, the number of youth hockey players in the area increased from 150 to more than 1,300.

1994

March: Ruskowski leads the Chill to its first playoff appearance in 1993–1994. The team would make the playoffs in five of their eight seasons.

March 14: NBC affiliate WCMH preempts prime time network programming to air the Chill's first home playoff game live, a rarity in minor league sports. The Chill is victorious over the Johnstown Chiefs, 9–4.

June: Ruskowski becomes the ECHL's first coach to be promoted to the Triple-A level when named the coach of the expansion Houston Aeros, of the International Hockey League. He is soon replaced on the Chill bench by Moe Mantha.

December 14: Spurred by the Chill's scheduling problems two years before, a Downtown arena feasibility study from the Chamber of Commerce is unveiled. The study states that with the Chill as the main tenant, the facility would break even financially, and Paitson verbally commits the Chill to play in the proposed arena.

1995

March 29: The Multi-Purpose & Sports Facility Work Group is formed by Mayor Greg Lashutka, the Franklin County Commissioners, Greater Columbus Area Chamber of Commerce, and the Franklin County Convention Facilities Authority. Paitson is among the 10 community leaders, and sole sports representative, appointed.

May: A Chill radio spot is selected as a national finalist for the Silver Microphone Award.

1996

April: Chill radio spot titled "Jingle" is awarded an ADDY, presented by the American Advertising Federation.

June 28: Paitson is named as part of a delegation that will go to New York to inform NHL commissioner Gary Bettman that Columbus is interested in an expansion franchise.

July 25: Mantha becomes the second Chill coach to be move to a higher level, taking the head coaching job with the Baltimore Bandits, of the AHL (later relocated as the Cincinnati Mighty Ducks). He spends four seasons with the organization, qualifying for the playoffs twice. Brian McCutcheon is named as his replacement.

1997

March 30: With a Chill 4–1 victory over the Toledo Storm, Columbus wins the North Division title, marking the first time Columbus pro hockey had won a division title.

April: The Chill and future Columbus Blue Jackets owner John McConnell sign a deal to build a second Chiller in the Easton Market area of northeast Columbus. Eventually, this results in the Central Ohio Ice Rinks, Inc., (Chillers) and the NHL club owning and managing eight sheets of ice in central Ohio (Chiller North was added in 2003 and the Chiller Ice Works in 2005).

April: Due to conflicts with the Ohio Expo Center, the Chill is forced to play its home playoff games about 55 miles west at the Nutter Center in Dayton, Ohio suburb Fairborn. Only one month before an arena/soccer stadium tax initiative (Issue 1) goes before votes, the controversy highlights Columbus' dire need for another facility to host sporting events.

May 6: In a monumental defeat, Issue 1 fails at the ballot box by 12 points. The loss seemingly ends any hope of Columbus receiving an NHL expansion franchise

May 17: McCutcheon named the 1997 ECHL Coach of the Year.

May 30: Paitson named 1997 ECHL Executive of the Year.

June 2: Nationwide Realty, Inc., unveiled plans to privately finance a $125 million Downtown Arena.

June 25: Five years and eleven months after the Chill is introduced, the NHL Board of Governors selects Columbus for an expansion franchise, scheduled to begin play in October 2000. Nashville (to begin play in 1998), Atlanta (1999), and Minnesota (2000) are also chosen. McConnell is named the principal owner of the Columbus franchise.

July/August: To clear the way for the Blue Jackets to have sole ownership of the hockey market, Paitson brokers a deal with the McConnell organization. Chill owner Horn Chen receives a small percentage ownership stake in the NHL expansion franchise and begins to search for a buyer for the ECHL team.

August 12: McCutcheon becomes the third Chill coach to move to the next level after being hired by the Buffalo Sabres organization and assigned as the head coach of their AHL affiliate the Rochester Americans. McCutcheon would later become associate head coach of the Sabres.

August 26: Inaugural season Chill player Don Granato returns to coach the team.

November 1: In what has become Columbus hockey folklore, the Chill dupes the media in the weeks leading to the announcement of the NHL expansion team's nickname into thinking the Chill moniker would be transferred to the new franchise when, in reality, the Chill is transformed into the "Mad Cows" for their home opener.

December: Chiller Easton is opened, making the Chill and the Anaheim Mighty Ducks the only franchises to own and operate two facilities.

1998:
September 24: It is announced that the Chill franchise has been sold to SMG, and the 1998–99 ECHL season will be the last in Columbus. The franchise will then be relocated to Reading, Pennsylvania.

1999
February 4: Bret Meyers becomes the first Chill player to start in an ECHL All-Star game.

March 14: The Chill wins a franchise-best 25th game at home and makes a bid for the Northwest Division title.

April 4: "Last Call:" The Columbus Chill plays its final regular season home game in front of its 191st sellout crowd of 5,846 on Easter Sunday. Christie scores the first goal, as the Chill defeat the rival Dayton Bombers, 5–0, to earn the Northwest Division title on the last day of the season. The Chill finished with an all-time regular season record of 280–215–48 and were 170–85–26 at home, including 3–1 at alternate "home" sites the first season of 1991–92.

The Legacy of the Columbus Chill

Chill Factor debuted as a No. 1 best seller in Amazon's Hockey and Sports Industry categories upon its release on March 3, 2015, thank you.

The book received very positive reviews including from sports news publications including *Columbus Business Journal*, the *Columbus Dispatch*, NHL.com, Joe Pelletier's Hockey Book Reviews by The Hockey Writers, *Boston Sun Times*, Taking Note with Greg Drinnan, *Utica Observer-Dispatch*, ECHL.com, and The Guy Who Reviews Sports Books.

Chill Factor has also been reviewed in academic journals Human Kinetics and the Journal of Sports History and has been utilized as required reading in numerous college and university sport management programs including Dayton, Findlay, Iowa, Ohio State, Ohio University, Otterbein, Neumann, New Haven, Northern Illinois, Sam Houston State, and Wilmington.

To stay current with the history of the franchise and updates on Chill players, coaches, and front office members follow the Columbus Chill Memories pages on Facebook and columbuschill.net.

A complete list of Chill player bio information and player statistics are available on ColumbusChill.net and updates on the Columbus Chill Memories Facebook Page. All updates as of May 1, 2020.

All-Time Chill Team (as selected by the fans in 1999)

Lance Brady (defenseman, 1993–95) was the head hockey coach at Assumption College for 10 seasons before beginning his first season as director of hockey operations for Merrimack College in the fall of 2018. He passed away on Feb. 5, 2019, at age forty-eight after battling cancer. The Northeast-10 Conference named its men's hockey coach of the year award after the "Duke" and the players' lounge at his alma mater (Holy Cross) is named for him as well. **Jason Christie (forward, 1991–93, 1998–99)** finished his third season as head coach of the Jacksonville Icemen of the ECHL in March 2020. He is the

ECHL's all-time leader in regular season victories with 633 following previous stints with the Peoria Rivermen (2000–2005), Utah Grizzlies (2005–2008), Ontario Reign (2011–2015) and Tulsa Oilers (2015–2017). "Smurf" was voted the 2010–11 Central Hockey League Coach of the Year after guiding Bloomington (Illinois) to a 32–27–7 record. He had 182 points (57 goals, 128 assists) in 159 Chill games.

Derek Clancey (forward, 1993–97) was inducted with the 2020 class into the ECHL Hall of Fame. He is the Chill career leader in points (313) and assists (218). He also added 95 goals in 221 games. In 1995–96, he had 109 points (32–77) in 67 games. He is in his 13th season in the front office of the Pittsburgh Penguins, helping them win the Stanley Cup three times (2009, 2013, and 2017). Clancey was the director of pro scouting from 2010 until being promoted to the Penguins' director of player personnel prior to the 2019–20 season.

Phil Crowe (enforcer, 1991–92) played in the NHL for the Los Angeles Kings, Philadelphia Flyers, Ottawa Senators, and the Nashville Predators between 1994 and 2000. He is the co-owner of Total Directional, which provides directional drilling services to oil and gas producers. He is based in Windsor, Colorado, about 60 miles north of Denver, where he is the vice president of sales and marketing. He played 32 games for the Chill and had 11 points (4–7) and 145 penalty minutes.

Barry Dreger (defenseman, 1991–93) is the head coach and general manager of the New Jersey Rockets of the National Collegiate Development Conference, one of two tuition free junior hockey leagues in the U.S. He has been there since March of 2019 after nearly seven years as head coach of the Los Angeles Jr. Kings. Prior to that he was head coach at Kennesaw (Georgia) State University. He had 663 penalty minutes in 94 games with the Chill (7.05 avg.).

Jeff Salajko (goalie, 1996–99) has been the goaltender coach for the Detroit Red Wings since May 2016. He previously spent three seasons with the Red Wings' American Hockey League affiliate as the goaltending development coach for the Grand Rapids Griffins. "Sal" was an assistant coach for the Ohio State men's hockey team from 2008–2011 before joining the Ohio AAA Blue

Jackets for one season. He was the goalie coach for the Ohio State women's team for a season prior to his Grand Rapids stint.

Rob Schriner (forward, 1992–96, 1998–99) is an assistant general manager at the Chiller ice rinks in central Ohio. The former Ohio State forward had 174 points (91–83) in 239 games with the Chill. At age forty-two, having not stepped onto the ice for a pro game in a dozen years, Schriner played a game for the ECHL's Cincinnati Cyclones in 2012, a feat covered by The Hockey News.

Coaches

All four Chill coaches would advance through the ranks, with two becoming NHL assistant coaches:

Terry Ruskowski (1991–94; 96–80–20, .541) lives in McKinney, Texas, about 30 miles north of Dallas. In the spring of 2020, he was named head coach of the McKinney North Stars AA 18U team, part of the Dallas Stars Travel Hockey League that competes in local and out-of-town tournaments. He is a certified USA Hockey coach who also works with the Stars' youth hockey programs through their Xtreme Team of mainly former NHL players who hosts camps and workshops. The Stars operate eight rinks (16 ice surfaces) in the Dallas-Fort Worth area. When "Roscoe" left the Chill, he spent 1½ seasons coaching the Houston Aeros expansion team in the IHL. From there he took over the first-year Knoxville Speed of the United Hockey League for two seasons followed by going to his fourth expansion franchise, the Laredo Bucks of the Central Hockey League, where he was the president, general manager and coach. He won championships there in 2003 and '05. He was with the Bucks from 2002 through the 2010–11 season before coaching the Rio Grande Valley Killer Bees (CHL) for one season prior to his Quad City stint. Prior to working with the Stars, his most recent coaching and general manager job with the ECHL's Quad City Mallards ended in January 2017 after 4½ seasons.

Moe Mantha (1994–96; 68–60–10, .529) retired as coach/general manager of the St. Cloud (Minnesota) Blizzard at the end of the 2019–20 season.

He had been involved with the Tier II junior team in the North American Hockey League since June 2017 when it was based in Brooking, SD. The Blizzard moved to St. Cloud prior to his last season in charge. Following his two seasons with the Chill, Mantha moved up to the AHL's Baltimore Bandits. After the 1996–97 season they became the Cincinnati Mighty Ducks and Mantha coached there three more seasons. Always known as a developer of talent, he coached the USA Hockey National Team Development Program's Under-17 team in Ann Arbor, Michigan, from 2000 to 2004 and later became minority owner, general manager, and head coach for the Michigan (Flint) Warriors of the NAHL from 2010 to 2015. He took the expansion team to the championship game in 2011. He later coached the Saginaw Spirit of the Ontario Hockey League and was GM/coach for the French River Rapids of the Northern Ontario Junior Hockey League before taking over the Blizzard.

Brian McCutcheon (1996–97; 44–21–5, .664. North Division title) resides in Ithaca, NY, where he first gained fame for Cornell, leading the Big Red in goals in 1969–70 when they became the only undefeated and untied (29–0–0) NCAA Division I hockey champion in history. He was head coach at his alma mater from 1987 to 1995 with a 108–105–24 record. McCutcheon was an assistant for the Los Angeles Ice Dogs (IHL) in 1995–96 before his one season with the Chill that earned him the ECHL Coach of the Year award. That success led to his promotion to Rochester (AHL), the top affiliate of the Buffalo Sabres. He spent three seasons with the Americans, reaching the Calder Cup final the final two years. He moved up to the Sabres as an assistant coach and later associate head coach from 2001 to 2011. He then coached in Italy and Germany through 2016. His son, Mark, was the fifth-round selection (146th overall) of the Colorado Avalanche in the 2003 NHL Entry Draft. He played four seasons at Cornell prior to a pro career in the AHL, ECHL, and Europe before retiring in 2015.

Don Granato (1997–99; 72–54–14, .564. Northwest Division title, 1998–99) completed his first season as an assistant coach for Buffalo in 2019–20. In September 2019 he developed a streptococcus bacterium in his blood that led to severe pneumonia and respiratory failure during his hospital stay, and at one point doctors said he had five minutes to live before medical procedures saved his life. He returned to coaching the Sabres two months later. After Granato's two seasons in Columbus he became the fourth consecutive Chill coach to reach a higher level, albeit with a stop in-between. Following the Chill's final season, he coached the Peoria Rivermen to the ECHL title in 1999–2000. That earned him a promotion to head coach of the St. Louis Blues' AHL affiliate, the Worcester IceCats. Granato was named AHL Coach of the Year during his inaugural campaign of a five-year stint. He was a Blues assistant coach for the 2005–06 season and head coach of the AHL's Chicago Wolves from 2008 to 2010 before he was named the USA Hockey National Team Development Program's U-17 head coach in August 2011—the same position once held by Mantha— and later the U-18 and U-20 head coaching positions. He joined his alma mater, Wisconsin, to become associate head coach to his brother, Tony, for the 2016–17 season then spent two seasons as an assistant coach for the Chicago Blackhawks. Don was inducted into the Illinois Hockey Hall of Fame in January 2020.

Players, Post-Chill

Development: Over the course of the team's history, more than 100 players moved up to the IHL or AHL and four made their NHL debuts after playing for the Chill. In all, eight players who wore a Chill uniform also skated in the NHL at some point.[31]

NHL Players

Blair Atcheynum (1993–94) was a longtime assistant coach for the Battlefords North Stars of the Saskatchewan Junior Hockey League. He played in 192 of his 196 NHL games after a short but epic stint in Columbus in which he registered 27 points (15–12) in 16 games.

---

[31] David Bumbry dressed as the backup goalie for the Minnesota Wild in November 2000, but did not play.

Cam Brown (1991–93) was inducted into the ECHL Hall of Fame in 2010. Brown played 46 games for the Chill over two seasons. His lone NHL game was March 3, 1991, for the Vancouver Canucks.

Phil Crowe (1991–92) See All-Time Chill Team Section.

Trent Kaese (1991–92) had a prolific stretch for the Chill with 50 points (28–22) in 28 games in the second half of the season. Tied a pro record with a hat trick in three straight games. "The Mighty" Kaese played one NHL game for the Buffalo Sabres on March 25, 1989, at the Quebec Nordiques.

Sasha Lakovic (1992–93) played a notable role in the film Miracle as "the Russian" and played a Russian soldier in the 2007 movie Afghan Knights. He passed away at the age of forty-five after a seven-month battle with brain cancer. "Pit Bull" played 19 games with the Calgary Flames in 1996–97 and 18 with the New Jersey Devils in 1997–98 and 1998–99. He had four assists and 117 penalty minutes in the NHL.

Eric Manlow (1996–97) a member of the Niagara (Canada) Regional Police. In 2016 helped coach the Niagara Falls novice AA hockey team to the Ontario Minor Hockey Association championship. In 37 NHL games (11 Boston, 26 New York Islanders) he had two goals and four assists for six points.

André Racicot (1995–96) only played one game for the Chill. The "Red Light" started his National Hockey League (NHL) career with the Montreal Canadiens, for whom he played from 1989 to 1993, and won a Stanley Cup in 1993.

Peter Vandermeer (1996–98) went undrafted but reached the highest level playing in two National Hockey League (NHL) games during the 2007–08 season for the Phoenix Coyotes. Now is the president of Vandermeer Ventures in Sylvan Lake, Alberta.

NHL Management, Coaching, Scouting, Etc.

Scott Bell (1995–96) has been a scout for the Toronto Maple Leafs since August 2018. Previously he was a scout for the Pittsburgh Penguins when they won the Stanley Cup in 2016 and '17.

Derek Clancey (1993–97) Pittsburgh Penguins Director of Pro Scouting. See All-Time Chill Team Section for additional details.

Jason Fitzsimmons (1992–93) as a pro scout for Washington he hoisted the Stanley Cup after the Capitals defeated the Vegas Golden Knights in 2018.

Don Granato (1991–93) has coached in the NHL as an assistant coach with the Buffalo Sabres (beginning 2019–20), Chicago Blackhawks and the St. Louis Blues as well as the head coach of the USA Hockey National Development Team.

David Hymovitz (1996–97) a scout for the New York Islanders from August 2007 to July 2016. Now the director of hockey operations for the Boston Junior Eagles.

Colin Muldoon (1997–98) has been the director of player development for the Carolina Jr. Hurricanes since September 2007.

Matt Oates (1994–99) is managing partner in O2K Worldwide Management Group which oversees sports management for numerous NHL players and other athletes. Oates had 247 points (80–167) in 257 games in a long and distinguished Chill career which included being captain.

Jeff Salajko (1996–99) Detroit Red Wings goaltender coach. See All-Time Chill Team Section for additional details.

Jamie Spencer (1995–96) is the executive vice president of business development for the Minnesota Wild. From 2011–14 he was the executive vice president of sales with the Tampa Bay Lightning. Prior to that, he was a founding staff member of the Wild in 1997.

Jason Taylor (1991–92) has been an agent/hockey advisor since 2002 with Newport Sports Management, working with such NHL players as Mark Stone, Evander Kane, Jordan Eberle and Brandon Sutter.

Brad Treliving (1991–93, 1994–95) has been the general manager of the Calgary Flames since April 28, 2014. He signed a multi-year contract extension on October 3, 2019.

Marty Wilford (1997–98) spent his second season as an assistant coach for the Anaheim Ducks in 2019–20, his ninth year with the organization.

Vince Williams (1998–99) is a scout for the Vegas Golden Knights.

Mark Yanetti (1997–98) is the director of amateur scouting for the Los Angeles Kings. He began with the organization in 2006 as a scout.

Players Who Made Their Homes in Columbus

Kevin Alexander (1991–93) is agency owner and operator of Search2Close real estate in Powell. He is the head hockey coach at Olentangy Liberty High School.

Darcy Cahill (1997–98), hockey coach at St. Francis DeSales High School. Previously, led Dublin Coffman High School to an appearance in the 2016 OHSAA state championship tournament.

Dan Cousineau (1998–99) is a coach in the Capital Amateur Hockey Association in central Ohio and has worked with AAA Blue Jackets system as well.

Marty LaRoche (1998–99) is a chief technology officer at Customized Girl in Columbus and has been a coach in the Ohio AAA Blue Jackets program for many years. He is also the player on the cover of Chill Factor.

Darwin McClelland (1993–95) is an assistant coach to Kevin Alexander at Olentangy Liberty High School and has spent more than a dozen years coaching at Columbus area schools.

Mike Ross (1993–95) is an account executive at Associated Agencies Inc., in Westerville. He had 130 points (58–72) in 131 games for the Chill and later was the ECHL MVP for the 1996–97 season for the South Carolina Stingrays.

Jeff Salajko (1996–99) See All-Time Chill Team Section.

Rob Sangster (1991–92) head coach at St. Charles Preparatory School in Bexley.

Rob Schriner (1992–96, 1998–99) See All-Time Chill Team Section.

Jim Slazyk (1993–94) the Chill and Ohio State goalie is DevOps senior engineer for BMW Financial Services in the Columbus area. He was the head coach for the 10U team for the Columbus Chill Youth Hockey Association in the 2019–20 season.

Front Office and Staff

Dr. David Paitson spent ten years with the Blue Jackets organization as vice president of marketing and ticket sales and concurrently served for two years president of the Arena Football League's Columbus Destroyers before moving on to a career in intercollegiate athletics at Sam Houston State University. He is currently the Director of Athletics at Lake Superior State University, home of the five-time national hockey champion Lakers (NAIA in 1972 and 1974; NCAA in 1988, 1992, and 1994). Dr. Paitson is also an emerging expert in intercollegiate athletics leadership theory, evolving from his dissertation Assessment of Leadership Traits Required for the Intercollege Athletic Director Position, and post dissertation research Critical Leadership in the Management and Marketing of University Athletics (Paitson, Zapalac, & Zhang, 2020), published in the book Sport Business in the United States: Contemporary Perspectives. He has had his research The State and Focus of U.S. Intercollegiate Athletics: Past, Present, and Future (Paitson, Zapalac, & Zhang) presented at the 2017 World Association for Sport Management conference in Kaunas, Lithuania.

His original Chill co-workers from Indiana went on to careers in sports as well: **Alan Karpick** is the president and publisher of Boilers, Inc., which publishes *Gold and Black Illustrated*, a publication that covers Purdue University athletics. **Larry Lane** left the Chill to launch the ECHL's Jacksonville Lizard Kings. He continued his career in sports with the World Golf Association, Wasserman Media Group, and the Jimmy V Foundation.

Brent Maurer moved on to head up communications for the AHL before returning to Columbus as PR director at Rahal Racing, serving as Danica Patrick's publicist and, later, in a similar position at Ford Racing. Maurer recently returned to private business in Columbus.

Columbus Blue Jackets: In addition to Paitson, eight additional people affiliated with the Chill organization ultimately joined the Blue Jackets: trainer Chris Mizer; equipment manager Jason Stypinski; front office members

Aylish Costello, Gary Kohn, Nora Ludwig and Jason Rothwell; Chiller ice technician Mike Sims, and legal counsel Greg Kirstein.

Also, team photo grapher Greg Bartram and several members of the minor officials crew moved over to the Blue Jackets in game-day roles, including: Jay Coyer, Dan Grassbaugh, Don Gullata, Steve Haller, Joe Mongolier, Ron Mongolier, Doug Reed, Don Supelak, and Larry Wilson.

Development: More than 30 other Chill employees, interns and game - management personnel continued their careers in sporting endeavors at all levels of competition, including: Dale Ball (ESPN), Amy Reese Blackmore (Buffalo Sabres, NHL; JP Morgan Chase), "Downtown" Billy Brown (Ohio State University), Mike Citro (Florida Panthers, NHL), Ken Cohn (NASCAR, Cagnazzi Racing), Brian Farr (Oklahoma State University, University of Texas), Julie Fry Maurer (Chillers), Andy Herron (Columbus Crew, MLS; McConnell Arts Center), Pam Gill Ivaldi (Chillers), Kristina Jameson (Chillers), Bruce Javitz (Mandalay Sports Properties, Los Angeles FC, MLS), Susie Churchill Karya (Indianapolis Ice, IHL), Anthony King (ECHL, Partner at Spertus, Landes & Umhofer), Sheryl Kolb (Central Hockey League), Nick Magistrale (Dublin Scioto High School), Jakki Moyer McMahon (Ohio State University), Jill McNeal Womsley (WXIN-TV), Andrea Navin (Anaheim Ducks, NHL; Minnesota United FC, MLS), Carol Guisti Parrish (University of Washington), Rusty Pearl (Philadelphia Flyers), David Peck (Jacksonville Jaguars, NFL; PepsiCo), Rusty Ranney (Live Technologies), Paul Schaeffer (Scranton Wilkes Barre Penguins), Brian Sells (Cincinnati Bengals, NFL), Angie Skinner (Ryan Newman Motor Sports), Mike Slates (Minnesota Vikings, NFL; Minnesota United FC, MLS), Brendan Smith (Jacksonville Lizard Kings), Pete Smith (Jacksonville Lizard Kings), Ron Stevens (TS Sports, Nations Wright, Top Golf), Noelle Bollinger Szydlyk (Indiana Sports Commission), Scott Woods, (International Hockey League), Jim Talamonti (Sporting News Radio), Joe Trotta (Anaheim Mighty Ducks), Chesa White (Polaris Amphitheatre), and Ted Van Zelst (New York Islanders, NHL; NASCAR; WWE; Detroit Pistons, NBA).

Notable staff that went on to careers outside sports include Josh Beachy (GE – Energy Management Director, Global Employee Communications for Nike), Briana Beauchesne (CCA Global Partners), Joe Engle (Chase), Courtney Hilbert (Express, Abercrombie & Fitch), Andrew Jahant (Centurylink), Lance Parker (Photography), and Jason Strouf (Main Street).

Leaderboard

Career Leaders

Games Played: **Beau Bilek** (266)
Goals: **Keith Morris** (104)
Assists: **Derek Clancey** (218)
Points: **Derek Clancey** (313)
Penalty Minutes: **Barry Dreger** (663)
Plus/Minus: **Darwin McCelland** (+32)

Single-Season Records

Points: **Derek Clancey** (109), 1995–96
Goals: **Keith Morris** (46), 1995–96
Assists: **Derek Clancey** (77), 1995–96
PIM: **Gary Coupal** (406), 1995–96
Wins: **Jeff Salajko** (35), 1996–97
GGA: **Jeff Salajko** (2.30), 1997–98

Yearly Standings

Year	Division	Games Played	Wins	Losses	Ties	Overtime Losses	Shootouts Lost	Points	Winning %	Head Coach
1991–92	West	64	25	30	0	6	3	59	.461	Terry Ruskowski
1992–93	West	64	30	30	0	1	3	64	.500	Terry Ruskowski
1993–94	North	68	41	20	0	1	6	89	.654	Terry Ruskowski
1994–95	North	68	31	32	0	5	0	67	.493	Moe Mantha
1995–96	North	70	37	28	0	0	5	79	.564	Moe Mantha
1996–97	North	70	44	21	0	0	5	93	.664	Brian McCutcheon
1997–98	North west	70	33	30	0	0	7	73	.521	Don Granato
1998–99	North west	70	39	24	0	0	7	85	.607	Don Granato

Chillers

Source: Central Ohio Ice Rinks, Inc.

One of the lasting legacies of the Chill was the philosophy from the start to build a base of hockey fans at the grassroots level and make ice skating available for generations to come. Today, the Chill's footprints are everywhere, as Chiller, LLC, which is owned and operated by the majority owner of the Blue Jackets (JMAC), which oversees five facilities in central Ohio and a sixth about 50 miles west in Springfield, Ohio, to bring the number of sheets of ice under its umbrella to nine:

- NTPRD Chiller (Springfield)
- OhioHealth Chiller Dublin
- OhioHealth Chiller Easton
- OhioHealth Ice Haus (adjacent to Nationwide Arena)
- OhioHealth Ice Works
- OhioHealth North Chiller North

In all, there are 14 sheets (ten year-round) with the inclusion of Nationwide Arena, Value City Arena, the OSU Ice Rink, and the Lou and Gib Reese Ice Arena in Newark, Ohio, and the NTPRD Chiller in Springfield, Ohio..

- The central Ohio facilities serve more than 3,200 adult men and women players among at least 220 clubs and six youth associations, with approximately 5,000 players. Whereas Columbus had one high school program (Upper Arlington) when the Chill started, there are thirty-two now spread across the varsity, junior varsity and club levels.
- In 2006, the Ohio High School Athletic Association, in partnership with the Blue Jackets, permanently moved its state hockey championship finals to Nationwide Arena.
- There have also been several prominent Division I hockey players and NHL draftees, including Connor Murphy, the son of former Columbus Blue

Jackets assistant coach Gord Murphy, who was raised in suburban Dublin and made his NHL debut with the Phoenix Coyotes on November 16, 2013. Other Columbus born alumni to graduate to the NHL include Sean Kuraly (Boston Bruins), Jack Roslovic (Winnipeg Jets), Kole Sherwood (Columbus Blue Jackets), and Kiefer Sherwood (Anaheim Ducks), as well as dozens of NCAA Division I & III players.

- The Columbus Blue Jackets Foundation awards college scholarship money to one high school hockey player each year. The Foundation also awards a quarter of its proceeds to promote the growth of youth hockey.
- The Chillers run one of the largest U.S Figure Skating programs in the country.
- Marcy Hinzmann first came to skating prominence as a figure skater at the Chiller Dublin and OSU Ice Arena. Marcy and her skating partner Aaron Parchem won the silver medal at the 2006 US Figure Skating Championships, qualifying for the 2006 Winter Olympic team. The pair finished 13th in Turin, Italy. Marcy went on to skate professionally. She married former NHL player Todd Simpson, and now lives in Kelowna, British Columbia.

Nationwide Arena[32]

- Opened September 9–10, 2000, with the Tim McGraw and Faith Hill Soul 2 Soul Tour.
- First Blue Jackets' regular season game was October 7, 2000, against the Chicago Blackhawks.
- Columbus hosted the 2007 NHL Draft.
- Columbus hosted the 2015 NHL All-Star Game (January 24–25).
- Columbus hosted the 2004 and 2016 World Cup of Hockey Team USA training camps and exhibition games vs. Canada and Russia; 2007 NHL Draft; Stanley Cup Playoff games in 2009, 2014, 2017, 2018, and 2019.

---

[32] Source: Nationwide Realty Investors

- Nationwide Arena was selected for early round NCAA men's basketball tournament games in 2004, 2007, 2012, 2015, and 2019; the NCAA women's basketball tournament in 2009; a finalist to host the 2016 Democratic Party convention and site of the 2018 NCAA Women's Final Four.
- Within seven years of debuting, the Blue Jackets and Nationwide Arena had an economic impact of more than $2 billion to the area, according to a study conducted by the John Glenn Institute of Public Affairs at Ohio State University.
- In 2009, Nationwide Arena and Ohio State reached an agreement to stop cannibalizing each other in bookings, whereas the Schottenstein Center (home of Value City Arena) management would sign and operate special events at both arenas.
- On March 30, 2012, arena owners Nationwide Insurance and the Dispatch Printing Company sold the facility to the Franklin County Convention Facilities Authority (FCCFA). As part of the deal, Nationwide Insurance will pay the Blue Jackets $28 million to retain the arena's naming rights until 2022, as well as $58 million to purchase 30 percent ownership stake in the franchise. The Blue Jackets, in turn, agreed to remain in the city until 2039 or pay $36 million in damages.

Arena District[33]

- The Arena District, developed by Nationwide Realty Investors, is nationally recognized as one of the country's leading developers of large, complex, mixed-use projects.
- The Arena District houses bars, clubs and world-class entertainment at Nationwide Arena, Express Live! concert venue, Huntington Park, and new Columbus Crew opens its new soccer specific stadium in the Arena District in July 2021.
- Nationwide continued its two-stage, $1.3 billion in development in 2011.

---

[33] Source: Nationwide Realty Investors

- Other Statistics (Source: Nationwide Realty Investors):
  - More than 6 million visitors per year
  - Greater Columbus Convention Center – 2,500,000 visitors
  - Nationwide Arena – 1,200,000 visitors
  - Huntington Park – 750,000 visitors
  - Express Live! – 300,000 visitors
  - More than 500 annual community events
  - Red White & Boom – 500,000 attendees
  - Jazz & Rib Fest – 400,000 attendees
  - Arnold Sports Festival – 175,000 attendees
  - By 2022, downtown Columbus will have more than 5,000 hotel rooms, 2,700 of which will be connected or adjacent to Nationwide Arena and the Greater Columbus Convention Center.
  - 1,000+ total residential units
  - Nearly 17,000 full - and part-time employees
  - 75 businesses
  - 15+ acres of park space
  - 2 million square feet of Class A office space
  - 300,000 square feet of retail and 20 restaurants
  - A 2008 report by Ohio State University estimated that area businesses posted annual sales of $1.6 billion and that consumer spending by 800 residents totaled nearly $32 million a year.
  - A Columbus Chamber of Commerce study in 2009 projected the area would generate $60 million a year in state and local taxes by 2018.
- History (Source: Nationwide Realty Investors):
  - The former site of the Ohio Penitentiary, "The Pen," opened in 1834, on 22-acres on West Spring St between West Street and Dennison Ave. (now known as Neil Ave.).
  - The Lofts Hotel occupies the 55 E. Nationwide Boulevard building, built in 1882 by wall covering manufacturer Charles Aler.
  - Built in 1913, the Ohio Moline Plow building was once home to Ohio's largest distributor of farm equipment.

- The Great Atlantic & Pacific Tea Company opened a grocery warehouse at Neil Ave. and Spring Street in 1926, now home to the North Bank Condominiums.
- The Union Station Arcade once sat atop the High Street viaduct where the Hyatt Regency Hotel stands today. One of the original Union Station arches now stands at McFerson Commons.
- The 40-story, 1.328 million-square foot Nationwide Tower, broke ground on July 12, 1974, at the corner of High Street and Nationwide Boulevard.
- "The Pen" closed in 1984, having been one of the oldest continuously operating inner-city maximum security facilities in the nation.
- In 1997, Nationwide Insurance announced plans to develop Nationwide Arena at the corner of Nationwide Blvd. and Front Street with an NHL franchise to call it home.

Columbus Blue Jackets[24]

- **June 25, 1997:** The NHL awards the city of Columbus an expansion franchise, along with Nashville, Tennessee; Atlanta, Georgia; and St. Paul, Minnesota.
- Their name, Blue Jackets, was chosen to celebrate patriotism, pride, and the rich Civil War history in the state of Ohio. It was President Abraham Lincoln who requested Ohio raise 10 regiments at the outbreak of the Civil War and the state raised 23 regiments for three months of service.
- **September 8, 2000:** The Blue Jackets open their training camp at the CoreComm Ice Haus, the only practice facility in the NHL where the team plays its games.
- **October 7, 2000:** Welcome to the NHL, Columbus! The Blue Jackets jump out to a 3–0 first period lead but suffer a 5–3 loss to the Chicago

---

[34] Source: Columbus Blue Jackets

Blackhawks before a sellout crowd of 18,136 in their inaugural NHL game. Bruce Gardiner scores the first goal in team history at 7:34 of the first period.

- **June 22–23, 2007:** The Blue Jackets and Nationwide Arena host the 2007 NHL Entry Draft.

- **April 21, 2009:** A Nationwide Arena record crowd of 19,219 is on hand for the first Stanley Cup Playoff game played in the state of Ohio. Detroit earns a 4–1 win in Game 3 of the Western Conference Quarterfinals Series.

- Columbus Blue Jackets Foundation has awarded more than $10.4 million in grants to various charitable and youth hockey organizations in Central Ohio since its inception in 2000.

- **January 24–25, 2015:** NHL All-Star Game and Weekend hosted at Nationwide Arena. The weekend included the NHL All-Star Skills Competition, in addition to the All-Star Game.

- **April 19, 2018:** A record crowd of 19,395 attended Game 4 of the Eastern Conference First Round vs. the Washington Capitals.

- **April 15, 2019:** In what was arguably the most unlikely first-round playoff upset in the NHL's modern history, the Blue Jackets, in their 18th season without a playoff series victory, shocked the Tampa Bay Lightning 7–3 to complete a 4-game first-round sweep. Tampa Bay had won an NHL league record tying 62 regular season games on their way to capturing the Presidents' Trophy. It was the first time a Presidents' Trophy winner was swept in the first round.